Lecture Notes in Computer Science 5767

Commenced Publication in 1973
Founding and Former Series Editors:
Gerhard Goos, Juris Hartmanis, and Jan van

Peter Y. A. Ryan   Berry Schoenmakers (Eds.)

E-Voting and Identity

Second International Conference, VOTE-ID 2009
Luxembourg, September 7-8, 2009
Proceedings

 Springer

Volume Editors

Peter Y. A. Ryan
University of Luxembourg
Luxembourg
E-mail: peter.ryan@uni.lu

Berry Schoenmakers
Technical University of Eindhoven
Eindhoven, The Netherlands
E-mail: berry@win.tue.nl

Library of Congress Control Number: Applied for

CR Subject Classification (1998): E.3, D.4.6, K.6.5, C.2, J.1, K.4.4

LNCS Sublibrary: SL 4 – Security and Cryptology

ISSN 0302-9743

ISBN 978-3-642-04134-1 Springer Berlin Heidelberg New York

springer.com

© Springer-Verlag Berlin Heidelberg 2009

Typesetting: Camera-ready by author, data conversion by Scientific Publishing Services, Chennai, India
Printed on acid-free paper   SPIN: 12748914   06/3180   5 4 3 2 1 0

Preface

These proceedings contain the papers presented at VoteID 2009, the Second International Conference on E-voting and Identity. The conference was held in Luxembourg during September 7–8, 2009, hosted by the University of Luxembourg.

VoteID 2009 built on the success of the 2007 edition held in Bochum. Events have moved on dramatically in the intervening two years: at the time of writing, people are in the streets of Tehran protesting against the claimed outcome of the June 12th presidential election in Iran. Banners bearing the words "Where is my vote?" bear testimony to the strength of feeling and the need for elections to be trusted. These events show that the search for high-assurance voting is not a purely academic pursuit but one of very real importance. We hope that VoteID 2009 will help contribute to our understanding of the foundations of democracy.

The Program Committee selected 11 papers for presentation at the conference out of a total of 24 submissions. Each submission was reviewed by at least four Program Committee members. The EasyChair conference management system proved instrumental in the reviewing process as well as in the preparation of these proceedings.

The selected papers cover a wide range of aspects of voting: proposals for high-assurance voting systems, evaluation of existing systems, assessment of public response to electronic voting and legal aspects. The program also included a keynote by Mark Ryan.

We would like to thank everyone who helped in making this conference happen. First of all thanks to the authors for submitting their work and thanks to the members of the Program Committee and the external reviewers for their efforts. Many thanks as well to the local organizers for hosting the conference, with special thanks to Hugo Jonker who served both as General Chair of the conference and as a member of the Program Committee. Finally, we should also like to thank the FNR in Luxembourg for their generous sponsorship of the workshop that allowed us to extend invites to the two speakers as well as fund a number of student stipends.

July 2009

Peter Ryan
Berry Schoenmakers

VOTE ID 2009

September 7–8, 2009, Luxembourg

General Chair

Hugo Jonker   University of Luxembourg, Luxembourg

Local Organization

Baptiste Alcalde   University of Luxembourg, Luxembourg
Ragga Eyjolfsdottir   University of Luxembourg, Luxembourg

Program Chairs

Peter Ryan   University of Luxembourg, Luxembourg
Berry Schoenmakers   Technical University of Eindhoven,
                                  The Netherlands

Program Committee

Mike Alvarez   Caltech, USA
Josh Benaloh   Microsoft Research, USA
Ian Brown   University of Oxford, UK
David Chaum   USA
Michael Clarkson   Cornell University, USA
Lorrie Faith Cranor   Carnegie Mellon University, USA
Peter Emerson   de Borda Institute, Ireland
Jeroen van de Graaf   Universidade Federal de Ouro Preto, Brazil
Dimitris Gritzalis   University of the Aegean, Greece
Bart Jacobs   Radboud University, The Netherlands
Hugo Jonker   University of Luxembourg, Luxembourg
Steve Kremer   LSV ENS Cachan, France
Robert Krimmer   evoting.cc, Austria
Olivier Pereira   Universite Catholique de Louvain, Belgium
Andreas Pfitzmann   Technical University of Dresden, Germany
Josef Pieprzyk   Macquarie University, Australia
Bart Preneel   Katholieke Universiteit Leuven, Belgium
Mark Ryan   University of Birmingham, UK
Ahmad-Reza Sadeghi   Ruhr University Bochum, Germany
Ronald Rivest   MIT, USA

Kazue Sako	NEC, Japan
Ted Selker	MIT, USA
Jacques Traoré	France Telecom, France
Melanie Volkamer	Technical University of Darmstadt, Germany
Dan Wallach	Rice University, USA

External Reviewers

Roberto Araujo
Rainer Boehme
Benjamin Kellermann
Stefan Köpsell
Lucie Langer
Dimitrios Lekkas
Hans Löhr
Olivier de Marneffe
Lilian Mitrou
Axel Schmidt
Matt Smart
Ben Smyth
Marianthi Theoharidou
Joe-Kai Tsay
Bill Tsoumas

Table of Contents

Not-So Hidden Information:
Optimal Contracts for Undue Influence in E2E Voting Systems

Jeremy Clark, Urs Hengartner, and Kate Larson

Cheriton School of Computer Science
University of Waterloo
Waterloo, ON, Canada, N2L 3G1
{j5clark,uhengart,klarson}@cs.uwaterloo.ca

Abstract. This paper considers coercion contracts in voting systems with end-to-end (E2E) verifiability. Contracts are a set of instructions that an adversary can dictate to a voter, either through duress or by offering payment, that increase the probability of a compliant voter constructing a vote for the adversary's preferred candidate. Using a representative E2E system, we place the attacks in game-theoretic terms and study the effectiveness of three proposed contracts from the literature. We offer a definition of optimality for contracts, provide an algorithm for generating optimal contracts, and show that as the number of candidates increases, the adversary's advantage through the use of contracts decreases. We also consider the use of contracts in a heterogeneous population of voters and for financially constrained adversaries.

1 Introduction

End-to-end verifiable voting systems (E2E systems) allow voters to independently verify the correctness of the final tally, without needing to trust the chain-of-custody over the ballots after the election in paper voting settings, nor any software or hardware used for vote capture and tallying in electronic and remote voting settings. E2E systems often use cryptographic primitives to achieve these properties while maintaining the secrecy of every cast ballot. A sample of recently proposed E2E systems include VoteHere [20], "Votegrity" [12], Prêt à Voter [14], "Benaloh-06" [7], Scratch and Vote [3], Punchscan [15,23], ThreeBallot [24], Scantegrity [10,11], Civitas [19], VoteBox [25] and Helios [1]. A common element of these systems is the production of some kind of obfuscation of each vote, which voters can retain, digitally or physically, as a privacy-preserving receipt of their vote. Since the receipt does not reveal which candidate the voter selected, it ostensibly cannot be used effectively in a scheme to buy votes or coerce voters into voting for a particular candidate. However this is not the case: even if votes are correctly obfuscated, undue influence can still be accomplished by paying or forcing voters to follow certain procedures in the construction of their receipts, such that the receipts become probabilistically biased toward a chosen candidate. We call these procedures, and consequences for not following

P.Y.A. Ryan and B. Schoenmakers (Eds.): VOTE-ID 2009, LNCS 5767, pp. 1–17, 2009.

them, a contract. In this paper, we argue that contracts are persistent enough in E2E systems to warrant further study and, in response, we conduct a detailed analysis in a representative E2E system—Punchscan.

Our contributions can be summarized as

- a new analysis of the effectiveness of three existing attacks [9,17,18] using coercion contracts in Punchscan with two candidates,
- a definition of optimality for contracts and a linear-time algorithm for generating optimal contracts,
- an analysis of multiple-candidate contracts showing that their effectiveness decreases with the number of candidates,
- an analysis of contracts in the setting where some voters have intentions other than accepting the highest payment available to them and hide their real intentions from the adversary, and
- an analysis of contracts in the setting where the adversary is financially constrained showing that the adversary must value the vote by, approximately, an order of magnitude more than the voter selling the vote.

2   Preliminaries

2.1   End-to-End Verifiability

Voting systems that offer end-to-end verifiability often use a variety of cryptographic techniques to simultaneously achieve ballot secrecy and tally correctness. One common construction includes, abstractly, these three critical steps:

i. The voter produces and retains an obfuscation of her vote, such that given only the obfuscated vote, it is not possible to determine the vote.
ii. Obfuscated votes are collected by the election authority, published publicly, and voters check that the obfuscation of their vote is included and correct in this collection.
iii. Obfuscated votes are collectively deobfuscated to produce a tally in a way that is verifiably correct and does not reveal the link between any obfuscated and deobfuscated votes.

While there is little room for variation within (ii), a variety of approaches to (i) and (iii) have been presented in the literature. The integrity of (i) is sometimes referred to as *ballot casting assurance* [2] or *voter initiated auditing* [5], while privacy is called *coercion resistance* [16] or *receipt freeness* [8]. The dominant mechanism for achieving obfuscation in (i) is encryption, but more recent literature includes use of permutations, code substitutions, information splitting, and vote swapping. When the obfuscation technique is encryption, the deobfuscation in (iii) is typically achieved through a mix network [13,22] or additive homomorphic encryption [6].

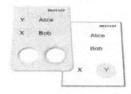

Fig. 1. A marked Punchscan ballot, showing top and bottom layers. In our notation, this ballot is of type {YX,XY} and the position marked is R. It represents a vote for Alice.

2.2 Undue Influence

The subject of this paper pertains to the privacy property in (i). We are interested in cases where given only an obfuscated vote, the voter's selection remains hidden; yet if certain decisions in the construction and verification of the obfuscated vote are dictated to the voter by an adversary, the voter's compliance results in a non-negligible probability that the voter selected the adversary's preferred candidate.[1] We call such a set of instructions a *contract* and this class of attack *contract-based attacks.*

Contract-based attacks have been proposed for a variety of E2E systems. In the experience of the first authors, they have also proven non-trivial to avoid in the design of Scantegrity, which has been specifically hardened against them. It is our belief that this category of attack is sufficiently wide-spread that a detailed analysis of contracts can provide value to voting system designers in understanding the mechanisms at play and the effectiveness of these attacks in a realistic setting. Instead of a light-touch on a range of systems, we have undertaken a very detailed analysis of contract-based attacks in one representative system—Punchscan [23]—which has been found to be vulnerable in this regard [9,17,18].

2.3 The Punchscan Voting System

In a Punchscan election, two-layer paper ballots are used (See Figure 1). Both layers have a serial number and a list of candidates. Additionally, a column of symbols is printed on the top layer beside the candidates' names and a row of symbols is printed on the bottom layer underneath the candidates. These bottom layer symbols are visible through circular holes in the top layer. A voter marks a ballot by finding the symbol in the bottom row that corresponds to the symbol

---

[1] Other types of manipulation may include forcing the voter to cast a random vote [16] or to vote *against* a particular candidate instead of *for* one. This latter distinction is called destructive manipulation, as opposed to constructive, and can be accomplished through a combination of constructive manipulations. Forming a strategy of constructive manipulations can be intractable in the worse-case for some scoring protocols but it is trivial for plurality voting [4].

beside their preferred candidate and daubs this position with a suitably-sized Bingo dauber such that the ink is clearly visible on both layers of the paper.

After marking the ballot, the voter separates the layers of paper and is allowed to keep either layer of paper as a receipt.[2] The other layer is shredded without anyone except the voter having seen its contents. The receipt is scanned and then retained by the voter, who can use it to perform steps (ii) and (iii) in the E2E construction from Section 2.1.

Both sets of symbols—the column on the top layer and the row on the bottom layer—are randomly ordered on a per ballot basis. In other words, the top symbols on a ballot could be X beside Alice and Y beside Bob or vice versa as in the ballot in the figure; similarly with the bottom symbols. Thus if shown the top layer in the figure, it is not possible to identify whether the symbols on the bottom layer were ordered XY (resulting in a vote for Bob) or YX (a vote for Alice).[3] The same property holds when shown only the bottom layer. For this reason, the voter can ostensibly show her receipt to anyone without violating her privacy. Furthermore, unlike in conventional optical scan voting systems, the scanner does not know which candidate the voter voted for (nor would anyone who hacks into the scanner).

3   Extensive Form of the Ballot Casting Process

To analyse the effective privacy of Punchscan ballot receipts, we will formalize the ballot casting process using game-theoretic conventions.[4] Contract-based attacks will ultimately involve three players—nature (N),[5] the voter (V), and the adversary or influencer (I), whose role will be outlined in the next section. For now, we consider the initial interaction between N and V in ballot casting. The extensive form of this interaction is shown in Figure 2.[6] Nature's first two moves are randomly drawn with equal probability from the action sets $A_{N_1} = \{$Top: XY, Top: YX$\}$ and $A_{N_2} = \{$Bottom: XY, Bottom: YX$\}$ and will define the layout of the ballot given to the voter.

Upon observing N's moves, V chooses a position to mark, left or right, from action set $A_{V_1} = \{$L, R$\}$. In particular, V will choose an action such that a particular candidate will be voted for. V then chooses to keep the top sheet

---

[2] It is important that either layer could be potentially kept. This is for security reasons that we are deliberately omitting, as they are not essential to the results of this paper. For full details, see [15,23].

[3] More properly, it is not possible without knowledge of a secret cryptographic key held by a committee of election trustees, which ties the serial number to the information needed to deobfuscate the vote and produce a verifiable tally.

[4] All game theoretic conventions employed in this paper can be found in most introductory textbooks on the subject (*e.g.*, [21]). Future footnotes will provide additional background on game theoretic concepts as they are used.

[5] When a game incorporates randomness, a special player called nature chooses random actions from a known distribution as needed.

[6] An extensive form diagram is a tree, with the root node defined as the first player to move and a vertex defined for each action the player can take for this move.

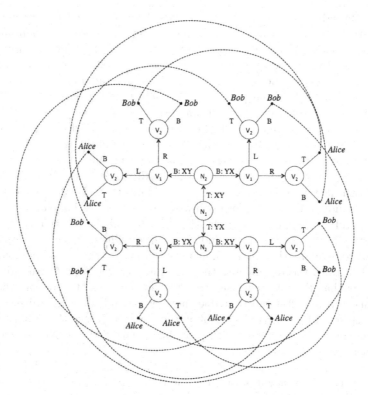

Fig. 2. Extensive form of the ballot casting process, involving the voter and nature, in a Punchscan election. The ballot casting process begins at N_1 and ends at a candidate. The dotted lines represent hidden information.

or bottom sheet: $A_{V_2} = \{T, B\}$. This decision does not influence, of course, which candidate was voted for, however the three previous moves all influence the outcome. This will become important in section 5.2.

The privacy of the receipt comes from the fact that this model contains hidden information. Depending on how V moves, either A_{N_1} or A_{N_2} will be hidden from any observer of the receipt. If one were to only observe V's receipt and not both moves by N, they could only determine the outcome to be in a set of outcomes joined with a dotted line in Figure 2 but not know which outcome. For all outcome sets, the state of the world could be a vote for Alice or Bob with equal probability. For this reason, the privacy of a Punchscan receipt appears very strong, however this does not imply coercion resistance.

4   Contract-Based Attacks

Despite appearances to the contrary, Punchscan receipts can be exploited to bias a voter's choice. This is accomplished through a contract, which is presented to V by the adversary. A contract specifies, for each possible receipt a voter can construct, a payoff the voter will receive for that receipt. Assuming V is utility-maximizing, V will construct her receipt in a way that maximizes her payoff. Using this property, the adversary seeks to offer a contract that will result, on balance, in more votes for his preferred candidate than the other candidates. We study three proposed contracts that accomplish this for two-candidate races, named for their authors: MN [18], BMR [9], and KRMC [17]. These three contracts are not central to their respective works, and thus certain subtleties are glossed over by the authors which we will fill in.

An alternative to contracts suggested in the same literature are scratch-off cards. A scratch-off card, in a race between Alice and Bob, would be a 2 × 2 matrix, with the rows marked X and Y, the columns L and R, and each cell would contain a random T or B underneath a scratch-off layer. The voter is given a new card and instructed to vote for Alice, scratch off the cell that corresponds to the letter beside Alice's name and the position where this letter appears on the ballot received by the voter. The voter then retains the top or bottom layer, as revealed. Both the receipt and the card must be returned to the adversary, who checks that they are consistent. If the voter does not vote for Alice, the voter must scratch off a cell that does not correspond to either Alice's symbol or the position of the asserted symbol on the bottom layer of the ballot. In both cases, the voter will be caught with probability 0.5—if the scratch reveals T in the former case or B in the latter.

Scratch-off cards are attractive since they fix the adversary's ability to gain votes for Alice, while we will show in Section 5.1 that contracts perform worse as the number of candidates increases. By contrast, contracts are attractive because they are informational and can be memorized by voters (especially in the case of voting buying, where the voter has such an incentive). This eliminates the risk of being caught using a scratch-off card or even giving the voter incriminating evidence of the undue influence. In addition, contracts do not need to be secure against physical tampering (scratch-off surfaces can be removed and reapplied). Finally, contracts do not necessarily require the voter to rendezvous with the adversary after the attack. The voter can simply report their serial number and the adversary can retrieve the information from the public record (this assumes the voter does not collude with other voters to misreport their serial number as the serial number of another voter's receipt that coincidently meets the conditions of the contract; a difficult task even if allowed). Our purpose is not to argue that contracts are better than scratch-off cards, merely that contracts have enough interesting advantages to warrant their own thorough study.

4.1   Voter Coercion and Vote-Buying

It is useful to distinguish between voter coercion and vote-buying. As mentioned, the contract will offer payoffs in the form of utility. These utilities are in either two or three amounts with strict ordering: $\{u_0, u_1, u_2 \mid u_2 > u_1 > u_0\}$. Generally, a vote-buying contract will promise positive utilities, such as $u_0 = \$0$, $u_1 = \$5$, and $u_2 = \$10$, while a coercive contract will threaten negative utilities, such as

u_0 as arson against a home, u_1 as slashed tires, and u_2 as nothing happening. Generally participation in vote-buying is voluntary, while coercion is involuntary as no rational voters would opt into a negative utility. We use the term **vote-buying** to refer to a voluntary contract with positive utilities and **coercion** to refer to an involuntary contract with at least one negative utility.

4.2   The MN Contract

The first contract we consider is due to Moran and Naor [18]. It is presented by the authors as a vote-buying contract and is w.l.o.g. biased toward Alice.[7] It is as follows:

$$\text{Contract}_{MN} = \begin{cases} u_1 = \pi_V(L) \\ u_1 = \pi_V(R, T \mid \{XY, \_\_\}) \\ u_1 = \pi_V(R, B \mid \{\_\_, XY\}) \\ u_0 \text{ otherwise} \end{cases}$$

In our notation, this means that V is given a payoff (π_V) equal to u_1 for any receipt where the left position is marked, or a top sheet with symbols XY and the right position marked, or a bottom sheet with symbol order XY and the right position marked. Any other receipt is given u_0. The underscores denote information that is hidden due to the choice of T or B.

The normal form of the contract is shown in Figure 3(a).[8] Since V, the row player, only moves after observing the move made by N, we consider V's best response to each of N's actions separately, which is the highest payoff to V (the first number in the pair of payoffs) in each column. This assumes the voter is utility-maximizing and is only interested in the highest payoff, a simplifying assumption that we will reconsider in Section 5.3.

The second payoff in the pair, with a slight abuse of notation, is to the influencer I and not to the column player N. I receives $+1$ when V votes for Alice and -1 when she votes for Bob. Since I's payoffs are not a function of how much money he is paying to V, this implicitly assumes that money is no object. This is a simplification that we will rectify in Section 5.4.

Recall that N chooses each column with equal probability: 0.25. If the first column is selected, the voter will receive u_1 in any case. It is difficult to interpret what these weakly dominant responses mean to a utility-maximizing voter but

---

[7] All the contracts considered in this paper will be presented in their pro-Alice form for consistency and easy comparison. Due to the symmetric nature of the ballot casting process, any contract can be adopted for Bob instead.

[8] The normal form of a game is a matrix with player 1's action set as the rows and player 2's action set as the columns. The elements contain a tuple: the payoff to player 1 and player 2 respectively for the selection of these actions (however note the deviation from convention in this case). A player's dominant strategy, if one exists, is the selection of an action that will always yield a higher payoff than any other action, and a weakly dominant strategy is the selection of an action that will yield at least as high of a payoff as any other action.

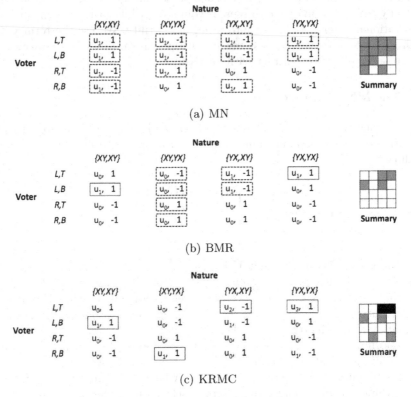

Fig. 3. Three pro-Alice contracts in normal form. Lined boxes are dominant best responses, while dotted boxes are weakly dominant best responses. The underlying game is sequential with the column player moving first; thus each column is a subgame. *Notational abuse:* the first element of the payoff is to the row player, V, while the second element is to the influencer I; not the column player N. This latter utility distinguishes votes for Alice (+1) and for Bob (-1). The summary captures the payoff to the row player, visualizing higher utilities as darker squares.

let us assume the voter will choose randomly between them. This is more problematic in the second column, where the voter has three options: two of which result in a vote for Bob and one for Alice. We could assume the voter, caring only for the payoff, (i) chooses randomly between the two candidates or (ii) chooses randomly between the three options. This has an effect on I's expected payoff. The third column is much like the second, while the final column is the interesting one: both options produce a vote for Alice. Thus I is guaranteed a vote for Alice whenever this column is chosen by N.

We can calculate the probability of this contract resulting in a vote for Alice to be 0.625 under interpretation (i) and 0.54 under interpretation (ii). For all outcomes, I will incur u_1, thus the purchase of a full vote for Alice requires manipulating 1.6 voters for a cost of $(1.6)u_1$ per vote under (i) and 1.85 voters under (ii) for a per vote cost of $(1.85)u_1$. Although proposed as a vote-buying contract, it also works for coercion.

4.3 The BMR Contract

The second contract is due to Bohli, Müller-Quade, and Röhrich[9], and is presented by the authors as a vote-buying contract:

$$\text{Contract}_{BMR} = \begin{cases} u_1 = \pi_V(L, T \mid \{YX, \_\}) \\ u_1 = \pi_V(L, B \mid \{\_, XY\}) \\ u_0 \text{ otherwise} \end{cases}$$

The normal form of the contract is shown in Figure 3(b). A curiosity here is the second column, which yields u_0 regardless. If used coercively, with probability 0.25, the voter cannot escape punishment: there is no way, given a ballot like this from N, to please I. For this reason, we rule out the BMR contract as viable for coercion. The probability of the contract resulting in a vote for Alice is 0.625. This outcome will cost I $(0.75)u_1$ (assuming u_0 is zero). The purchase of a full vote for Alice requires manipulating 1.6 voters for a cost of $(1.2)u_1$ per vote. Thus this contract is better than the MN contract for vote-buying.

4.4 The KRMC Contract

The final contract is due to Kelsey, Regenscheid, Moran, and Chaum [17], and is presented by the authors as a vote-buying contract:

$$\text{Contract}_{KRMC} = \begin{cases} u_2 = \pi_V(L, T \mid \{YX, \_\}) \\ u_1 = \pi_V(L, B \mid \{\_, XY\}) \\ u_1 = \pi_V(R, B \mid \{\_, YX\}) \\ u_0 \text{ otherwise} \end{cases}$$

The normal form of the contract is shown in Figure 3(c). The contract is similar to BMR, only it uses graduated payoffs and includes an additional clause to resolve the ambiguity in the second column of BMR. Every column contains a strongly dominant response, leaving no ambiguity to a utility-maximizing voter. It works for coercion, as well as vote-buying. The probability of the contract resulting in a vote for Alice is 0.75. This outcome will cost the influencer $(0.5)(u_1 + u_2)$. The purchase of a full vote for Alice requires manipulating 1.3 voters for a cost of $(0.5)(u_1 + u_2)$. Since u_2 needs to be only epsilon greater than u_1, this contract is more effective than BMR and MN; more applicable than BMR; and has less ambiguity than BMR and MN.

4.5 The Optimal Contract

We have seen three contracts with different properties and expected votes for Alice. KRMC is the best contract, and we seek to prove that it is optimal for the two-candidate case. We also demonstrate that using more than three levels

Contract Clause		MN	BMR	KMRC
L,T | {XY,__}		u_1	u_0	u_0
L,T | {YX,__}		u_1	u_1	u_2
R,T | {XY,__}		u_1	u_0	u_0
R,T | {YX,__}		u_0	u_0	u_0
L,B | {__,XY}		u_1	u_1	u_1
L,B | {__,YX}		u_1	u_0	u_0
R,B | {__,XY}		u_1	u_0	u_0
R,B | {__,YX}		u_0	u_0	u_1
Perfect:				

Fig. 4. A summary of the three contracts, delimitated by possible clauses

of utility does not increase the expected votes, independent of the number of candidates. Consider Figure 4. The leftmost column shows every possible (most specified) clause that could appear in a contract. While clauses do not have to be fully specified in each variable, such as the first clause in MN, such general clauses are some combination of the most specified clauses: the combination of the first, second, fifth, and sixth clauses in this case.

For each clause, the second column of the figure contains a small grid. This grid is intended to be a visualization of the payoff matrix, like the summaries in Figure 3. Let C be the number of candidates. The rows of the grid represent the voter's binary choice between the top or bottom layer as well as the C-way choice of which position to mark; hence, $2C$ rows. The columns represent the order of the symbols on the ballots. These orderings are random rotations, not full permutations which simplifies the tallying process of Punchscan. There are C^2 possible orderings, not $C!$, and hence C^2 columns. Black cells represent the positions in the payoff matrix that will be affected by adding the clause. For example, if a contract offers a payoff of u_1 for receipts matching the first clause in the figure, u_1 will be added to the two indicated cells in the payoff matrix for the contract: cells (1,1) and (1,2). MN in Figure 3(a) is an example of contract that includes such a clause.

The next three columns summarize the three contracts in the literature and the payoffs they award for each clause. This information can be combined into a concise visualization of the contract by layering the grids associated with each clause on top of each other, where the darker squares represent a higher payoff to V for that outcome. The concise form is shown in the bottom row of each contract.

As a reminder of which outcomes result in a vote for Alice, these outcomes are marked with black cells in the perfect contract in the bottom-left of the figure (*i.e.*, the elements in Figure 3 with payoffs of 1 to I). We refer to these cells as the Alice region of the grid (and the inverse set of cells as the Bob region). The perfect contract is not possible to achieve with the available clauses; however an optimal contract will resemble it as closely as possible.

Continue to consider a contract as a grid, with rows $0 \leq j \leq 2C - 1$ and columns $0 \leq k \leq C^2 - 1$. Each element contains u_i with $i \geq 0$. We note three properties:

P1: For each clause with utility u_i in the contract, a column $\hat{k}$ has u_i added to it in the Alice region.
P2: In P1, u_i is always added to the region of each additional candidate in the same row and some column other than $\hat{k}$.
P3: In P2, the (set of) column(s) is either $\{k | \lfloor \frac{k}{C^2} \rfloor = \lfloor \frac{\hat{k}}{C^2} \rfloor\}$ or $\{k | k \equiv \hat{k} \mod C\}$.

Most specified clauses include a top or bottom layer, T or B, and a marked position that we will now call P_m, where $0 \leq m \leq C-1$, instead of the two-candidate specific terms left and right. Clauses also include an ordering of symbols to appear on the receipt. Consider an arbitrary ordering to be the canonical ordering $\hat{o}$. The other possible orderings are generated by rotating this ordering right or left, which we denote with functions $\texttt{ror}()$ or $\texttt{rol}()$. For example, if $\hat{o} = XY$ then $\texttt{ror}(\hat{o}) = YX$. This set has closure, such that $\texttt{ror}^C(\hat{o}) = \hat{o}$ (*i.e.*, $\texttt{ror}$ applied C times to an ordering is the same ordering).

With these notational conventions, we construct a simple, $\mathcal{O}(C)$ greedy algorithm to select an optimal contract. An optimal contract should have three properties: (**O1**) the highest expected votes for Alice from utility-maximizing voters, (**O2**) no ambiguity (unlike MN), and (**O3**) no columns with all u_0 (unlike BMR). The algorithm selects a contract, w.l.o.g., for the first listed candidate (*i.e.*, a pro-Alice contract). There are many contracts satisfying the properties for optimality—this algorithm finds one instance. It is given in Algorithm 1.

For analysis of the algorithm, we explain each line in terms of the visualization of a contract as a grid. Line 1 of the algorithm adds u_1 to the Alice region in column 1 of the contract's grid. All clauses will add u_1 to the Alice region somewhere (**P1**), thus this clause is no worse than any other clause with respect to **O1**, and it is strictly better than adding no clauses with respect to **O3**.

Algorithm 1. Optimal Contract Generation

---

1 Add to contract: $u_1 = \pi_V(P_0, B | \{\_\_, \hat{o}\})$
2 **for** m *from* 1 *to* $C - 1$ **do**
3 $\quad\lfloor$ Add to contract: $u_1 = \pi_V(P_m, B | \{\_\_, \texttt{ror}^m(\hat{o})\})$

4 **for** m *from* 1 *to* $C - 1$ **do**
5 $\quad\lfloor$ Add to contract: $u_2 = \pi_V(P_m, T | \{\texttt{rol}^m(\hat{o}), \_\_\})$

6 Add to contract: $u_0 = $ otherwise

Lines 2-3 add u_1, on each iteration, to the Alice region in a new column, which is strictly better than not adding additional clauses with respect to **O2**. Each clause never adds u_1 to more than one column, whether in the Alice region or not (following $\{k|k \equiv \hat{k} \mod C\}$ in **P3**), thus it is no worse than any other group of clauses that could be provided. After completion of the loop, every column contains exactly one u_1, satisfying **O3**.

Lines 4-5 add additional clauses. To ensure **O2**, additional clauses have payoff u_2 and are non-overlapping in the columns that they affect. On each iteration, a clause adds u_2 to the Alice region, making it the best response over the u_1 already present in the column. Furthermore, the distribution of the added clauses follows $\{k||\lfloor \frac{k}{C^2} \rfloor = \lfloor \frac{\hat{k}}{C^2} \rfloor\}$ in **P3**, which ensures that the set of each u_2 added to another candidate's region (**P2**) is disjoint from the set of columns where Alice is the best response. Taken together, the addition of these clauses is strictly better than not adding the clause with respect to **O1**.

Line 6 suggests that no more clauses can be added that would improve the contract with respect to **O1** and the contract should be closed. Consider the addition of a clause with u_i. By **P1**, this would add u_i to the Alice region in some column. For it to improve the contract with respect to **O1**, the Alice region of this column must not already contain the highest utility and i must be greater than the highest utility present. All such columns contain u_2; thus all candidate clauses must be u_3. However by **P2**, this would also add u_3 to the regions of the other candidates in other columns. Given the distribution of this addition by either type in **P3**, this would add u_3 to a column that contains u_2 in the Alice region, making Alice no longer a best response for that column. Thus additional clauses cannot improve the contract with respect to **O1**.

Recall that Algorithm 1 finds one instance of the many contracts satisfying the properties for optimality. Running this algorithm for the two-candidate case produces the following contract:

$$\text{Contract}_{opt} = \begin{cases} u_2 = \pi_V(R, T \mid \{YX, \_\}) \\ u_1 = \pi_V(L, B \mid \{\_, XY\}) \\ u_1 = \pi_V(R, B \mid \{\_, YX\}) \\ u_0 \text{ otherwise} \end{cases}$$

This contract is equivalent to KRMC with respect to **O1**, **O2**, and **O3**. Therefore since the output contract is optimal, KRMC is as well.

5   Extending the Base Model

5.1   Multiple-Candidate Contracts

For our first extension to the basic contract, we consider the optimality of a contract as the number of candidates is increased from two to an arbitrary number, C, of candidates. **P1**, **P2**, and **P3** still hold. For an arbitrary C, an optimal contract for Alice can be constructed from the union of the first C columns with payoff u_1 and every additional C^{th} column with payoff u_2.

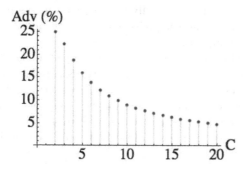

Fig. 5. The advantage of an optimal contract over a random selection as C, the number of candidates, grows. As seen, the advantage appears asymptotic to 0 in the number of candidates.

Figure 5 shows that the advantage an optimal contract offers over forcing a utility-maximizing voter to vote for a random candidate. The two-candidate case had a probability of 75% of resulting in a vote for Alice, which is a 25% advantage over a random choice between two candidates. The probability of a vote for Alice in the three-candidate case is 56%, which is only a 22% advantage (over a random choice between three candidates). Likewise, as C increases, the adversary's advantage decreases.

5.2   Reordering the Game

We now consider the order of play. If V were to choose either R or L prior to N choosing the ballot layout, the candidate voted for would be random. Enforcing this in a contract, without any additional clauses, could be an effective denial of service attack—but it is no better than simply paying the voter to not vote at all. Thus if V is to vote with intention, she can only choose between R and L after observing the moves by N. However the outcome of the game is invariant to whether V chooses T or B, therefore this move could be safely relocated in the sequence of events. If it was chosen by V prior to observing the moves by N, then no contract can be formed that would favour Alice or another candidate. In other words, this simple change solves the problem.

To see why, consider again the properties in Section 4.5. In this new extensive form, **P1** and **P2** still hold. However **P3** does not. If the top sheet is selected, then the set of columns in **P3** will only be $\{k \| \lfloor \frac{k}{C^2} \rfloor = \lfloor \frac{\hat{k}}{C^2} \rfloor\}$. Likewise, if the bottom sheet is selected, the set of columns will only include $\{k | k \equiv \hat{k} \mod C\}$. With this symmetric pairing of columns, there is no way to asymmetrically win a column for Alice without losing one to another candidate.

Requiring the voter to select the top or bottom layer before seeing the ballot is a known solution, and the Punchscan procedure has been subsequently modified to reflect this change. However this change does cause the privacy of the system to be contingent on poll worker procedure, which is a weak foundation for something as critical as ballot secrecy. From the first author's experience, poll workers may not follow procedures exactly, especially when deviation does not affect the voters ability to cast their ballot and the poll-workers do not have a solid mental model of why a procedure is important.

In general, removing decisions that a voter must make during the voting process, especially arbitrary choices made after observing the actions selected by nature can help resolve issues of coercion. However one choice can never be eliminated: selecting a candidate to vote for. For some obfuscation mechanisms in E2E systems, this decision alone may be exploitable. Thus, there is no simple trick—vote casting procedures must always be carefully examined.

5.3   Voter Types

So far, we have considered V to be utility-maximizing and thus follows the contract fully. However, this is not necessarily the case, especially for vote-buying. There may be some voters who will forgo payment and always vote for Alice or Bob. In this case, they are still utility-maximizing: they receive utility that is external to the contract from their political convictions or expected benefits from an elected candidate. Our use of the term utility-maximizing should be interpreted as maximizing only the utility internal to the contract. There may be other "vengeful" voters who would punish the adversary whenever possible: for example, by always choosing to vote contrary to the adversary when given the choice. In the next section, we also consider opportunistic voters who will sell their vote if they are already intending to vote for the adversary's candidate. In all of these cases, the true type of the voter is hidden from the influencer.

Consider a simple split between the fraction of utility-maximizing voters (α) and vengeful voters $(1 - \alpha)$ in the coercion model. The adversary will accept any payoff in the set of best responses. In MN, the expected votes for Alice from a vengeful voter is 0.25. Thus to make ground for Alice, the following expression should hold: $(0.54)\alpha + (0.25)(1 - \alpha) > 0.5$. The means $\alpha > 0.86$ or at least 86% of the voters need to be utility-maximizing for the attack to work. Using the same analysis for BMR, recall that in BMR it is possible for V to obtain a layout from N that has u_0 as a payoff for all moves by V. As a result, a vengeful V can always vote for Bob, even if the payoff is u_0 since V could have plausibly received a bad ballot type. As a result, $\alpha > 0.769$ which means BMR can tolerate a higher proportion of vengeful voters than MN while maintaining profitability. For KRMC, a vengeful voter can at best vote for Bob on half of the columns (by receiving u_1 on the fourth column). Thus any $\alpha > 0$ will produce profitability for KRMC, making it the most resilient of the three.

5.4   Money Is an Object

Consider the vote-buying model. In this case, voters could simply choose to reject the contract, receive u_0, and vote for either Alice or Bob. However, occasionally such strategies will coincidentally allow them to meet the terms of the contract and be paid. Say that the fraction of voters rejecting the contract and voting for Alice is p_a and for Bob is p_b. The fraction that are utility-maximizing and opt into the contract is, as before, α, and the vengeful voters make up the remainder. Unlike in the coercive case, vengeful voters will accept u_0 and thus act like voters in p_b. For KRMC, the expected amount of money paid by the adversary to a voter of a hidden type is,

$$0.5(u_1)(p_a) + 0.25(u_2)(p_a) + 0.25(u_1)(p_b) + 0.25(u_2)(p_b) + 0.5(u_1)(\alpha)$$
$$+0.5(u_2)(\alpha) + 0.5(u_1)(1 - p_a - p_b - \alpha) + 0.25(u_2)(1 - p_a - p_b - \alpha)$$

Before we assumed that money was no object, so the value of this expression is irrelevant. However if money does matter, then the adversary must ensure that he is not paying more for a vote than it is worth to him. The difference between a voter in p_a and α can be rephrased: the latter place less value on their vote and thus will choose to accept a payoff that is higher than the amount of value they place on their vote. Let U_v be the value of u_1 such that α voters will accept the contract; in other words, the maximum value a voter in α places on their vote. Since u_2 only needs to be marginally greater than u_1 (*i.e.*, $u_2 = u_1 + \epsilon$), we can assume for simplicity that they are equivalent. Furthermore, assume that p_a is the same as p_b, since close elections will more plausibly have attempts at undue influence. This reduces the equation above to

$$U_v(0.75 - 0.25(p_a) + 0.25(\alpha)).$$

For it to be profitable for the vote buyer, he expects to influence a share of $0.75(\alpha)$ votes in favour of Alice, and if a vote is worth on average U_b to the buyer then

$$U_v(0.75 - 0.25(p_a) + 0.25(\alpha)) < U_b(0.75(\alpha)).$$

This expression forms a ratio between how much a vote is worth to the coercer and how much it is worth to the voter, and how large the ratio must be for KRMC to be profitable. For example, if $p_a = p_b = 0.45$ and $\alpha = 0.10$, the ratio is 8.17. This means that if 10% of voters value their vote at less than, say, \$10, the buyer should only exploit this opportunity if a vote gained is worth at least \$82 to him. For three candidates, $p_a = p_b = p_c = 0.30$ and $\alpha = 0.10$, the vote should be worth at least \$96 to him.

6   Future Work and Concluding Remarks

We have shown how game theoretic-models can be applied to analysing coercion contracts in E2E voting systems. We developed an algorithm for devising optimal contracts, proved that KRMC is optimal in the two candidate case, and found that the effectiveness of contracts decrease with the number of candidates are added. We also show that no more than two levels of utility are needed and that contracts are costly for the adversary.

We conclude with a few avenues for future work. In paper-based elections, where unrecoverable errors are possible, voters are typically given the option to spoil a ballot and receive a new one. Future work could examine the impact of spoiling on coercion contracts in realistic scenarios, like being allowed up to two spoiled ballots: some voters will spoil to try and receive higher payoffs, others may spoil to avoid meeting the adversary's demands. Voters must strategize whether spoiling is likely to increase or decrease their fortunes when the payoffs are ternary or when there are multiple contests on the ballot, each with its own payoff. It may also be plausible for the adversary to observe when the voter spoils a ballot, and he may adjust his own strategies accordingly.

Our definition of optimality assumes voters are utility-maximizing, and we later study the performance of these contracts in a setting for which they were not optimized: voters with hidden types. We conjecture that reoptimizing the contracts for this setting would not change the contract; however, we leave proof of this for future work. A final topic for further exploration is the potential for adversaries to employ screening techniques to differentiate between voters with hidden types. For example, the payoff could include a contribution to one candidate's campaign to prevent supporters of another candidate from accepting the contract if their receipt coincidentally meets its conditions.

We hope our study of contracts in Punchscan, and the tools we have used in our analysis, is of assistance to the designers of E2E systems. The more we understand these attacks, the easier it will be to design against them.

Acknowledgements. The authors acknowledge the support of this research by the Natural Sciences and Engineering Research Council of Canada (NSERC)—the first author through a Canada Graduate Scholarship, and the second and third through Discovery Grants.

References

1. Adida, B.: Helios: web-based open-audit voting. In: USENIX Security Symposium (2008)
2. Adida, B., Neff, C.A.: Ballot Casting Assurance. In: Electronic Voting Technology Workshop, EVT (2006)
3. Adida, B., Rivest, R.L.: Scratch & vote: self-contained paper-based cryptographic voting. In: Workshop on Privacy in Electronic Society (2006)
4. Bartholdi, J., Orlin, J.: Single transferable vote resists strategic voting. Social Choice and Welfare 8(4) (1991)
5. Benaloh, J.: Ballot Casting Assurance via Voter-Initiated Poll Station Auditing. In: Electronic Voting Technology Workshop, EVT (2007)
6. Benaloh, J.: Secret sharing homomorphisms: Keeping a secret secret. In: Eurocrypt 1986 (1986)
7. Benaloh, J.: Simple veriable elections. In: Electronic Voting Technology Workshop, EVT (2006)
8. Benaloh, J., Tuinstra, D.: Receipt-free secret-ballot elections. In: ACM Symposium on Theory of Computing, STOC (1994)
9. Bohli, J., Müller-Quade, J., Röhrich, S.: Bingo Voting: Secure and Coercion-Free Voting Using a Trusted Random Number Generator. In: Alkassar, A., Volkamer, M. (eds.) VOTE-ID 2007. LNCS, vol. 4896, pp. 111–124. Springer, Heidelberg (2007)

10. Chaum, D., Carback, R., Clark, J., Essex, A., Popoveniuc, S., Rivest, R., Ryan, P., Shen, E., Sherman, A.: Scantegrity II: End-to-End Verifiability for Optical Scan Election Systems using Invisible Ink Confirmation Codes. In: Electronic Voting Technology Workshop, EVT (2008)
11. Chaum, D., Essex, A., Carback, R., Clark, J., Popoveniuc, S., Sherman, A., Vora, P.: Scantegrity: End-to-End Voter Verifiable Optical-Scan Voting. IEEE Security & Privacy 6(3) (2008)
12. Chaum, D.: Secret-Ballot Receipts: True Voter-Verifiable Elections. IEEE Security & Privacy 2(1) (2004)
13. Chaum, D.: Untraceable electronic mail, return addresses, and digital pseudonyms. Communications of the ACM (1981)
14. Chaum, D., Ryan, P.Y.A., Schneider, S.: A practical, voter-verifiable election scheme. Technical Report CS-TR-880, University of Newcastle upon Tyne (2004)
15. Fisher, K., Carback, R., Sherman, A.T.: Punchscan: introduction and system definition of a high-integrity election system. In: Workshop on Trustworthy Elections, WOTE (2006)
16. Juels, A., Catalano, D., Jakobsson, M.: Coercion-Resistant Electronic Elections. In: Workshop on Privacy in Electronic Society (2005)
17. Kelsey, J., Regenscheid, A., Moran, T., Chaum, D.: Hacking Paper: Some Random Attacks on Paper-Based E2E Systems. Frontiers of Electronic Voting (2007)
18. Moran, T., Naor, M.: Split-Ballot Voting: Everlasting Privacy With Distributed Trust. In: ACM Conference on Computer and Communications Security, CCS (2007)
19. Myers, A.C., Clarkson, M., Chong, S.: Civitas: Toward a secure voting system. In: IEEE Symposium on Security and Privacy (2008)
20. Neff, C.A.: A Veriable Secret Shufe and its Application to E-Voting. In: ACM Conference on Computer and Communications Security, CCS (2001)
21. Osbourne, M.J.: An introduction to game theory. Oxford University Press, Oxford (2003)
22. Park, C., Itoh, K., Kurosawa, K.: All/Nothing Election Scheme and Anonymous Channel. In: Eurocrypt 1993 (1993)
23. Popoveniuc, S., Hosp, B.: An introduction to Punchscan. In: Workshop on Trustworthy Elections, WOTE (2007)
24. Rivest, R., Smith, W.D.: Three Voting Protocols: ThreeBallot, VAV, and Twin. In: Electronic Voting Technology Workshop, EVT (2007)
25. Sandler, D.R., Derr, K., Wallach, D.S.: VoteBox: a tamper-evident, veriable electronic voting system. In: USENIX Security Symposium (2008)

Masked Ballot Voting for Receipt-Free Online Elections

Roland Wen and Richard Buckland

School of Computer Science and Engineering
The University of New South Wales
Sydney 2052, Australia
{rolandw,richardb}@cse.unsw.edu.au

Abstract. To prevent bribery and coercion attacks on voters, current online election schemes rely on strong physical assumptions during the election. We introduce Masked Ballot, an online voting scheme that mitigates these attacks while using a more practical assumption: untappable channels are available but only *before* the election. During the election voters cast ballots over completely public channels without relying on untappable channels, anonymous channels or trusted devices. Masked Ballot performs only the voting part of an election and is designed to integrate with counting schemes that compute the final election result.

Keywords: Receipt-freeness, online elections, voting schemes.

1   Introduction

The secret ballot is a fundamental instrument for protecting the freedom of choice of voters. It mitigates bribery and coercion because nobody knows whether voters are lying about how they voted. Replicating the secret ballot in a virtual setting is one of the greatest challenges of designing online election schemes. Although many innovative cryptographic solutions have been put forward, the required high level of secrecy forces these schemes to rely on strong physical assumptions during the election and sometimes also before the election. In this paper we develop a new approach to constructing online voting schemes. Our approach shifts strong assumptions from the election itself to a registration stage before the election so that the voting can take place over insecure public networks such as the Internet.

The underlying difficulty in online elections arises from reconciling confidentiality with verifiability. To prevent bribery and coercion, online elections must be receipt-free, which means voters cannot prove how they voted [2]. Receipt-freeness is an intrinsic property of most traditional elections, where the conventional secret ballot ensures that the votes are completely confidential and that voters have no evidence of how they voted. But online elections must also be both individually verifiable and universally verifiable. Individual verifiability means each voter can confirm the ballot cast corresponds to the intended vote, while universal verifiability means any observer can confirm that the authorities conducted the election

P.Y.A. Ryan and B. Schoenmakers (Eds.): VOTE-ID 2009, LNCS 5767, pp. 18–36, 2009.

correctly. To achieve these strong notions of verifiability, the voting process must publicly expose the ballots to some extent. Then to satisfy receipt-freeness the public ballots must appear ambiguous to conceal the votes. Given a public ballot, the voter's transcript of the ballot construction for a genuine vote must be *indistinguishable* from a fake transcript for any other possible vote.

Receipt-free voting schemes typically provide indistinguishability through the use of secret randomness. In general the ballot construction must contain an element of randomness that remains secret from the voter. Otherwise the ballot transcript suffices as a receipt that unequivocally corresponds to a unique vote. For example suppose that a voter constructs a ballot by probabilistically encrypting a vote. Then the ballot transcript contains the encrypted vote, the plaintext vote and the randomness for the encryption. Anyone can confirm whether the transcript is genuine simply by encrypting the vote with the given randomness and comparing the ciphertext with the ballot. But if the randomness is secret from the voter, then genuine and fake transcripts are indistinguishable.

The dilemma with using secret randomness is that while indistinguishability must hold, the voter must still learn the actual vote that corresponds to the ballot. The authorities could construct the ballots and then secretly reveal the votes to the voters. However a powerful coercive adversary who intercepts all communication between the voters and authorities would learn all the information that a voter knows. In this case the adversary could distinguish between genuine and fake ballot transcripts. To enable voters to generate fake ballot transcripts, receipt-free schemes require physical assumptions that limit the adversary's knowledge of the genuine transcripts. All previous schemes rely on one of the following three alternative assumptions.

1. During the election voters and election authorities have access to untappable channels. The adversary cannot intercept any secret data transmitted via these channels.
2. During the election voters have access to anonymous channels. In addition, before the election voters and election registrars have access to untappable channels.
3. During the election voters have secure access to trusted randomisers that generate secret randomness. In practice the randomisers are trusted devices such as smart cards.

Each approach has practical limitations, for instance untappable channels are difficult to implement over the Internet. To achieve receipt-freeness some strong assumption appears inevitable. However for practical Internet elections it is desirable to avoid such assumptions during the voting.

1.1 Contributions

We introduce Masked Ballot, an online voting scheme that achieves receipt-freeness under a more practical physical assumption: before the election there are one-way untappable channels from a registrar to the voters. As a registration stage in advance of an election is orders of magnitude longer than the voting stage, offline implementations of untappable channels become feasible, for instance by post or face-to-face communication. During the election voters submit their ballots over insecure public channels. In this setting attacks such as forced abstention and forced random voting are unavoidable. The stronger property of coercion-resistance [11] prevents these attacks but additionally requires anonymous channels during the voting. Hence under our assumptions only receipt-freeness is possible. We prove receipt-freeness using Moran and Naor's formal model [15].

Masked Ballot is purely a voting scheme and as such is independent of the vote encoding and counting method. The idea behind the scheme is to disguise each vote with a secret mask. Each voter receives a single-use mask during a registration stage before the election. The registration is a trusted process and voters can generate fake mask transcripts for any possible mask. Then during the election voters construct ballots by combining their votes with their masks. Any party can subsequently unmask the votes in a universally verifiable manner.

The secret mask ensures receipt-freeness. An adversary can force a voter to reveal the masked vote. However the voter can generate a fake mask transcript such that the masked vote is consistent with any fake vote.

1.2 Organisation

Section 2 discusses contemporary approaches to constructing receipt-free online voting schemes. Section 3 defines the security model, Section 4 summarises Moran and Naor's definition of receipt-freeness and Section 5 covers the necessary cryptographic building blocks. Section 6 describes the details of the Masked Ballot voting scheme and Section 7 analyses the security and complexity of the scheme.

2   Related Work

There is extensive literature on receipt-free online voting schemes. We classify the schemes according to the three different physical assumptions and analyse the practical challenges of each approach.

2.1   The Untappable Channels Approach

Many voting schemes use untappable channels during the election [2,9,18,20]. A voter constructs a ballot by interacting with the authorities. The voter and authorities can exchange secret information, such as the vote and zero-knowledge proofs, via untappable channels. Since voters can plausibly lie about this secret information, they can generate fake ballot transcripts for any vote.

Untappable channels pose several challenges. First, implementing completely untappable channels can be problematic. Although in some cases it could be reasonable to assume the Internet provides sufficient protection against eavesdropping, in general a powerful adversary can potentially intercept all communication. Hence it is hard to *guarantee* that eavesdropping is impossible.

Another difficulty is resolving disputes about messages sent via untappable channels. If a voter claims that the secret values sent by an authority are invalid, then only the voter and the authority know which party is dishonest. The inability to resolve such disputes can potentially disrupt the entire election process.

The final concern is the extent of trust in the authorities. Even when the trust is distributed among multiple authorities, a voter must know at least one honest authority in order to safely generate a fake ballot transcript [9]. An adversary potentially knows the genuine transcripts for all communication between the voter and the possibly corrupt authorities. Hence voters can only generate fake transcripts for their communication with known honest authorities. In some cases it might be reasonable to assume that each voter does know an honest authority. For example if each candidate acts as an authority, then a voter's preferred candidate is presumably trustworthy. However in general voters cannot trust any particular authority. For this reason schemes relying on untappable channels typically assume that an adversary cannot corrupt or collude with any authorities to compromise receipt-freeness.

2.2   The Anonymous Channels Approach

Another approach is to use anonymous channels during the election and untappable channels before the election [17]. In contrast to the untappable channels approach, the secret randomness is in an anonymous credential rather than the ballot. During a registration stage before the election, registrars send credentials to the voters via untappable channels. The voter can generate a fake credential transcript for any possible credential and an adversary cannot distinguish between genuine and fake credentials. The voter can use the same credential for multiple elections. During the election each voter submits a credential-ballot pair via an anonymous channel. The credential-ballot pair consists of an encrypted credential and an encrypted vote. Although voters cannot generate fake ballot transcripts, they can submit additional credential-ballot pairs with fake credentials. The anonymous channels ensure the adversary cannot otherwise trace credential-ballot pairs to the voters. All credential-ballot pairs are public but only those with genuine credentials contribute to the election result.

The existence of untappable channels before the election is still a fairly strong physical assumption but the possibility of offline implementations makes it more practical than the use of untappable channels during the election. Resolving disputes is still problematic but at least there is now an opportunity to find a solution before the election begins. However there remains an issue with trust in the registrars. As in the untappable channels approach, a voter must know at least one honest registrar, and so the general assumption is that all the registrars are honest. In addition distributing the trust among multiple registrars can pose an inconvenience for voters, for instance if the voter must exchange data in person with each registrar. For simplicity and convenience, schemes often assume that there is a single trusted registrar [11]. This is fairly reasonable as some degree of trust in the registrar is unavoidable even in traditional elections.

During the election the use of anonymous channels is more practical than the use of untappable channels. Solutions such as public terminals or mix-nets can often provide a sufficient degree of anonymity. However it is hard to guarantee complete anonymity in all cases. For example a mix-net can only conceal the correspondence between its input and output messages. Achieving receipt-freeness would still require the assumption of untappable channels between the voters and the mix-net. Otherwise an adversary who intercepts all communication between the voters and the mix-net can potentially identify the voters and force them to reveal their votes. Furthermore the first server in the mix-net can similarly identify the voters and their votes. Hence the first mix server must be honest.

A limitation with the anonymous channels approach is that a subtle coercion attack is possible by a fully adaptive adversary who can coerce voters at any time, including after the voting period. In contrast to the untappable channels approach, a voter cannot lie about any arbitrary vote. The voter can only submit an appropriate ballot with a fake credential in response to an adversary's instructions during the voting period. If the adversary only coerces a voter after the voting is complete, for instance to check who voted for the local Mafia boss, then the voter cannot reveal a plausible ballot. To counter such attacks a voter must always submit a credential-ballot pair for each possible vote, using the genuine credential only for the desired vote. While this may be acceptable when the number of possible votes is small, it is impractical in the general case.

2.3   The Trusted Randomisers Approach

The final approach is to use trusted randomisers during the election [1,12,13]. A voter constructs a ballot by interacting with a randomiser via an untappable channel. Then the voter submits the ballot over public channels. This is similar to the untappable channels approach, but now a randomiser provides the secret randomness.

In practice randomisers can be implemented by tamper-resistant devices such as smart cards. The untappable channel thus becomes a local channel rather than a network communication channel. Hence this approach can be much more feasible than the untappable channels approach. However smart cards have several drawbacks. Currently, suitable smart cards and card readers are relatively expensive and are not yet widespread. More concerning is the failure model for these devices. Equipment failure may prevent voters from voting, since it can take time to obtain a replacement smart card. Furthermore an adversary who compromises the devices could commit large-scale fraud.

3   Security Model

3.1   Participants

A voting scheme has three types of participants.

Voters. A voter is a participant who can vote in the election. Voters cast ballots and then take no further part in the election.

Registrar. A trusted registrar maintains the electoral roll and ensures that only eligible voters can participate. The registrar interacts with voters before the election but takes no part in the election itself. Although it is possible to distribute the trust among multiple registrars, for simplicity we generally consider only a single registrar.

Authorities. An authority helps to conduct the election. Multiple authorities collaborate to process the ballots and compute the election result. As Masked Ballot performs only the voting and not the subsequent counting, the authorities have a passive role in our scheme.

We assume that the registrar and authorities have large computational, communication and storage resources, but voters might only have limited resources.

3.2 Communication Model

The participants communicate by sending messages via two types of channels.

Untappable channel. An untappable channel ensures that communication is completely private and no eavesdropping is possible. We assume untappable channels provide authentication of both senders and receivers.

Bulletin board. A bulletin board is a public broadcast channel with memory. Participants can post messages but no party can delete or modify posted messages. Any party can read all posted messages. We assume the bulletin board provides authentication of senders.

Before the election each voter can receive messages from the registrar via a one-way untappable channel. During the election voters and authorities post messages to the bulletin board via public channels such as the Internet.

3.3 Adversary Model

We model cheating by a central adversary with the following powers.

Active corruption. The adversary has complete control of corrupt participants. It can privately communicate with corrupt participants and always knows their internal states. The adversary can instruct corrupt participants to arbitrarily deviate from the protocol in any way it desires.

Adaptive corruption of voters. The adversary can corrupt any voter at any time before, during or after the election.

Static corruption of authorities. The adversary can corrupt any authority only at the start of the election.

Threshold corruption. The adversary can corrupt any number of voters but only up to a threshold of authorities.

Adaptive coercion. The adversary can coerce a voter at any time before, during or after the election. It can privately communicate with coerced participants but has no knowledge of their internal states.

Eavesdropping. The adversary can intercept all communication apart from messages sent via untappable channels.

We assume coercion occurs remotely, and the voting environment and device are both secure. The adversary cannot observe voters physically (through cameras or shoulder surfing) or electronically (through malware).

3.4 Security Requirements

The voting scheme must satisfy the following requirements.

Receipt-Freeness. Voters cannot prove how they voted. We provide a formal definition in the next section.

Authenticity. Only eligible voters can participate.

Uniqueness. Each voter has only one vote.

Vote Independence. A voter cannot cast a vote that is some function of another voter's vote. For instance a voter cannot copy another vote without knowing the actual vote.

Individual Verifiability. Each voter can confirm the cast ballot corresponds to the intended vote.

Universal Verifiability. Any observer can confirm the voting is correct.

Robustness. The voting tolerates the corrupt or faulty behaviour of any group of authorities up to a threshold.

4 Receipt-Freeness

Moran and Naor provide a simulation-based definition of receipt-freeness. The definition explicitly permits null vote (abstention and invalid ballot) attacks and random vote attacks, but otherwise captures the full range of attacks by an adaptive adversary. This section summarises the definition. A detailed description appears in Chapter 5 of Moran's thesis [14].

The simulation paradigm establishes the security of a protocol by comparing an ideal specification of the protocol's functionality in an ideal world with the execution of the protocol in the real world. In the ideal world a trusted third party, known as the ideal functionality, accepts inputs from the participants via completely secure channels and then performs the specified computation. In the real world the participants follow the protocol to perform the computation. A protocol is secure if all attacks by an adversary in the real world are also possible in the ideal world. In other words the protocol securely emulates the ideal functionality.

Moran and Naor's definition extends the standard simulation model to capture receipt-freeness. Under this definition a receipt-free protocol requires a coercion-resistance strategy that specifies how coerced voters in the real world respond to the adversary's queries and commands. A scheme is receipt-free if the adversary cannot distinguish whether a coerced voter follows the coercion-resistance strategy or follows the adversary's instructions.

Note that an adversary can still potentially coerce voters by examining only the output of an ideal counting process. For example suppose the counting output includes all the (anonymised) votes. For a plurality election it might be reasonable to assume that the output is receipt-free in almost all cases, but for a preferential election coercion is possible through signature attacks [6]. We address this issue in other work on preferential counting [21].

4.1 The Ideal World

There are n voters $V_1, \ldots, V_n$. Each voter has three secret inputs.

1. An intended vote that the voter wishes to cast.
2. A fake vote that the voter will reveal when resisting coercion.
3. A coercion-response bit that determines whether a voter complies with or resists coercion.

Each voter V_i submits a cast vote v_i to the ideal functionality, which then computes $f(v_1, \ldots, v_n)$ and broadcasts the result. For an honest voter the cast vote is the intended vote. For corrupt or coerced voters, the cast vote may be altogether different. The ideal adversary $\mathcal{I}$ can adaptively corrupt and coerce voters in the following manner.

Corrupting a voter V. V reveals the intended vote to $\mathcal{I}$ and follows $\mathcal{I}$'s instructions to cast any forced vote.

Coercing a voter V. If the coercion-response bit is $c = 1$ then V complies with coercion by revealing the intended vote to $\mathcal{I}$. If $c = 0$ then V resists coercion by revealing the fake vote to $\mathcal{I}$. After coercing the voter, $\mathcal{I}$ can also instruct V to cast any forced vote. If the forced vote is a null vote $\perp$ or random vote $*$, then V complies regardless of c. Otherwise if $c = 1$ then V complies by casting the forced vote and if $c = 0$ then V resists by casting the intended vote.

$\mathcal{I}$'s view contains the intended votes of corrupt voters, either the intended or fake votes of coerced voters (depending on their coercion-response bits), any forced votes of corrupt or coerced voters, the output of the ideal functionality, and the randomness it used.

4.2 The Real World

There are n voters $V_1, \ldots, V_n$ each with an intended vote, fake vote and coercion-response bit as in the ideal world. The voters follow the real-world protocol to submit the cast votes $v_1, \ldots, v_n$ and compute $f(v_1, \ldots, v_n)$. The real-world adversary $\mathcal{A}$ can adaptively corrupt and coercer voters in the following manner.

Corrupting a voter V. $\mathcal{A}$ can send commands and queries to V, who follows $\mathcal{A}$'s instructions exactly. Hence $\mathcal{A}$ can learn V's entire internal view.

Coercing a voter V. $\mathcal{A}$ can send commands and queries to V. If the coercion-response bit is $c = 1$ then V behaves exactly as a corrupt voter. If $c = 0$ then V follows the coercion-resistance strategy to respond to commands and queries.

$\mathcal{A}$'s view consists of the views of corrupt voters, all its communication with coerced voters, all public communication, and the randomness it used.

4.3   Definition of Receipt-Freeness

Definition 1 (Receipt-Freeness). *A protocol is receipt-free if for every real adversary $\mathcal{A}$ there exists an ideal adversary $\mathcal{I}$ who corrupts and coerces exactly the same participants as $\mathcal{A}$, and the following condition holds: for any intended votes $v_1, \ldots, v_n$, fake votes $v'_1, \ldots, v'_n$ and coercion-response bits $c_1, \ldots, c_n$, $\mathcal{I}$ can simulate a view in the ideal world that is indistinguishable from $\mathcal{A}$'s view in the real world, where the distributions are over the randomness used by $\mathcal{I}$, $\mathcal{A}$ and the voters.*

5   Cryptographic Preliminaries

The Masked Ballot voting scheme requires a threshold homomorphic cryptosystem and compatible zero-knowledge proofs to prove certain properties of encrypted messages.

5.1   Threshold Homomorphic Cryptosystem

A homomorphic cryptosystem is a public-key cryptosystem that enables any party to efficiently compute an encryption of the sum or product of two messages given only the encryptions of the individual messages. Suitable candidates are the Paillier cryptosystem [19] and the ElGamal cryptosystem [7].

For concreteness we describe the scheme using Paillier, which is semantically secure under the Decisional Composite Residuosity Assumption. The public key is (g, n), where $n = pq$ is an RSA modulus and $g = n + 1$. All plaintext operations are modulo n and all ciphertext operations are modulo n^2. For simplicity we omit the modular reduction in the notation.

A message $m \in \mathbb{Z}_n$ is encrypted by randomly generating $r \in \mathbb{Z}_n^*$ and computing the ciphertext

$$\llbracket m \rrbracket = g^m r^n \in \mathbb{Z}_{n^2}^* \ .$$

The Paillier cryptosystem is additively homomorphic. For the plaintexts $m_1, m_2 \in \mathbb{Z}_n$,

$$\begin{aligned} \llbracket m_1 \rrbracket \boxplus \llbracket m_2 \rrbracket &= (g^{m_1} r_1^n) \times (g^{m_2} r_2^n) \\ &= g^{m_1 + m_2} (r_1 r_2)^n \\ &= \llbracket m_1 + m_2 \rrbracket \ . \end{aligned}$$

In the threshold version of Paillier [5,8], each authority has a share of the private key. A quorum of authorities must collaborate to decrypt any ciphertext.

5.2   Non-interactive Zero-Knowledge Proofs

Masked Ballot uses two types of non-interactive zero-knowledge proofs: a proof of plaintext knowledge [3] and a designated-verifier proof of correct encryption. A proof of correct encryption [5] shows that a given ciphertext $\llbracket m \rrbracket$ is an encryption of the given plaintext m. Converting this into a designated-verifier proof [10] enables the prover to convince only a specific verifier that the proof is valid. The prover constructs the proof using the verifier's public key and the verifier can generate a fake proof using its private key.

6   The Masked Ballot Voting Scheme

The Masked Ballot voting scheme has three stages: registration, voting and unmasking. The registration stage takes place in advance of the election, and the election itself consists of the voting and unmasking stages. Apart from the use of one-way untappable channels during the registration stage, all communication is via the authenticated bulletin board.

At a conceptual level Masked Ballot is essentially a hybrid of the Juels-Catalano-Jakobsson (JCJ) scheme [11] and the Cramer-Gennaro-Schoenmakers (CGS) scheme [4]. During the registration stage voters obtain secret masks in the same way as credentials in the JCJ scheme. Then during the voting stage voters cast ballots as in the CGS scheme. The important difference is that rather than submitting encrypted votes, voters submit encrypted masked votes. The masked vote combines a mask and a vote using a standard additive secret sharing technique, much like in Moran and Naor's paper-based election scheme [16]. To unmask a ballot the authorities use the homomorphic property of the cryptosystem to combine the encrypted mask from the registration stage with the masked ballot from the voting stage.

Note in the following protocol descriptions we sometimes abuse notation to have $[\![x]\!]$ refer to a variable that contains an encryption of x.

6.1   Initialisation

First the authorities perform the necessary initialisation steps.

1. Set up an authenticated bulletin board and establish access mechanisms for the registrar, authorities and voters.
2. Set up the threshold cryptosystem. Each authority has a secret share of the private key.
3. Publish the public key and any system parameters.

6.2   Registration Stage

In advance of the election, the trusted registrar provides each voter with a secret mask using Protocol 1. The input is the voter's identifier V and public key pk. Voters must only use their masks for a single election.

The untappable channels and designated-verifier proofs prevent other parties from learning any information about the masks. We assume that voters know their private keys, and so they can generate fake mask transcripts for any possible mask. Alternatively voters can provide proofs of knowledge of their private keys [9]. A more simple option is that voters could generate a single-use key pair for

```
1: register(V, pk)
2:     m ← random element of Z_n
3:     ⟦m⟧ ← encrypt(m)
4:     d ← designated-verifier proof for pk that ⟦m⟧ is an encryption of m
5:     post(V, ⟦m⟧) to the bulletin board
6:     send(m, d) to the voter via a one-way untappable channel
```

Protocol 1: Registering a voter

the election and then reveal their private keys to the registrar immediately after they receive their masks.

Distributing the registration among multiple registrars is possible. In this case each registrar follows the single registrar protocol to provide a voter with a mask share. The voter's combined mask is simply the sum of the shares. The homomorphic cryptosystem enables any party to compute the encrypted mask from the posted encryptions of the mask shares. As long as at least one registrar is honest, the mask remains secret. However, as discussed in Section 2, the voter must still know an honest registrar and there must be some procedure for resolving disputes.

6.3   Voting Stage

During the voting stage each voter casts a masked ballot using Protocol 2. The inputs are the voter's secret mask $m \in Z_n$ and vote $v \in Z_n$.

```
1: vote(m, v)
2:     ⟦v − m⟧ ← encrypt(v − m)
3:     p ← proof of plaintext knowledge of ⟦v − m⟧
4:     post(⟦v − m⟧, p) to the bulletin board
```

Protocol 2: Casting a masked ballot

The intuition for receipt-freeness is that $(v - m)$ is identical to any fake vote v' and fake mask m' such that $v' - m' = v - m$. A coerced voter responds to the adversary using the coercion-resistance strategy in Protocol 3.

Since the voting is non-interactive and the adversary cannot observe the voter during the voting, we can consider the voting protocol as an atomic operation. The adversary only knows a voter has completed the voting when the voter posts the ballot. Hence the coercion-resistance strategy varies according to whether coercion of a voter starts before or after the ballot is cast.

Before the ballot is cast the adversary can specify the coerced voter's ballot. The adversary can instruct the voter to abstain or cast an invalid ballot, resulting in a null vote attack. Alternatively the adversary can instruct the voter to cast a valid ballot for a prescribed random value instead of $(v - m)$, resulting in a

---

Coercion-resistance strategy

1: **if** before ballot is cast
2:     $m' \leftarrow$ random element of $\mathbb{Z}_n$
3: **else**
4:     $m' \leftarrow v' - (v - m)$
5: $d' \leftarrow$ fake designated-verifier proof that $[\![m]\!]$ is an encryption of m'
6: follow the adversary's instructions exactly except with fake (m', d') instead of genuine (m, d)

Protocol 3: Coercion-resistance strategy

random vote attack. Otherwise the adversary can instruct the voter to cast a ballot for a forced vote. In this case the voter uses a fake random mask, and so the ballot again contains a random vote. Notice attempts to coerce the voter to cast a forced vote without having the voter commit to the mask are futile.

After the ballot is cast the adversary cannot influence the coerced voter's ballot. The adversary can only learn the fake mask for any given fake vote.

6.4   Unmasking Stage

After the voting stage any party can verify the ballots and unmask the valid ballots using Protocol 4. The input is the voting transcript $\mathbb{T}$, which is the list of public voter transcripts. Each public voter transcript is of the form $(V, [\![m]\!], [\![v - m]\!], p)$, where V is a voter's identifier, $[\![m]\!]$ is the encrypted mask, $[\![v - m]\!]$ is the masked ballot and p is the proof of plaintext knowledge.

1: **unmask**($\mathbb{T}$)
2:     **for** each $(V, [\![m]\!], [\![v - m]\!], p) \in \mathbb{T}$
3:         **if** p is incorrect
4:             post(V, invalid) to the bulletin board
5:         **else**
6:             $[\![v]\!] \leftarrow [\![v - m]\!] \boxplus [\![m]\!]$
7:             post($V, [\![v]\!]$) to the bulletin board

Protocol 4: Unmasking the ballots

6.5   Counting

After unmasking the ballots the authorities use an appropriate counting scheme to compute the election result in accordance with a prescribed electoral system. Intermediate integration steps may be necessary to transform the ballots into a valid form for the counting. The precise integration procedure is specific to each counting scheme.

7 Analysis

7.1 Security

The Masked Ballot scheme satisfies the common security requirements for online voting schemes. We prove receipt-freeness in the next subsection. The proof also implies correctness and robustness.

Authenticity and Uniqueness. The authenticated bulletin board ensures that only eligible voters can submit ballots and that each voter submits only a single ballot.

Vote Independence. The proof of plaintext knowledge ensures that the voter knows the plaintext masked vote.

Individual Verifiability. In the registration stage the proof of correct encryption convinces the voter that the mask is correct. In the voting stage the voter can use the private data to reconstruct the ballot and compare it to the posted ballot.

Universal Verifiability. The unmasking stage requires only deterministic operations on posted messages. Any observer can perform these operations and verify the correctness of the posted results.

7.2 Proof of Receipt-Freeness

To prove receipt-freeness under Definition 1, we construct a simulator in the ideal world and show that an adversary's real-world view is indistinguishable from the simulated view.

In the ideal world, an ideal adversary $\mathcal{I}$ can interact with the ideal voting functionality $\mathcal{F}_{\text{VOTING}}$ (Protocol 5). As Masked Ballot is purely a voting scheme and does not consider the counting, the output of $\mathcal{F}_{\text{VOTING}}$ is simply the list of voters who cast non-null votes.

$\mathcal{I}$ runs a black-box simulation (Protocol 6) using oracle access to the real adversary $\mathcal{A}$. Whenever $\mathcal{A}$ corrupts a voter in the real world, $\mathcal{I}$ corrupts the corresponding voter in the ideal world and learns the intended vote. Whenever $\mathcal{A}$ coerces a voter in the real world, $\mathcal{I}$ coerces the corresponding voter in the ideal world and, depending on the voter's secret coercion-response bit, learns either the intended or fake vote. For corrupt and coerced voters, $\mathcal{I}$ also learns any forced vote provided by $\mathcal{A}$. $\mathcal{I}$ simulates the necessary parts of the voters' real-world views using its knowledge of the votes for corrupt and coerced voters, and all communication with $\mathcal{A}$.

In the real world a voter's view consists of the mask transcript $\mathbb{M}$ and the ballot transcript $\mathbb{B}$. The mask transcript is $\mathbb{M} = (\llbracket m \rrbracket, m, d, pk, sk)$ where:

$\llbracket m \rrbracket$ is the encrypted mask,
m is the mask,

d is the designated-verifier proof that $[\![m]\!]$ is an encryption of m, and

(pk, sk) is the key pair for the proof d.

The ballot transcript is $\mathbb{B} = ([\![v - m]\!], p, v - m, r)$ where:

$[\![v - m]\!]$ is the masked ballot,

p is the proof of plaintext knowledge,

v is the vote,

m is the mask, and

r is the randomness for the encryption $[\![v - m]\!]$ and the proof p.

The voter's public transcript is $\mathbb{P} = ([\![m]\!], [\![v - m]\!], p)$ and the remaining values in $\mathbb{M}$ and $\mathbb{B}$ form the voter's internal view. We need not explicitly consider the unmasking transcript because it is a known, deterministic function of $\mathbb{P}$.

We assume the registration is secure. To generate fake proofs of correct encryption, the designated-verifier property of the proofs must hold. Furthermore the registrar must be honest, otherwise receipt-freeness would be broken. However the encryption of the masked vote and the zero-knowledge property of the proof of plaintext knowledge ensure honest voters would still retain privacy of their votes.

We also assume that the threshold cryptosystem is semantically secure and that some threshold of authorities is corrupted statically but a quorum remains honest. Then the corrupt authorities cannot compromise the protocol execution in any way.

Lemma 1 (Indistinguishability). *$\mathcal{I}$'s simulated view in the ideal world and $\mathcal{A}$'s view in the real world are computationally indistinguishable.*

Functionality $\mathcal{F}_{\text{VOTING}}$	
Vote, V, v	Accept this command from an honest voter V or the adversary if V is corrupt. Store (V, v) and disregard subsequent **Vote** commands for V. If the command is from the voter then notify the adversary that V has voted.
Vote, $V, *$	Accept this command from the adversary if the voter V is coerced. This represents a random vote so randomly choose a vote v, store (V, v) and disregard subsequent **Vote** commands for V.
Vote, $V, \perp$	Accept this command from the adversary if the voter V is corrupt or coerced. This represents an abstention so store a null vote $(V, \perp)$ and disregard subsequent **Vote** commands for V.
BeginVoting	Start accepting **Vote** commands.
EndVoting	Stop accepting **Vote** commands and then output the list of voters who cast non-null votes.
RevealVotes	Reveal the stored non-null votes pairs (V, v) to an ideal counting functionality.

Protocol 5: The ideal voting functionality $\mathcal{F}_{\text{VOTING}}$

Ideal world simulation

Initialisation

$\mathcal{I}$ simulates the generation of the authorities' public key and their shares of the private key. Notice $\mathcal{I}$ can decrypt messages using the authorities' shares of the private key.

Registration Stage

For each voter, $\mathcal{I}$ simulates the generation of the key pair (pk, sk). Notice $\mathcal{I}$ can generate fake proofs with the voter's private key. In addition $\mathcal{I}$ simulates the registration process using Protocol 1 to generate the mask m. Then $\mathcal{A}$ learns $[\![m]\!]$.

Voting Stage

At the beginning of the voting stage send **BeginVoting** to $\mathcal{F}_{\text{VOTING}}$ and then simulate the voters' views.

Honest voter. As the intended vote is unknown, $\mathcal{I}$ randomly selects a vote v and uses the mask m to simulate V's view using Protocol 2. Then $\mathcal{A}$ learns $([\![v - m]\!], p)$ and hence V's public transcript $\mathbb{P} = ([\![m]\!], [\![v - m]\!], p)$.

Corrupt voter. $\mathcal{A}$ can corrupt a voter V either before or after V casts a vote.

1. *Before the vote is cast.* At this point $\mathcal{A}$ only knows $[\![m]\!]$. $\mathcal{I}$ uses the mask m to simulate V's view according to $\mathcal{A}$'s instructions. If any of the instructions cause a null or random vote, then $\mathcal{I}$ submits (**Vote**, $V, \perp$) or (**Vote**, $V, *$) to $\mathcal{F}_{\text{VOTING}}$. Otherwise $\mathcal{A}$ instructs V to submit a valid ballot $([\![v - m]\!], p)$. Then $\mathcal{I}$ derives the forced vote $v = \texttt{decrypt}\,([\![v - m]\!]) + m$ and submits (**Vote**, V, v) to $\mathcal{F}_{\text{VOTING}}$. $\mathcal{A}$ learns V's mask transcript $\mathbb{M} = ([\![m]\!], m, d, pk, sk)$ and ballot transcript $\mathbb{B} = ([\![v - m]\!], p, v, m, r)$.

2. *After the vote is cast.* Originally $\mathcal{I}$ simulated V's view using a random vote v and the mask m. The original transcripts are $\mathbb{M} = ([\![m]\!], m, d, pk, sk)$ and $\mathbb{B} = ([\![v - m]\!], p, v, m, r)$ but at this point $\mathcal{A}$ only knows $\mathbb{P} = ([\![m]\!], [\![v - m]\!], p)$. Now $\mathcal{I}$ learns the intended vote v' and must update the transcripts. It constructs a fake mask $m' = v' - (v - m)$ and a fake proof d' that $[\![m]\!]$ is an encryption of m'. Then $\mathcal{A}$ learns V's updated transcripts $\mathbb{M}' = ([\![m]\!], m', d', pk, sk)$ and $\mathbb{B}' = ([\![v' - m']\!], p, v', m', r)$. Since $v' - m' = v - m$, the updated transcripts match the original public transcript.

Coerced voter. $\mathcal{A}$ can coerce a voter V either before or after V casts a vote.

1. *Before the vote is cast.* The simulation is the same as for a corrupt voter before the vote is cast. The only difference is instead of submitting (**Vote**, V, v) to $\mathcal{F}_{\text{VOTING}}$ for a forced vote, $\mathcal{I}$ submits (**Vote**, $V, *$).

2. *After the vote is cast.* The simulation is the same as for a corrupt voter after the vote is cast. The only difference is the revealed vote could be either the intended or fake vote.

At the end of the voting stage send **EndVoting** to $\mathcal{F}_{\text{VOTING}}$.

Protocol 6: Ideal world simulation

Proof (Sketch). For each voter, the simulated transcripts in Protocol 6 are computationally indistinguishable from the real-world transcripts.

Case 1 (Honest voter). The simulated and real-world public transcripts are $\mathbb{P}_S = (\llbracket m_S \rrbracket, \llbracket v' - m_S \rrbracket, p_S)$ and $\mathbb{P}_R = (\llbracket m_R \rrbracket, \llbracket v - m_R \rrbracket, p_R)$. The difference is that $\mathbb{P}_S$ is for a random vote v' whereas $\mathbb{P}_R$ is for the intended vote v. The semantic security of the cryptosystem ensures the transcripts are computationally indistinguishable.

Case 2 (Corrupt voter: before vote cast). The simulated transcripts are $\mathbb{M}_S = (\llbracket m_S \rrbracket, m_S, d_S, pk_S, sk_S)$ and $\mathbb{B}_S = (\llbracket v - m_S \rrbracket, p_S, v, m_S, r_S)$. These transcripts are consistent with the forced vote v. Then the simulated and real-world transcripts are identical because they are both consistent transcripts for the same forced vote.

Case 3 (Corrupt voter: after vote cast). The simulated ballot transcript $\mathbb{B}_S = (\llbracket v - m'_S \rrbracket, p_S, v, m'_S, r_S)$ is consistent with the intended vote v. However the simulated mask transcript $\mathbb{M}_S = (\llbracket m_S \rrbracket, m'_S, d'_S, pk_S, sk_S)$ is inconsistent because it contains an encryption of m_S instead of m'_S, and a fake proof of correct encryption d'_S. The semantic security of the cryptosystem ensures that even given m'_S, the encryption $\llbracket m_S \rrbracket$ is computationally indistinguishable from any $\llbracket m'_S \rrbracket$. In addition the designated-verifier property of the proof ensures that d'_S is computationally indistinguishable from a genuine proof. Hence such inconsistent transcripts are computationally indistinguishable from consistent transcripts. Then the simulated transcripts are computationally indistinguishable from the consistent real-world transcripts.

Case 4 (Coerced voter: before vote cast). The simulated transcripts are $\mathbb{M}_S = (\llbracket m_S \rrbracket, m_S, d_S, pk_S, sk_S)$ and $\mathbb{B}_S = (\llbracket v - m_S \rrbracket, p_S, v, m_S, r_S)$. The transcripts are consistent with the forced vote v. There are two different sets of real-world transcripts depending on the voter's coercion-response bit c.

If $c = 1$ then the voter behaves exactly as a corrupt voter and casts the forced vote v. As in Case 2 the simulated and real-world transcripts are identical because they are both consistent transcripts for the same forced vote.

If $c = 0$ then the voter follows the coercion-resistance strategy and casts a random vote. The real-world transcripts $\mathbb{M}_R = (\llbracket m_R \rrbracket, m'_R, d'_R, pk_R, sk_R)$ and $\mathbb{B}_R = (\llbracket v - m'_R \rrbracket, p_R, v, m'_R, r_R)$ are for the forced vote v. This is the reverse of Case 3: here the simulated transcripts are consistent but the real-world transcripts have the same inconsistency as the simulated transcripts in that case. Then for the same reasons the simulated and real-world transcripts are computationally indistinguishable.

Case 5 (Coerced voter: after vote cast). The simulated transcripts are $\mathbb{M}_S = (\llbracket m_S \rrbracket, m'_S, d'_S, pk_S, sk_S)$ and $\mathbb{B}_S = (\llbracket v - m'_S \rrbracket, p_S, v, m'_S, r_S)$. There are two different sets of real-world transcripts depending on the voter's coercion-response bit c.

If $c = 1$ then the voter behaves exactly as a corrupt voter and reveals the intended vote v. Since the real-world transcripts are consistent with v, the simulated and real-world transcripts are exactly the same as in Case 3. Then for the same reasons they are computationally indistinguishable.

If $c = 0$ then the voter follows the coercion-resistance strategy and reveals the fake vote v. The real-world transcripts are $\mathbb{M}_R = (\llbracket m_R \rrbracket, m'_R, d'_R, pk_R, sk_R)$ and $\mathbb{B}_R = (\llbracket v - m'_R \rrbracket, p_R, v, m'_R, r_R)$. Now both simulated and real-world transcripts have the same inconsistency as the simulated transcripts in Case 3. Then such transcripts are computationally indistinguishable from consistent transcripts, and hence indistinguishable from each other.

Finally the corrupt and coerced voters who cast null votes are identical in the ideal and real worlds. Hence the voting output (the list of voters who cast non-null votes) is identical in the ideal and real worlds.   □

Corollary 1 (Receipt-Freeness of Masked Ballot). *Under the stated assumptions, the Masked Ballot voting scheme is receipt-free.*

7.3   Complexity

Using typical costs of the underlying cryptographic primitives, we provide estimates of the computational and communication complexity. We use modular multiplication as the unit of measure and assume that a modular exponentiation costs $O(k)$ multiplications for a security parameter k. Encrypting a message and constructing (or verifying) a proof each requires a constant number of exponentiations. The number of modular multiplications performed has the same asymptotic complexity as the number of bits transferred, and so the computational complexity below also refers to the communication complexity.

The cost for each voter is $O(k)$. In the registration stage a voter verifies a designated-verifier proof, which costs $O(k)$. In the voting stage the voter encrypts a vote and constructs a proof of knowledge, which each costs $O(k)$.

In an election with V voters, the cost for the registrar is $O(Vk)$. The cost of performing or verifying the unmasking is also $O(Vk)$.

8   Conclusion

We introduced the Masked Ballot online voting scheme, which achieves receipt-freeness under the physical assumption that there are one-way untappable channels only before the election. Such channels can be realised through offline communication.

Masked Ballot presents a different set of trade-offs from previous receipt-free schemes. The main advantage of our approach is that it particularly suits Internet voting from any light-weight device with network access. A drawback is the need for the voter to securely obtain a single-use mask before each election.

Although several different physical assumptions can be used to construct receipt-free election schemes, none is ideal given the current state of widespread technology. Each approach has its own trade-offs, with advantages in certain settings but practical shortcomings in the general case. In the future tamper-proof smart cards, completely anonymous channels or untappable channels may be easier to implement. But at present these physical assumptions are not generally practical for large-scale elections. Given that there are cryptographic solutions, the challenge is to make them more practical for widespread use.

Acknowledgements

We are grateful to Berry Schoenmakers and Tal Moran for very helpful discussions. We also thank the anonymous referees for many valuable comments.

References

1. Baudron, O., Fouque, P.A., Pointcheval, D., Stern, J., Poupard, G.: Practical multi-candidate election system. In: PODC, pp. 274–283 (2001)
2. Benaloh, J.C., Tuinstra, D.: Receipt-free secret-ballot elections (extended abstract). In: STOC, pp. 544–553 (1994)
3. Cramer, R., Damgård, I., Nielsen, J.B.: Multiparty Computation from Threshold Homomorphic Encryption. In: Pfitzmann, B. (ed.) EUROCRYPT 2001. LNCS, vol. 2045, pp. 280–299. Springer, Heidelberg (2001)
4. Cramer, R., Gennaro, R., Schoenmakers, B.: A Secure and Optimally Efficient Multi-Authority Election Scheme. In: Fumy, W. (ed.) EUROCRYPT 1997. LNCS, vol. 1233, pp. 103–118. Springer, Heidelberg (1997)
5. Damgård, I., Jurik, M.: A Generalisation, a Simplification and Some Applications of Paillier's Probabilistic Public-Key System. In: Kim, K. (ed.) PKC 2001. LNCS, vol. 1992, pp. 119–136. Springer, Heidelberg (2001)
6. Di Cosmo, R.: On Privacy and Anonymity in Electronic and Non Electronic Voting: the Ballot-As-Signature Attack (2007),
   http://www.pps.jussieu.fr/~dicosmo/E-Vote/
7. ElGamal, T.: A public key cryptosystem and a signature scheme based on discrete logarithms. IEEE Transactions on Information Theory 31, 469–472 (1985)
8. Fouque, P.A., Poupard, G., Stern, J.: Sharing Decryption in the Context of Voting or Lotteries. In: Frankel, Y. (ed.) FC 2000. LNCS, vol. 1962, pp. 90–104. Springer, Heidelberg (2001)
9. Hirt, M., Sako, K.: Efficient Receipt-Free Voting Based on Homomorphic Encryption. In: Preneel, B. (ed.) EUROCRYPT 2000. LNCS, vol. 1807, pp. 539–556. Springer, Heidelberg (2000)
10. Jakobsson, M., Sako, K., Impagliazzo, R.: Designated Verifier Proofs and Their Applications. In: Maurer, U.M. (ed.) EUROCRYPT 1996. LNCS, vol. 1070, pp. 143–154. Springer, Heidelberg (1996)
11. Juels, A., Catalano, D., Jakobsson, M.: Coercion-resistant electronic elections. In: Atluri, V., di Vimercati, S.D.C., Dingledine, R. (eds.) WPES, pp. 61–70. ACM, New York (2005)
12. Lee, B., Boyd, C., Dawson, E., Kim, K., Yang, J., Yoo, S.: Providing Receipt-Freeness in Mixnet-Based Voting Protocols. In: Lim, J.-I., Lee, D.-H. (eds.) ICISC 2003. LNCS, vol. 2971, pp. 245–258. Springer, Heidelberg (2004)
13. Lee, B., Kim, K.: Receipt-Free Electronic Voting Scheme with a Tamper-Resistant Randomizer. In: Lee, P.J., Lim, C.H. (eds.) ICISC 2002. LNCS, vol. 2587, pp. 389–406. Springer, Heidelberg (2003)

14. Moran, T.: Cryptography by the People, for the People. PhD thesis, The Weizmann Institute of Science (2008),
    http://people.seas.harvard.edu/~talm/papers/thesis.pdf
15. Moran, T., Naor, M.: Receipt-Free Universally-Verifiable Voting with Everlasting Privacy. In: Dwork, C. (ed.) CRYPTO 2006. LNCS, vol. 4117, pp. 373–392. Springer, Heidelberg (2006)
16. Moran, T., Naor, M.: Split-ballot voting: everlasting privacy with distributed trust. In: Ning, P., di Vimercati, S.D.C., Syverson, P.F. (eds.) ACM Conference on Computer and Communications Security, pp. 246–255. ACM, New York (2007)
17. Niemi, V., Renvall, A.: How to Prevent Buying of Votes in Computer Elections. In: Safavi-Naini, R., Pieprzyk, J.P. (eds.) ASIACRYPT 1994. LNCS, vol. 917, pp. 164–170. Springer, Heidelberg (1995)
18. Okamoto, T.: Receipt-Free Electronic Voting Schemes for Large Scale Elections. In: Christianson, B., Crispo, B., Lomas, T.M.A., Roe, M. (eds.) Security Protocols 1997. LNCS, vol. 1361, pp. 25–35. Springer, Heidelberg (1998)
19. Paillier, P.: Public-Key Cryptosystems Based on Composite Degree Residuosity Classes. In: Stern, J. (ed.) EUROCRYPT 1999. LNCS, vol. 1592, pp. 223–238. Springer, Heidelberg (1999)
20. Sako, K., Kilian, J.: Receipt-Free Mix-Type Voting Scheme - A Practical Solution to the Implementation of a Voting Booth. In: Guillou, L.C., Quisquater, J.-J. (eds.) EUROCRYPT 1995. LNCS, vol. 921, pp. 393–403. Springer, Heidelberg (1995)
21. Wen, R., Buckland, R.: Minimum Disclosure Counting for the Alternative Vote. In: Ryan, P.Y.A., Schoenmakers, B. (eds.) VOTE-ID 2009. LNCS, vol. 5767. Springer, Heidelberg (2009)

Improving and Simplifying a Variant of Prêt à Voter*

Ralf Küsters, Tomasz Truderung, and Andreas Vogt

University of Trier, Germany
{kuesters,truderun,vogt}@uni-trier.de

Abstract. Recently, Xia et al. proposed a variant of Prêt à Voter which enjoys several attractive properties. Their protocol is among the few verifiable and receipt-free paper-based voting protocols resistant against randomization attacks. Trust is distributed among several authorities and the voter interface is relatively simple. Also, approval and ranked elections are supported.

In this paper, we improve and simplify the protocol by Xia et al. Among others, we propose a simpler way of producing ballots, which only involves the encryption and re-encryption of candidate names; homomorphic encryption and proxy re-encryption are not needed. Also, no machine involved in the production of ballots needs to store a secret key. Moreover, unlike the protocol by Xia et al., in our protocol all authorities can be held accountable in case they misbehave in an observable way.

1 Introduction

In the last few years many paper-based voting protocols have been proposed that are designed to achieve (various forms of) verifiability [10] and receipt-freeness/coercion resistance [4], with protocols by Chaum [7], Neff [18], and Prêt à Voter [22,9,24,23,16] being the first such protocols; other protocols include Scratch&Vote [3], PunchScan [6,19], ThreeBallot, VAV, and Twin [21], Split Ballot [17], BingoVoting [5], a protocol by Riva and Ta-Shma [20], and Scantegrity II [8]. Intuitively, verifiability means that the voter is assured that her vote is actually counted as cast. A voting protocol is coercion resistant if it prevents voter coercion and vote buying. In other words, a coercer should not be able to influence the behavior of a voter.

However, only very few of the paper-based protocols proposed so far are resistant against a specific kind of coercion, namely so-called randomization attacks [13] (see, e.g., [21,8,26]). In such an attack the adversary forces the voter to vote in a random way. For example, the voter could be forced to always mark the ballot at a specific position and the coercer may be able to check whether the

---

* This work was partially supported by the *Deutsche Forschungsgemeinschaft* (DFG) under Grant KU 1434/5-1 and 1434/4-2, and the Polish Ministry of Science and Education under Grant 3 T11C 042 30. The second author is on leave from University of Wrocław, Poland.

P.Y.A. Ryan and B. Schoenmakers (Eds.): VOTE-ID 2009, LNCS 5767, pp. 37–53, 2009.

voter marked the ballot as instructed by looking at the voter's receipt. The candidate corresponding to such a mark may change from ballot to ballot. So, the vote may be "random". But this is still a serious manipulation of the election as this attack could be carried out on a large scale and the coercer can check after the election whether or not voters followed his instructions.

The recently proposed protocol by Xia et al. [26], which is a variant of Prêt à Voter that resists randomization attacks, is particularly interesting as it distributes trust among several authorities while at the same time allows for a relatively simple voter interface and supports several electoral systems.

Contribution of this Paper. In this paper, we improve and simplify the protocol by Xia et al. In a nutshell, our protocol works as follows. Ballots are produced by a sequence of printers. This process merely involves the encryption and re-encryption of candidate names under the joint public key of tallying tellers. Ciphertexts printed on the ballot have to be covered by scratch strips. The final ballot has only one covered ciphertext per candidate, plus the printed name of the candidate. The voter interface is very simple. To vote, a voter enters a voting booth, chooses one or more candidates and marks or ranks them, by putting crosses or numbers next to the candidate names, and separates the left and the right-hand sides of the ballots. This does not involve a machine. Scanning of ballots and printing receipts can then be done outside of the voting booth in public, with the assistance of the clerks, if necessary. Tallying the ballots is done by the tallying tellers using a mixnet and distributed decryption. The main features of our protocol are the following:

1. **Distributed trust.** In all stages of the election, trust is distributed among several authorities.
2. **Simple production of ballots.** The production of ballots involves only basic cryptographic tasks, namely public key encryption and re-encryption. The machines (printers) involved in this process are rather simple and do not have to store secret keys. This reduces failures and security leaks.
3. **Simple voter interface.** The voter interface does not involve any complex task. Tasks such as uncovering scratch strips, scanning ballots, and printing receipts are done, under the assistance of clerks, using quite simple machines. This, again, increases the reliability and usability of the protocol. Just as the protocol by Xia et al., our scheme is best suited for elections with a small number of candidates.
4. **Supporting several electoral systems.** Several electoral systems, including approval and ranked elections, are supported.
5. **Coercion resistance.** Coercion resistance, including resistance against randomization attacks, kleptographic attacks, and chain voting, is guaranteed under weak assumptions: We only require one honest member in every group of authorities. The voting terminals for scanning ballots/printing receipts and posting them on the bulletin board may be dishonest. Dishonest parties may cooperate with the coercer. In fact, we identify them with the coercer. Also, the voter may freely communicate with the coercer during the whole voting

process, even in the voting booth. We only assume that the voter may lie about what she sees and does. (So, no pictures or videos may be taken by the voter. But talking on the phone would not be a problem.)

6. Verifiability. Verifiability can be ensured (with high probability), by the proofs authorities have to provide and the audits that are performed by voters, clerks, and auditors.

7. Accountability. Our protocol guarantees accountability of authorities, i.e., single authorities can be held accountable for their misbehavior.

The protocol by Xia et al. enjoys some of the above features. However, there are crucial differences. First, the production of ballots in the protocol by Xia et al. is much more complex, and hence, less reliable and harder to implement: Besides performing re-encryptions, it also needs homomorphic encryption and proxy re-encryption. Moreover, machines are required to decrypt ciphertexts obtained by proxy re-encryption. In particular, these machines need to store secret keys.

In the work by Xia et al., accountability has not been considered. However, it is clear that their protocol does not achieve the same level of accountability as ours. For example, if in their protocol the audit in the production of ballots reveals that the re-encryption has not been performed correctly, then this cannot be traced back to specific participants, only to a group of participants. For this reason, some participants may have a higher tendency to misbehave, and hence, spoil the outcome of the election.

Unlike in this paper, Xia et al. do not provide a security analysis of their protocol. It seems that arguments for verifiability and coercion resistant similar to the ones presented here carry over to the protocol by Xia et al. However, the exact security guarantees are not clear. For example, while our protocol has an explicit mechanism to prevent chain voting attacks, this is not the case in the protocol by Xia et al., although, presumably, such a mechanism could be added.

2   Our Protocol

In this section, we describe our protocol. It consists of four stages: initialization, preparation of ballots, voting phase, and tallying phase. For simplicity of presentation, we first assume that a voter votes for exactly one candidate. Choosing more or no candidate would result in an invalid ballot. We will see in Section 2.8 that this assumption is not necessary. In fact, as already mentioned in the introduction, our protocol supports a wide range of electoral systems.

Before going into the details of the protocol, we provide a brief description of how the election looks like from the voter's point of view.

2.1   Voting from the Voter's Point of View

When a voter enters the polling place, clerks provide her with what we call a *multi-ballot*. A multi-ballot contains exactly one *simple ballot* for each of the possible candidates. An example of a multi-ballot for an election with two candidates is depicted in Figure 1.

Fig. 1. A multi-ballot consisting of two simple ballots for a two candidate election

A simple ballot consists of two parts which can be easily separated. On the left-hand side of a simple ballot a candidate name is printed. This side does not contain any other information. On the right-hand side a serial number and a box is printed, which the voter can mark. There is also a scratch strip which covers some information, namely the encryption of the candidate name, as explained later. Every simple ballot in one multi-ballot has printed on it the same serial number.

Once the voter is provided with a multi-ballot, she enters the voting booth. She marks the box on exactly one of the simple ballots and for *every* simple ballot, including the ones not marked, she separates the left-hand side from the right-hand side and discards the left-hand sides. Note that up to this point, the voter does not have to use any device or machine, which makes this process less error-prone and relatively easy to perform. This is a big advantage in practice.

At this point the voter steps out of the voting booth with the right-hand sides of all simple ballots in her hand. The rest of the process is done in public, under the eyes of and possibly with the help of the clerks. Basically, the scratch strip is removed (by hand or using a machine) and all (right-hand sides of the) simple ballots are scanned and posted on the bulletin board. The voter gets a copy of all of these ballots as her receipt.

2.2 Cryptographic Primitives

We start the detailed description of our protocol with a brief introduction of the cryptographic primitives that we use.

We will use an encryption scheme that allows for random re-encryption and distributed decryption (see, e.g., [11,25,1]). In such a scheme, a group of agents can collectively generate a public key K which can be used to encrypt messages. To decrypt a ciphertext, the participation of all parties involved in generating K is necessary and the parties are required to provide proofs of compliance.

We will also use a universally verifiable re-encryption mixnet. A re-encryption mixnet consists of a set of mix servers $T_1, \ldots, T_m$, where T_1 gets as input an ordered set $\{c_1, \ldots, c_r\}$ of messages encrypted under the public key K and then successively each of $T_1, \ldots, T_m$ in turn applies a random re-encryption to every ciphertext c_i. These re-encryptions are then forwarded in a random order to the next mix server. The output of the mixnet is the output of T_m. This output is a permutation of re-encryptions of $c_1, \ldots, c_r$, if every mix server behaved correctly. As long as the mixnet contains at least one honest server, it should be infeasible to trace a message from the input to the output. In a universally verifiable mixnet the mix servers publish additional information so that for any observer it is possible to ensure that the servers behaved correctly (see, e.g., [12,2]).

2.3 Participants

Beside the voters, the following principals/machines participate in the protocol. Their tasks will be explained in more detail later on.

1. *Bulletin board* BB: This is a kind of write-only, publicly accessible memory. We assume that every message posted by a principal on the bulletin board is signed by that principal.
2. *Auditors* $A_1, \ldots, A_{m_a}$: They perform several kinds of audits.
3. *Printers* $P_1, \ldots, P_{m_p}$: These machines print the ballots. They may be run by different institutions at different locations.
4. *Bundlers* $B_1, \ldots, B_{m_b}$: They perform the final step in compiling multi-ballots.
5. *Clerks* $C_1, \ldots, C_{m_c}$: They conduct the voting process, including issuing multi-ballots to voters and ensuring the correctness of the procedure.
6. *Voting terminals* VT: These machines scan ballots cast by the voters, make copies (receipts) for the voters, and, after the voting phase is finished, post the scanned ballots on the bulletin board.
7. *Tellers* $T_1, \ldots, T_{m_t}$: They tally the ballots in a way specified later.

2.4 Initialization

In the initialization phase, all participants generate their private and public keys, as far as necessary, and put their public keys on the bulletin board, possibly along with a proof that they know the corresponding private key and signatures by some certification authority.

As mentioned in Section 2.2, the tellers $T_1, \ldots, T_{m_t}$ will perform distributed decryption in the tallying phase. Their joint public key, which we denote by K, can be computed publicly from the public keys every teller put on the bulletin board.

Finally, the set of allowed serial numbers is posted on the bulletin board as well as the list of candidates. This can be done by some election supervisors, which we do not specify in detail here.

2.5 Preparation of Ballots

We now describe how multi-ballots are produced. This is done in two steps. First, ballots are printed by the printers $P_1, \ldots, P_{m_p}$. Then, bundlers $B_1, \ldots, B_{m_b}$ do the final compilation. The whole process is audited by the auditors $A_1, \ldots, A_{m_a}$.

Printing of Multi-Ballots. As already mentioned in Section 2.1, a multi-ballot consists of a set of simple ballots, one simple ballot per candidate. Each multi-ballot has a unique serial number. This number is printed on every simple ballot within a multi-ballot.

Initially, the sheets of paper on which simple ballots are printed are a bit larger than in the final ballots in order to accommodate additional information needed for the production of the ballots. However, the additional parts of the (extended) simple ballots are cut off in the last step of the ballot preparation.

Each multi-ballot is prepared by the printers $P_1, \ldots, P_{m_p}$, which iteratively process the multi-ballots. Typically different printers would belong to different institutions in different locations in order to distribute trust. Let us look at the production of one multi-ballot with the serial number sid.

First, P_1 prints, for each candidate name name, an (extended) simple ballot which contains the serial number sid, the candidate name name, and an encryption s_1 of the candidate name name under the joint public key K of the tellers, as depicted in Figure 2, (a); the randomness used for the encryption is chosen freshly for every encryption. Then, P_1 covers the candidate name with a scratch strip (see Fig. 2, (b)).

In this way, P_1 prepares an (extended) simple ballot for each candidate. Together they form a multi-ballot. Before giving this multi-ballot to the next printer P_2, P_1 shuffles the simple ballots within the multi-ballots. In praxis, P_1 would of course not only send one but the set of all multi-ballots prepared by P_1 to P_2.

Now, when P_2 receives a multi-ballot from P_1, P_2 computes re-encryptions of the ciphertexts printed on the simple ballots contained in the multi-ballots, everytime using fresh randomness. For each simple ballot, the corresponding re-encryption is then printed next to the previous ciphertext. In addition, the old ciphertext is covered by a scratch strip. Figure 2, (c) shows a simple ballot after the re-encryption has been printed, where s_1 is the old ciphertext and s_2 is its re-encryption. Figure 2, (d) shows this simple ballot after the old ciphertext s_1 has been covered.

As in the case of P_1, P_2 shuffles the simple ballots of a multi-ballot before giving the multi-ballot to the next printer P_3. Then, P_3 processes the multi-ballot in the same way, and so on.

The last printer P_{m_p} obtains multi-ballots containing simple ballots of the form depicted in Figure 2, (e). It re-encrypts s_{m_p-1}, obtaining s_{m_p}, prints s_{m_p} next to s_{m_p-1} (see Fig. 2, (f)), and then covers both s_{m_p-1} and s_{m_p}, resulting in a simple ballot as depicted in Figure 2, (g).

We assume that independent auditors $A_1, \ldots, A_{m_a}$ make sure that in the process of printing ballots, scratch strips on ballots are never removed. They also make sure that ballots do not get lost or are replaced. However, the auditors do not get to see how exactly the ballots are shuffled. Of course, printers also keep the randomness they use for the encryption (in case of P_1) and re-encryption (in case of $P_2, \ldots, P_{m_p}$) secret.

In case a simple ballot in a multi-ballot is tampered with, this ballot is destroyed and the serial number of this ballot is marked invalid. This fact would then be reported by the auditors on the bulletin board. Potentially, a printer accountable for this tampering could be excluded from the group of printers.

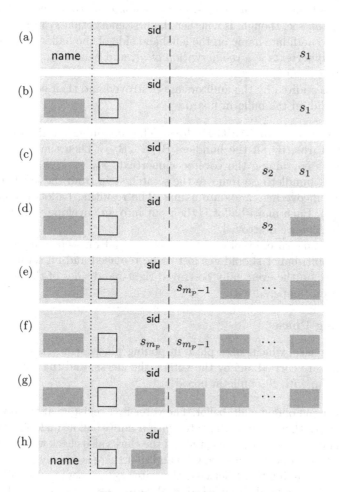

Fig. 2. Preparing ballots

Auditing of Printed Ballots. Beside this "physical auditing" of the printing process, auditors $A_1, \ldots, A_{m_a}$ (or a group of auditors different to the group
mentioned above), check, after the printing process is finished, whether the information printed on the ballots is as specified.

For this purpose, $A_1, \ldots, A_{m_a}$ jointly and randomly (every auditor contributes
her own randomness) pick a fraction of multi-ballots from the set of all printed
multi-ballots.

The auditors remove all scratch strips on these ballots and ask the printers to
reveal the randomness that they have used to perform the encryption (in case of P_1)
and the re-encryption (in case of $P_2, \ldots, P_{m_p}$) in the production of these ballots.

The auditors can then check (in public) whether these ballots have been produced as specified. Of course, they cannot see whether the randomness that the
printers used is really random. However, as we will see in Section 3, as long as

one printer is honest, and hence, uses real randomness, this is no problem. What the auditor *can* see, though, is whether the first encryption s_1 in Figure 2 in fact encrypts the candidate name on the left-hand side of the ballot and whether the rest of the ciphertexts is a re-encryption of s_1, and hence, s_{m_p} is an encryption of the correct candidate name.

All ballots audited by the auditors are destroyed and their serial numbers are marked invalid on the bulletin board.

Final Preparation of Multi-Ballots. The remaining multi-ballots are then shuffled, in turns, by all the bundlers $B_1, \ldots, B_{m_b}$. Then the right-hand sides of the ballots containing the covered ciphertexts $s_{m-1}, \ldots, s_1$ are cut off, say by B_{m_b}. This bundler also removes the scratch strip from the left-hand sides of the ballots, uncovering candidate names. The resulting ballots are depicted in Figure 2, (h). Each multi-ballot is then put into an envelope. The parts cut off from the ballots are destroyed.

Auditors make sure, by physical inspection, that all steps are performed correctly. No multi-ballot should get lost or be replaced and all scratch strips, including those on the eventually destroyed right-hand sides of the ballots should not have been tampered with.

2.6 Voting Phase

The voting phase, which takes place in polling places, consists of the following steps, which are carried out by the voters, the clerks, and the voting terminals, in conjunction with the bulletin board.

V1. Register and obtain multi-ballot. The voter first registers at the polling place. The clerks then provide the voter with a multi-ballot, making sure that the serial number is valid. The voter and the clerks also check whether the multi-ballot has not been tampered with and that there is exactly one simple ballot for every candidate. Otherwise, the voter gets a new multi-ballot and the old one is destroyed and marked invalid on the bulletin board. (The incident is reported and investigated.)

Clerks also record the serial number of the multi-ballot issued to a voter. (Later they make sure that the voter casts a ballot with the same serial number.)

V2. Entering the voting booth and choosing a candidate. The voter enters a voting booth and marks the box of exactly one candidate. All other boxes are left blank. In an election with two candidates, the multi-ballot would now look like the one depicted in Figure 3, (a).

V3. Separating left-hand and right-hand sides. The voter then separates the two parts of every simple ballot, not just the one that she marked (this can be done manually or using a simple cutter). She keeps only the right-hand sides. The left-hand sides can be thrown away. The right-hand sides should be shuffled. The result of this step is depicted in Figure 3, (b).

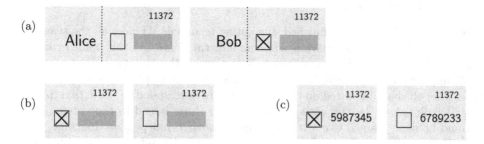

Fig. 3. An example of a multi ballot consisting of two simple ballots for a two candidate election: (a) after step V2, (b) after step V3, (c) after step V5. Note that a copy of (c) is given to the voter as a receipt. The number "5987345" is supposed to be a randomized encryption of "Bob".

Now, the voter leaves the voting booth. We emphasize that up to this point the voter did not have to use any machine or device. All steps performed by the voter thus far were relatively basic and simple, and hence, less error-prone and less susceptible to manipulation.

The rest of the voting process takes place in public.

V4. Auditing by clerks. The clerks check that the voter in fact has separated the left- and the right-hand sides of all simple ballots and that the scratch strips are untouched. The clerks also make sure that the ballots are separated in such a way that there are no visible signs that would allow an observer to match corresponding right- and left-hand sides. Otherwise, the ballots are destroyed, the serial number is marked invalid, and the voter may start the voting process all over again (beginning with step V1) or leave the polling place without voting.

V5. Removing scratch strips. The voter, possibly with the assistance of the clerks or some machine, may now remove the scratch strips from all (right-hand sides) of the simple ballots in her multi-ballot, resulting in a multi-ballot (with only right-hand sides) of the form depicted in Figure 3, (c).

V6. Casting the ballot and obtaining a receipt. The voter, in presence of the clerks, now casts her ballots, i.e. she inserts all the (right-hand sides of) the simple ballots into the voting terminal VT. The clerks make sure that the serial number of these ballots is the same as the one recorded in step V1.

The terminal scans the ballots and checks whether the markings made by the voter are correct, i.e. comply with the election system. If the markings are correct, the terminal provides the voter with a copy of the ballots. Otherwise, the voter is informed that the marking was invalid, without being given a receipt.

As mentioned at the beginning of Section 2, for now we assume that a voter marks exactly one simple ballot. So the terminal would only accept the multi-ballots with exactly one marked box. In this particular case, a voter could cast only the marked simple ballot.

2.7 Tallying Phase

After the voting phase is finished, the voting terminals VT post all the scanned multi-ballots with valid markings on the bulletin board. At this point or later, a voter can check, whether all her ballots (i.e. all the ballots she has receipts of) appear on the bulletin board. Also, at each pooling place, the clerks check whether the ballots posted on the bulletin board correspond to the actual (physical) ballots kept by the voting terminals and those issued to the voters. This could be done manually or with the help of another, independent machine.

Then, the tellers $T_1, \ldots, T_{m_t}$ shuffle and decrypt the set of published ballots, as described below. Recall that each of the published ballots contains a serial number, a ciphertext, and possibly a marking, where the markings of multi-ballots comply with the electoral system used.

Mixing. From the published ballots, the serial numbers are discarded. The ballots are then grouped according to their markings. In our simple setting, we have two groups, one group of ballots with markings and one without. If the marks were numbers, the ballots would be grouped according to these numbers. Every group of ballots is now put through a universally verifiable re-encryption mixnet (see Section 2.2), where the tellers $T_1, \ldots, T_m$ serve as mix servers. (In our simple setting, ballots without marks can be discarded. They do not need to be shuffled or decrypted.) The result of the whole mixing procedure is a list of shuffled and re-encrypted ballots posted by the last teller, one list for each group.

Decrypting. Finally, the tellers collectively decrypt the shuffled and re-encrypted ballots within each group of ballots. The results as well as proofs of compliance of the decryption are posted on the bulletin board.

2.8 Supporting Other Electoral Systems

Up to now, we have assumed, for simplicity of presentation, that every voter marks exactly one of the simple ballots within a multi-ballot. However, it is straightforward to support many other electoral systems, where voters may vote for many candidates or even rank candidates by assigning numbers.

We only need to assume that the pattern of marks (crosses or numbers) chosen by a voter does not reveal any information, e.g., to the clerks in the voting phase, about how a voter voted. If, for example, voters may make either one or two marks, then a clerk can see how many marks a voter made. Therefore, for our protocol to be coercion resistant, we assume that the electoral system is such that only one pattern of markings is allowed.

In case the electoral system allows for different marking patterns one can simply add to a multi-ballot enough of what we call dummy simple ballots, which do not belong to any candidate. For example, if the electoral system allows to vote for zero, one, or two candidates, a multi-ballot could contain two dummy simple ballots and every voter is required to mark exactly two simple ballots. To vote for one candidate, for example, a voter would mark her candidate and one dummy simple ballot.

We assume also that for tallying simple ballots the context of the multi-ballot it belonged to is not relevant. For some electoral systems that might not be true. In this case, the mixing and decryption of ballots should keep simple ballots grouped in multi-ballots. This could for example be done by leaving the serial numbers on the ballots, but encrypting and re-encrypting them in the mixing phase. However, we omit the details.

3   Security Analysis

In this section, we argue that our protocols enjoys verifiability, accountability, and coercion resistance.

3.1   Accountability

We say that a protocol is *accountable* if the following is true: If there is an observable deviation from the protocol (i.e., a participant does not send messages as expected, proofs of compliance are invalid, or an audit step fails), then this deviation can be traced back to every single party who misbehaved, not just an anonymous group of parties. This property is important. Without it there would be a higher tendency to misbehave, and hence, a higher probability for the result of the election to be spoiled. Accountability justifies the assumption that authorities, even if dishonest, do not misbehave in an observable way, if this is likely to be noticed by (honest) auditors/clerks or external observers who can check proofs of compliance of authorities.

To argue about accountability we assume the following:

A1. The bulletin board is honest and there is at least one honest participant in the group of auditors and clerks, respectively.

Accountability of auditors and clerks follows from the assumption that they watch each other and that there is at least an honest member in every group. Misbehavior of bundlers and voting terminals is observed by the checks that clerks and auditors do. Individual tellers can be held accountable due to the proof of compliance each teller has to provide. Misbehavior of printers is detected by auditors. For example, auditors make sure, at least for a fraction of the ballots, that printers can provide the randomness they have used for the encryption or re-encryption of candidate names. Since the encryption and re-encryption performed by every printer is recorded on the (extended) simple ballot, misbehavior can be traced back to every single printer. We note that in the protocol by Xia et al. [26], this is not the case.

3.2   Verifiability

We now show that our scheme is *verifiable* in the following sense. First, a voter, under some weak assumptions (see below), can make sure that her vote is included in the final tally as intended (*individual verifiability*). Second, under slightly stronger assumptions, it can be made sure that the outcome of the election corresponds to the intended votes of all legitimate voters; we call this property *complete verifiability*. Complete verifiability involves that (1) legitimate voters can cast ballots, (2) these ballots are tallied as expected by the tellers, and (3) no other ballots are tallied.

The assumption we need to obtain individual verifiability is the following:

S1. The multi-ballots checked by the auditors in the ballot production phase are chosen randomly and ballots are not altered or replaced before being issued to the voters.

Let us emphasize that this assumption is rather weak. It is, for example, implied by the assumption that there is one honest member in the group of auditors and clerks, respectively.

By assumption S1, the voter can be almost sure, that her ballot is formed correctly. (If t ballots are not formed correctly and 10% of the ballots are audited, then the probability that none of the ill-formed ballots is detected is $\leq 0.9^t$.) Now, universal verifiability of the mixnet plus the proofs provided by the tellers in the decryption phase guarantee that all ballots on the bulletin board are decrypted correctly. So, with the voter's receipts, individual verifiability follows.

To avoid the above assumptions, one could change the protocol in such a way that the voters themselves check whether multi-ballots are formed correctly: They are given two multi-ballots, say, possibly with still extended simple ballots, and randomly choose one of the two multi-ballots to be audited in a publicly verifiable way.

To obtain complete verifiability of our protocol, we, in addition to S1, assume:

S2. There is at least one honest clerk at each polling place.

From this assumption, (1) and (3) from above follow easily by the task that clerks have to perform. Condition (2) follows with S1 as before.

3.3   Coercion Resistance

Intuitively, a voting protocol is coercion-resistant if it prevents voter coercion and vote buying. In other words, a coercer should not be able to influence the behavior of a voter. Below we present a more accurate, but still informal definition of coercion resistance, inspired by the (formal) definition given in [15].

This definition has two parameters. The first one is the goal γ of the coerced voter. This goal is what the voter would try to achieve in absence of coercion. Typically the goal is to vote for some particular candidate (or some particular ranking of candidates). The second parameter of the definition is a set of runs α, which contains almost all runs of the system, except for those that are unlikely to happen and would reveal to the coercer whether or not the coerced voter followed his instructions. For instance, if a particular candidate did not obtain any vote, it is clear that the coerced voter did not vote for this candidate, even though the coercer might have instructed the coerced voter to do so. Therefore, such (unlikely) runs are excluded from the set α.

In the definition of coercion resistance we imagine that the coercer provides the coerced voter with a *coercion strategy* or *instructions* v which the coercer wants the coerced voter to carry out. We do not restrict the set of possible coercion strategies in any way. The coercion strategy may, for instance, simply require the voter to follow the instructions given by the coercer over some communication channel, e.g., a phone. However, the setup is such that the coercer does not get direct access to the interface of the voter in the voting booth. Hence, the voter can lie about what she sees and does in the booth. Now, coercion resistance is defined as follows.

Definition 1 (informal). A voting protocol is *coercion resistant* in α with respect to γ, if for each coercion strategy v that can be carried out by the coerced voter there exists a counter strategy v' that the coerced voter can carry out instead such that

(i) the coerced voter, carrying out v', achieves his own goal γ (with high probability) regardless of the actions of the remaining participants,

(ii) the coercer cannot distinguish (or only with negligible probability) whether the coerced voter carries out v or v', for runs in α.

To prove coercion resistance for our protocol, we make the following assumptions:

C1. The bulletin board is honest and there is at least one honest participant in each of the following groups: auditors, clerks, printers, bundlers, and tellers. We do not assume the voting terminals to be honest. Dishonest participants may cooperate with the coercer.

C2. A voter can freely communicate with the coercer, even in the voting booth. But, in the voting booth, she can lie about what she sees and does.
For example, our protocol is still coercion resistant if a voter talks on the phone with the coercer, even in the voting booth. But a voter should not be able to take pictures or make videos in the voting booth (unless she could manipulate them on the fly, which, however, is unrealistic).

Assumption C2 is justified if electronic devices are forbidden in the voting booth. The use of such devices may even be detectable from outside the voting booth. However, some kind of communication or non-interactice procedure, e.g., by means of scratch cards [14], can still be possible. Our security analysis shows that this kind of communication does not undermine the coercion resistance of our protocol as it is captured by the free communication between the voter and the coercer we allow even in the voting booth. For example, the coercer can just tell the coerced voter what she would see on the scratch card.

Now, we will define γ and α for our protocol and show that for these parameters Definition 1 is satisfied. While we consider only one coerced voter, from theorems shown in [15], the results easily carry over to the case where multiple voters are coerced.

To define γ, we first observe that our protocol, as basically any other paper-based protocol, is prone to forced abstention attack: The coercer may instruct the coerced voter not to vote. To enforce this, the coercer could, for instance, observe the polling place or cooperate with dishonest clerks. Hence, it would be too strong to formulate the goal γ of a voter simply as "the voter successfully votes for a candidate of her choice". The protocol can at most guarantee that *if* the coerced voter casts a valid multi-ballot, she votes for a (ranking of) candidate(s) of her choice, even though the coercer might have instructed her to vote for a different candidate.

However, this is still too strong. If a teller would misbehave in an observable way, i.e., is not able to provide information that shows the compliance of the teller, then voters cannot hope for their votes to be counted correctly. The same is true if a voting terminal misbehaves in an observable way, i.e., if clerks or voters discover that not all scanned ballots have been posted on the bulletin board.

These observations lead to the following specification of γ. For a valid choice (ranking) of candidates z, we say that γ_z is achieved in a given run, if this run satisfies the following condition: If the coerced voter, having cast her multi-ballot, obtains a receipt (which implies that the marking on her multi-ballot is correct) and if the tellers and voting terminals do not misbehave in an observable way as explained above, then she successfully votes for z (i.e. her ballots are published and, when decrypted, show the choice z).

The set α consists of all the runs such that for each valid choice z there exists an honest voter who casts a multi-ballot according to z.

Now, we can prove the following theorem.

Theorem 1. *The protocol proposed in this paper is coercion resistant in α with respect to γ_z, for any valid choice z.*

This theorem implies, for example, that if the coercer wants the coerced voter to vote for some candidate c, then the coerced voter, by performing the counter strategy, can nevertheless vote for her candidate z without being caught by the coercer, given that the run belonged to α. Conversely, the voter cannot prove to the coercer that she voted as intended by the coercer (resistance to vote buying). The theorem also implies that the protocol is not prone to randomization, chain voting, and kleptographic attacks. If these attacks were possible, the coerced voter could not vote for her choice without being detected by the coercer, contradicting the definition of coercion resistance.

Proof sketch of Theorem 1. Let v be a coercion strategy. We construct a counter strategy v' such that the conditions (i) and (ii) of Definition 1 hold for v and v'. The counter strategy v' works as follows: When in the voting booth, the coerced voter follows v in her head. If following v would result in an invalid ballot (e.g., the marking is invalid or the coerced voter is instructed to leave the booth without separating the two parts of the ballots), then the coerced voter performs v. Otherwise, the coerced voter fills in the multi-ballot according to *her own choice* z. (We assume that this can be done quickly.)

Condition (i) of Definition 1. To prove this condition, let us consider a run in which the coerced voter carries out v'. If the coerced voter does not obtain a receipt or if a teller or a voting terminal misbehaves in an observable way, then the goal γ_z is clearly achieved. Otherwise, according to the definition of v', the coerced voter prepares a (valid) multi-ballot according to her own choice z. This multi-ballot must be the one obtained from the clerks, since otherwise the serial number would be wrong (with high probability). Moreover, since by assumption C1 there is at least one honest member in the group of auditors and clerks, respectively, it follows, from the results shown in Section 3.2, that this multi-ballot is formed correctly (with high probability), i.e., candidate names printed in clear and encrypted on simple ballots coincide. Since the voting terminal and the tellers do not misbehave in an observable way, the multi-ballot cast by the coerced voter appears on the bulletin board and is counted correctly.

Condition (ii) of Definition 1. We argue that the information available to the coercer does not allow him to distinguish whether the coerced voter carries out v or v'. First, note that the information available to the coercer, including the information available from dishonest parties, before the coerced voter enters the voting booth is the same in both cases, as up to this point, the coerced voter follows the instructions of the coercer. The same is true for the information the coercer (including dishonest clerks) has right after the coerced voter leaves the booth: If the multi-ballot is not prepared correctly, v' is the same as v, and hence, the information the coercer has is the same independently of whether v or v' is performed. Clearly also all remaining steps will be identical in this case. So, we may from now on assume that the ballot is prepared correctly. Then, right after leaving the voting booth, there is no visible difference between the two cases, because, as we have assumed, all valid markings have the same pattern and all ciphertexts are still covered. Moreover, the serial number has to be the one issued to the coerced voter by the clerks at the beginning of the voting phase, as otherwise the multi-ballot would be invalid.

Now, consider the information available to the coercer (including dishonest clerks and the voting terminal) after the scratch strips are removed from the (valid) multi-ballot of the coerced voter. Due to the auditing in the ballot preparation phase, by (honest) auditors, and the voting phase, by (honest) clerks, the multi-ballot issued to the coerced voter was not manufactured by the coercer and the coercer did not get a chance to uncover scratch strips. Moreover, the honest printer, together with the way candidate names and ciphertexts are covered, make sure that the coercer looses the connection between a candidate name and the ciphertext printed on a simple ballot. Also note that the coercer cannot simply decrypt ciphertexts, as this requires the participation of the honest teller, which we assume in C1.

In the tallying phase, the coercer looses the connections between the ciphertexts on the simple ballots cast by the coerced voter (and printed on the receipts) and the decrypted candidate names, again due to the honest teller.

It is easy to see that information obtained in audits also does not help the coercer to distinguish between carrying out v and v'.

Finally, consider the information sent directly to the coercer by the coerced voter. By the construction of the counter strategy v', this information corresponds to the one provided when carrying out v. Here we use that the coerced voter can lie about what she is actually doing in the voting booth (Assumption C2).

References

1. Abe, M.: Universally Verifiable Mix-net with Verification Work Indendent of the Number of Mix-servers. In: Nyberg, K. (ed.) EUROCRYPT 1998. LNCS, vol. 1403, pp. 437–447. Springer, Heidelberg (1998)
2. Adida, B.: Advances in Cryptographic Voting Systems. PhD thesis, MIT Department of Electrical Engineering and Computer Science (2006)
3. Adida, B., Rivest, R.L.: Scratch & vote: self-contained paper-based cryptographic voting. In: Workshop on Privacy in the Electronic Society (WPES 2006), pp. 29–40 (2006)
4. Benaloh, J.C., Tuinstra, D.: Receipt-free secret-ballot elections (extended abstract). In: Proceedings of the Twenty-Sixth Annual ACM Symposium on Theory of Computing (STOC 1994), pp. 544–553. ACM Press, New York (1994)
5. Bohli, J.-M., Müller-Quade, J., Röhrich, S.: Bingo Voting: Secure and Coercion-Free Voting Using a Trusted Random Number Generator. In: Alkassar, A., Volkamer, M. (eds.) VOTE-ID 2007. LNCS, vol. 4896, pp. 111–124. Springer, Heidelberg (2007)
6. Chaum, D.: http://punchscan.org/
7. Chaum, D.: Secret-Ballot Receipts: True Voter-Verifiable Elections. IEEE Security & Privacy 2(1), 38–47 (2004)
8. Chaum, D., Carback, R., Clark, J., Essex, A., Popoveniuc, S., Rivest, R.L., Ryan, P.Y.A., Shen, E., Sherman, A.T.: Scantegrity II: End-to-End Verifiability for Optical Scan Election Systems using Invisible Ink Confirmation Codes. In: Dill, D.L., Kohno, T. (eds.) USENIX/ACCURATE Electronic Voting Technology (EVT 2008). USENIX Association (2008)
9. Chaum, D., Ryan, P.Y.A., Schneider, S.: A practical, voter-verifiable election scheme. In: de di Vimercati, S.C., Syverson, P.F., Gollmann, D. (eds.) ESORICS 2005. LNCS, vol. 3679, pp. 118–139. Springer, Heidelberg (2005)
10. Chaum, D.: Untraceable Electronic Mail, Return Addresses, and Digital Pseudonyms. Commun. ACM 24(2), 84–88 (1981)
11. Gennaro, R., Jarecki, S., Krawczyk, H., Rabin, T.: Secure Distributed Key Generation for Discrete-Log Based Cryptosystems. J. Cryptology 20(1), 51–83 (2007)
12. Jakobsson, M., Juels, A., Rivest, R.L.: Making Mix Nets Robust for Electronic Voting by Randomized Partial Checking. In: Boneh, D. (ed.) Proceedings of the 11th USENIX Security Symposium, pp. 339–353 (2002)
13. Juels, A., Catalano, D., Jakobsson, M.: Coercion-resistant electronic elections. In: Proceedings of Workshop on Privacy in the Eletronic Society (WPES 2005). ACM Press, New York (2005)
14. Kelsey, J., Regenscheid, A., Moran, T., Chaum, D.: Scratch off attacks on end-to-end voting systems. In: Rump Session of the 28th Annual International Cryptology Conference, CRYPTO 2008 (2008)
15. Küsters, R., Truderung, T.: An Epistemic Approach to Coercion-Resistance for Electronic Voting Protocols. In: 2009 IEEE Symposium on Security and Privacy (S&P 2009), pp. 251–266. IEEE Computer Society, Los Alamitos (2009)

16. Lundin, D., Ryan, P.Y.A.: Human Readable Paper Verification of Prêt à Voter. In: Jajodia, S., Lopez, J. (eds.) ESORICS 2008. LNCS, vol. 5283, pp. 379–395. Springer, Heidelberg (2008)
17. Moran, T., Naor, M.: Split-ballot voting: everlasting privacy with distributed trust. In: ACM Conference on Computer and Communications Security (CCS 2007), pp. 246–255 (2007)
18. Neff, C.A.: Practical High Certainty Intent Verification for Encrypted Votes, http://www.votehere.com/old/vhti/documentation/vsv-2.0.3638.pdf
19. Popoveniuc, S., Hosp, B.: An introduction to PunchScan. In: IAVoSS Workshop on Trustworthy Elections, WOTE 2007 (2007)
20. Riva, B., Ta-Shma, A.: Bare-Handed Electronic Voting with pre-processing. In: USENIX/ACCURATE Electronic Voting Technology, EVT 2007 (2007)
21. Rivest, R.L., Smith, W.D.: Three Voting Protocols: ThreeBallot, VAV and Twin. In: USENIX/ACCURATE Electronic Voting Technology, EVT 2007 (2007)
22. Ryan, P.Y.A.: A variant of the Chaum voter-verifiable scheme. In: Water, Innovation, Technology & Sustainability (WITS 2005), pp. 81–88 (2005)
23. Ryan, P.Y.A.: Prêt à Voter with Paillier Encryption. Technical Report CS-TR 1014, University of Newcastle upon Tyne (2008)
24. Ryan, P.Y.A., Schneider, S.A.: Prêt à Voter with Re-encryption Mixes. In: Gollmann, D., Meier, J., Sabelfeld, A. (eds.) ESORICS 2006. LNCS, vol. 4189, pp. 313–326. Springer, Heidelberg (2006)
25. Sako, K., Kilian, J.: Receipt-Free Mix-Type Voting Scheme — A practical solution to the implementation of a voting booth. In: Guillou, L.C., Quisquater, J.-J. (eds.) EUROCRYPT 1995. LNCS, vol. 921, pp. 393–403. Springer, Heidelberg (1995)
26. Xia, Z., Schneider, S.A., Heather, J., Traoré, J.: Analysis, Improvement, and Simplification of Prêt à Voter with Paillier Encryption. In: Dill, D.L., Kohno, T. (eds.) USENIX/ACCURATE Electronic Voting Technology (EVT 2008). USENIX Association (2008)

Implications of Graphics on Usability and Accessibility for the Voter

Benjamin Smith[1], Sharon Laskowski[2], and Svetlana Lowry[2]

[1] Laboratory for Automation Psychology, University of Maryland
3111 Biology-Psychology Building, College Park, MD 20742 USA
bsmith@lap.umd.edu
[2] National Institute of Standards and Technology
100 Bureau Drive, Gaithersburg, MD 20899 USA
{sharon.laskowski,svetlana.lowry}@nist.gov

Abstract. This paper explores the impact of graphics on the usability and accessibility of voting systems. Graphical elements, as part of voting systems, include both photographs and party logos that indicate specific candidates or political parties, informational icons such as arrows and alert symbols, and animations or other video. After an overview of the history of graphics on ballots, usability and accessibility issues concerning graphics are discussed in detail. The question of whether certain types of graphics would help people with cognitive disabilities vote is then considered in light of research and best practices for usability and accessibility.

Keywords: Accessibility, Animation, Ballots, Graphics, Icons, Logos, Usability, Voter Interface, Voting System.

1 Introduction

The purpose of this paper is to explore the practice of using graphical elements on ballots, the implications for the usability and accessibility of voting systems, and the impact on voters, especially those with cognitive disabilities. It describes the positive and negative impacts of the use of graphics, based on published research literature. The intention is that the findings in this paper will provide a foundation for further research.

There are two major classes of graphical elements: (1) those that that indicate specific candidates or political parties and (2) those used to assist the voter in the process

---

Disclaimer: This paper describes research performed in support of voting system standards and test methods as part of the National Institute of Standards and Technology (NIST) work on the Voluntary Voting System Guidelines for the US Election Assistance Commission. It does not represent a consensus view or recommendation from NIST, nor does it represent any policy positions of NIST. Certain commercial entities, equipment, or material may be identified in the document to describe an experimental procedure or concept adequately. Such identification is not intended to imply recommendation or endorsement by NIST, nor is it intended to imply that these entities, materials, or equipment are necessarily the best available for the purpose.

P.Y.A. Ryan and B. Schoenmakers (Eds.): VOTE-ID 2009, LNCS 5767, pp. 54–74, 2009.
© Springer-Verlag Berlin Heidelberg 2009

of voting. The pictures, icons, and images in the first category are used to accompany the names of the candidates and parties that appear as written text on paper or electronic ballots. The second class includes informational icons and navigational features such as alert symbols, arrows, or animations and videos. Some discussion of ballot design is included to better understand the context in which graphical elements appear, but note that this paper is not intended as a general discussion of ballot design issues.

2 History and Variety of Graphics on the Ballot

Although voting has existed in various forms since ancient times, graphics have only been a part of voting systems for the past two centuries. This section examines the history of voting systems and graphics used in the United States and describes a variety of voting systems employing graphics from other countries as well.

2.1 Ballots in the United States

The word ballot comes from the Italian ballotta, a small ball that was dropped in a specified container to indicate a voter's choice. The container with the most "ballotte" indicated the winner. Variants of this system using corn and beans were used in colonial America but were replaced by other systems (Evans, 1917). Voice votes and the showing of hands were also popular in early America, but aside from party caucuses in a few states, systems like these have been eliminated in US elections due to a lack of secrecy (Reynolds & Steenburgen, 2006). Paper ballots were eventually adopted by every State after the American Revolution and subsequent voting systems have been attempts to improve on this system. The first paper ballots were scraps of paper on which voters wrote the names of their preferred candidates.

By the 1820s, there were so many elected offices that it became difficult to write the names of each candidate, and by the 1830s, the use of printed ballots became legal in some states. These ballots, or tickets, were mass produced by political parties and distributed to voters to cast into the ballot box on Election Day. Citizens did not need to know how to read or write in order to vote. The parties began to print tickets on colored paper, print in color, and use various pictures on the ballot. In some places, new laws required that ballots be cast unfolded and in plain view. These changes eliminated the secrecy of the ballot by allowing partisan observers to determine the votes by looking at the colors or graphics, which enabled vote-selling and coercion (Evans, 1917). The graphics on these ballots included patriotic images like the bald eagle and the American flag, ornate, abstract decorations, and names of political parties in fancy letters. They also included likenesses of the candidates for President and Vice President, although not for lesser offices. Ballots for Abraham Lincoln included pictures of naval battles and trains. Political slogans or cartoons might be included, some of which would be considered offensive by today's standards (Goodrich, 2004). Some ballots were printed with the name of one party, but the names of the candidates from the other party (Smithsonian, 2004).

These and other controversial voting practices led to a reform movement in the late 1800s. A product of that movement was the Australian ballot system. Beginning in the 1880s, election officials printed blanket ballots that contained the names of every candidate for every office. Voters received, marked, and cast ballots at the polling place on Election Day. This restored secrecy to the ballot, and simplified, but did not eliminate the use of graphics. In some places, party symbols were placed next to the name of the party, often in a row across the top of the ballot, with the candidates listed below the name and symbol of the corresponding party (See Figure A, Appendix). This allowed illiterate voters to indicate their choice by marking next to the symbol of their party. Some blanket ballots did not contain party symbols, although these were controversial at the time because they were considered by some to be illegal tests of literacy (Smithsonian, 2004; Evans, 1917).

The graphics used as party symbols were not uniform from one place to another. Although these ballots were in use after the famous Thomas Nast cartoons that led to the modern political party symbols of the Democratic donkey and the Republican elephant, these symbols had not been adopted by the parties and were not on these ballots. Democrats most often used a star and Republicans an eagle (Smithsonian, 2004).

In the 1890s, gear and lever voting machines were introduced and became the dominant voting technology in the US. They were similar to the blanket ballot, but the results could be counted immediately and unambiguously. Like the paper ballots, candidates from a single party were grouped together. Party symbols were still some-times used, but were smaller than on the paper blanket ballots. In places like New York, these continued to be the star and eagle for the two major parties. The eagle was simplified to be recognizable at such a small size, and looks more like a modern icon than the elaborate illustrations of earlier ballots. In some cases, tiny copies of the party symbol were placed next to the name of each candidate. Figure B in the Appen-dix shows an absentee ballot modeled on the lever machines used in New York. These machines often featured pictures of hands pointing to the levers that represent each party. Versions of the pointing finger still exist on many ballots.

Punch cards and optical-scan ballots were introduced in the 20th century to enable computers to count ballots. In punch card systems, voters punch holes in a card to indicate their choices using an external tool and are guided by an external ballot struc-ture indicating which parts of the card to punch for each candidate. In many cases, the cards themselves contain no such information. Optical-scan systems are marked using a pencil on a paper ballot, by filling in a circle or completing an arrow, and are very similar in principle to the original paper blanket ballot but enable counting by com-puter. Some optical scan ballots include illustrations showing how to mark the ballot properly. Instructions for the punch card systems typically appear separately from the ballot itself due to space constraints. The Votomatic punch card system contained arrows that pointed from the candidates' names to the proper place to punch the card, although these arrows appeared misleading to some voters in the 2000 Florida elec-tion. Party symbols could be used on either of these systems, but were rarely used in punch-card systems due to limited space. Oregon recently switched to an all-postal voting system. The Oregon system uses a standard optical-scan ballot without party symbols or candidate photos, but voters are mailed a voter's pamphlet by the state, featuring information about each candidate, supplied by the candidate, and featuring a black-and-white photo of the candidate.

Touch screen or DRE (Direct Record Electronic) systems replace the paper ballot with an electronic display and recording system. These systems have become the second most popular voting technology in the US (Herrnson, et al. 2008). They generally do not feature party symbols, although this would be possible on some of these systems. Voters generally make their selections by touching a computer screen near or on the name of their preferred candidate, or by using external buttons, or an external input device designed for voters with disabilities. The voter's choice is indicated by a checkmark or "X", often colored differently from other elements on the screen. DRE systems are based on personal computer technology and graphical user interfaces. For example, some of these systems rely on user interface elements such as scroll bars and scroll arrows when there is more information to display than will fit on the screen. They also sometimes feature interface metaphors like a virtual three-dimensional button that reacts when touched by having the border colors invert, to suggest that the button has been pushed back, changing how it reflects ambient light.

2.2 Ballots Outside of the US

There are a variety of ballots and voting systems in use outside of the US. The form of government and the needs of the voters determine many aspects of the ballots. It is informative to consider the use of graphics in different contexts to see the degree to which they support usability and accessibility for their voters.

The Guinea-Bissau ballot paper in Figure C simply shows the candidate names and photos.

In South Africa, full-color photographs of the candidates are printed on paper ballots, along with full-color party logos, and the names of the parties. This practice assisted the large population of people who were voting for the first time in 1994, many of whom cannot read. Late changes to the ballot were made by attaching stickers printed with the new candidates' names, photos, and party logos to spaces at the bottom of the ballots. Figure D shows a South African sample ballot from 1994; the actual ballot was similar.

Zimbabwe, in its recent, controversial election, used ballot papers with the names of the candidates and their parties (Figure E), along with photographs of the candidates and detailed party symbols (Kroeger, A., 2008).

New Zealand uses Mixed Member Proportional representation, a system in which people vote twice, on the same full-color paper ballot, for both a party and a specific local candidate for Parliament (Elections New Zealand, 2008). The parties are arranged in one column, and the candidates in another (Figure F). Although the local candidates are often affiliated with a party, a voter may, by splitting the ticket, support a local candidate in a party other than their preferred party, without reducing the proportion of seats held by their preferred party. On these ballots, party symbols appear next to both the names of candidates and the parties, to make it easier to see the relationship between the candidate and the party. Candidate photos are not used. Two informational icons appear at the top of the ballot, each with a sample check mark, and an arrow pointing to the column of blank spaces where the voter is supposed to make their mark. The two check marks are intended to emphasize that the voter should make one mark in each column.

Brazil uses a portable electronic device with a numerical keypad. Voters indicate their choices by entering a number associated with their candidates. The numbers are publicized before the election, and campaign posters feature pictures of the candidates along with the numbers used to select them. The voting system itself does not use graphics of any kind (BBC News, 2002).

3 Usability Issues for Graphics on Ballots

The use of graphics on ballots has been controversial from the beginning. Although many issues surrounding the use of graphics and the implications for the voter have been resolved, new issues have emerged related to the use of electronic voting technologies as well as modern printing capabilities. This section describes arguments for and against adopting graphics as part of voting systems, particularly in the US.

3.1 General Issues Concerning the Use of Graphics on Ballots

In favor. Graphics may help people with low reading ability to vote. This is the main reason party symbols were used on the blanket ballot (Evans, 1917). Voters who know the party they wish to support, and that party's symbol, or who can recognize the faces of their preferred candidates, do not need to read the words on the ballot to find their choices.

Graphics may speed voting even for people with good reading ability. People have a remarkable ability to find visual objects, and graphics could help them find the party symbol or candidate of their choice quickly. Graphical user interfaces take advantage of this ability and have become the dominant form of computer interface (Ware, C., 2004).

Against. Graphics cannot replace words entirely. Although voting instructions should be kept as simple as possible, some necessary instructions cannot be clearly explained with graphics. Furthermore, ballot questions are often quite complex and cannot be fairly translated into pictures.

Graphics are no longer the only way for people who cannot read to vote secretly. The Help America Vote Act of 2002 requires polling places in the United States to have at least one accessible voting station that includes an audio interface for voters who cannot see the ballot. Voters who have difficulty reading can also use these stations to vote independently.

Graphics will appear different on different media and in different environments. Although both paper-based systems and electronic screens usually feature black text on a white background, paper and electronic systems are not identical. Lighting conditions, visual angle, settings, and wear and tear can alter images on an electronic display. Alignment errors, variations in ink level, quality, and color blends, and storage conditions can alter the appearance of printed images. Thus, it is difficult to ensure that graphics will appear similar on all machines, paper ballots, and absentee ballots. Voters who rely on this information might have difficulty voting if the images do not appear as expected or changed from election to election.

Space is at a premium on ballots. When many candidates appear on the ballot for a single race, it is often difficult to fit all of them on at once and still have the text be legible. Space, and thus font size, was the reason that Florida's infamous 2000 butterfly ballot featured presidential candidates in two columns, which led to the confusion (Smithsonian, 2004). In elections like the California gubernatorial recall, there were so many candidates that they had to be displayed on multiple pages, complicating the voting procedure and potentially placing certain candidates at a disadvantage. Any graphics to appear on a ballot must be small, which can interfere with how recognizable the graphic is (Darcy & Schneider, 1989). Different digital formats resize differently, potentially impacting the quality of graphics printed at different sizes.

Additional elements violate the principle of making ballots as simple as possible. Usability experts agree that it is best to keep interfaces free of extraneous features which can be confusing (Norman, D. A. 1988, Nielsen, 2000). On a ballot, poorly designed graphics can make it difficult for voters to find the candidates they prefer. If the graphics do not help, they should not be included.

Providing graphics places extra burdens on candidates and election officials. Candidates must send the graphics they want to all of the election officials preparing ballots featuring that candidate's contest, and election officials must make sure to design the ballot include these graphics properly. This costs money and takes time. Further, it increases the possibility of errors on the ballot and voter confusion. Voter errors due to poorly designed ballots can be difficult to detect, but can be high enough to affect the outcome of an election.

3.2 Party Logos

Account executive: So, who'd you vote for?
Creative Director: Obama, he's got cool logos.
-- New York Ad Agency, Midtown (overheardinnewyork.com, 2008)

In favor. Party logos can help voters find their preferred party's candidates. Humans process images quickly, and do not necessarily need to fixate on an image in order to see it (Ware, 2004). This could help people find their preferred party without having to read the party label of each candidate. This might also help voters quickly determine whether particular parties are running in a specific race.

Party logos can help little-known parties convey a visual message. This could be interpreted as good or bad, but symbols can quickly get simple ideas across.

Against. Party logos are not standardized. Although we often see the Democratic donkey and Republican elephant in the US, these symbols are not at all standard on ballots. Niemi and Herrnson (2003) detail that, in nine states that use party symbols on the ballot, the symbols are different for each state. Competing parties sometimes use similar symbols. Within the past decade, Democrats have used a star, the flag, the Statue of Liberty, roosters, eagles, and donkeys. In the same time frame, Republicans have used eagles and elephants. The Libertarian Party used the Statue of Liberty in some states, but in Missouri, used a mule as their ballot symbol, to force the Democrats to give up the Statue and switch to the well-known donkey. The Reform and Constitution parties use eagles in some places, and in Oklahoma, the Reform party use a star that looked very similar to a star used by the Democratic Party in some states. In Michigan, both the Democratic and Republican parties use symbols that combine the printed name of the party, the flag, and tiny portraits of popular Presidents from their party. Many State parties use symbols that are specific to their state, including outlines of the state map by the Libertarian Party in Utah and state symbols by the Green Party in New Mexico.

Party symbols emphasize political parties over individual candidates. In countries like New Zealand where voters choose parties and candidates separately, symbols are used to help voters identify which candidates represent which party. In the US, political parties are almost always included on the ballot alongside the candidate's name, but it is ultimately a candidate that is elected, not a party.

Some candidates would prefer to use their own logos. Candidates for high office hire graphic designers to create campaign logos and signs (Heller, 2008a, 2008b), and might want to use versions of these symbols in place of generic party symbols. They might want to do this to take advantage of a nationwide visual identity campaign that they believe is effective, or because they wish to play down their association with their political party, due to a hostile political involvement, or to portray themselves as an "independent". But other candidates in the same party, or even a different party, might then want to use the same logo as the candidate at the top of the ticket, to indicate an alliance with that candidate. Voters could be confused that different candidates in the same party have different logos, which could lead to "roll-off," the phenomenon in which people vote for the top office and not lower offices, skewing the outcomes of elections (Darcy & Schneider, 1989).

It is hard to control how a political symbol is used. National parties are protective of their symbols and might be upset by a local candidate with views outside the party's mainstream using their symbol. The Republican Party recently sued cafepress.com for selling goods featuring its elephant logo (Smith, 2008). Further intellectual property disputes would be likely if party logos became an even more important aspect of the electoral process.

Party symbols can be controversial, misleading, or misunderstood. For example, in New York, the Right to Life Party uses a picture of a fetus in the womb as its ballot symbol. The Marijuana Reform Party uses a leaf, presumably representing a marijuana leaf. Many parties simply use the initials of the party name as their ballot symbol, which may have alternative interpretations. New York election law regulates party emblems, but the regulations do not ensure that parties choose symbols or symbols that are consistent across States in the US. Nor can regulations ensure that the symbols do not frustrate, upset, or confuse voters. It is difficult to predict the effect a symbol may have on a voter's performance. For example, does the logo help or hinder voters with poor reading ability or with different cultural backgrounds?

3.3 Candidate Photographs

In favor. Candidate photos can help voters find their preferred candidate. Humans are especially good at recognizing faces, in part due to specialized brain structures devoted primarily to face recognition (Kanwisher, et al., 1997).

Against. Graphical variations can have particularly strong effects on photographs. The factors that may contribute to graphics appearing differently are explained above, but if they made pictures unrecognizable, this could skew the election even more than hard-to-identify party symbols. Viewing an LCD screen from an odd angle can cause colors to invert. Excessive ink in a print run could make a candidate's features impossible to make out. Misaligned color printing is commonplace and could be expensive to correct.

The cost of professional photographs may place a burden on local candidates. Candidates who could not afford a professional photograph would use a lower-quality photograph or no photograph, placing themselves at a disadvantage. Photographs also make late changes to the ballot more difficult.

Photographs invite prejudices and uninformed decisions. In a recent series of experiments (Todorov, et al., 2005, Willis & Todorov, 2006, Ballew & Todorov, 2007), people were shown pictures of actual candidates in US Senate and House elections. Although the participants were not familiar with the candidates, they were able to make judgments about them based on viewing their photographs for a fraction of a second. The surprising finding is that these judgments, particularly the judgment of competence, were significantly correlated with the proportion of votes each candidate received in the actual election, and strongly predicted the winner. Even looking at a photo for a tenth of a second was enough for people to make judgments and predict election winners. The competence judgment was not a substitute for ethnicity or gender, and predicted the winner even when these were the same for both candidates. Placing photographs on the ballot could encourage snap decision making based on superficial information. It could also facilitate voting based on prejudices about ethnicity, gender, age, and anything else that can be gleaned from a photograph.

Candidates might manipulate photos or use visual codes. Candidates might use photographs from when they were younger, or try to make themselves look older to avoid age bias. Changes to appear more competent would probably be useful in light of the findings mentioned above. Politicians routinely have their photographs taken in front of the flag. Candidates can also use backdrops to portray cultural or regional alliances, or use props like a stethoscope or various pins or ribbons to indicate life experience or policy positions, or send coded messages. This could encourage voters to make their decision by looking at the pictures, rather than informing themselves ahead of time about the candidates. In Oregon, where voting is done by mail and voters get a pamphlet from the State featuring photos of the candidates, election officials sometimes have to edit the photos they receive from candidates to make sure they conform to the rules. Notably, an official photograph of George W. Bush was edited to replace a flag in the background with solid gray (Oregon Secretary of State, 2006). Finally, lookalike candidates could run as spoilers, either to intentionally draw votes from a particular candidate, or as a publicity stunt.

3.4 Informational Icons and Illustrations

Although icons are commonly used as interactive parts of a graphical user interface like Mac OS X or Windows, in the context of voting systems, we are using the term icon to mean a small picture meant to convey a concept (Shneiderman & Plaisant, 2005). In this sense, icons are as common on paper ballots as they are on electronic touch-screen systems. This section concerns informational icons, those designed to assist and instruct the voter, not graphics used to represent a particular party or candidate, which are discussed above. Informational icons include arrows and pointing fingers, as well as alert symbols like an exclamation point in a circle.

In favor. Some concepts are more easily explained graphically than in words. A picture of an oval being filled on an optical scan ballot, or an arrow pointing to a critical part of the ballot can get these concepts across quickly and clearly. Text and pictures can reinforce one another to help avoid confusion caused by ambiguous instructions or illustrations. A checkmark or "X" is one of the simplest and clearest ways of indicating how to select a candidate.

Icons can be used to call attention to important instructions. People tend to ignore instructions unless they get stuck (Galitz, W., 2007). An example ballot by Design for Democracy (2007) uses an alert icon, a circle with an exclamation point inside it, next to the unusual instruction to vote for three candidates in a contest that will have three winners instead of the usual one.

Icons can be used to illustrate quantity without using numbers. The bars indicating mobile phone reception are a common example. In a voting context, the settings on an electronic system can be illustrated with icons. In a prototype voting interface, Bederson (described in Herrnson, et al., 2008) used a combination of colors and numbers to show how many contests had been voted.

Many informational icons are cross-cultural, and do not need to be translated when ballots have to be translated, although there are important exceptions noted below.

Against. Icons can be misinterpreted. Icons based on small illustrations of real objects depend on the viewer being familiar with that object. Fernandes (1995) notes that some objects differ in their appearance regionally and internationally; as do the meanings of common hand gestures. The common pointing finger seen in many ballots could be offensive in places where it is rude to point, or where the left hand is taboo (the left hand is often shown pointing to each row of candidates). While these cultural preferences may not apply to systems used in the US, it is important to be careful in the use of symbols to avoid confusion. Even symbols that are not offensive may be ambiguous. A raised index finger can be pointing up or indicating the number one, depending on the context, and would be a poor choice for an interface that should be as simple as possible.

Illustrations must be made carefully to be as clear as possible. This usually means clean and simple line drawings that accurately reflect the actual system in use, not photographs.

Icons and illustrations, like all graphics, add to the visual complexity of a screen or page. An illustration of every step of a process, or an icon next to every element, will distract the voter and slow the voting process.

Icons have to be designed in accordance with good design principles and verified with usability testing to establish that the meanings are easily understood by voters. Confusion such as, "Can I press this alert icon for more information? Should I fill the circular icons on this paper ballot? Do I need to press this arrow to see more candidates or contests?", distracts voters from accurately completing their ballots.

3.5 Animations and Video

In favor. Short, simple animated sequences are often used in computer interfaces to illustrate actions. This technique has been adopted by some manufacturers of electronic voting systems to illustrate unfamiliar techniques. For instance, some systems require the voter to insert a card into a slot on or near the machine as a security measure. This is somewhat akin to inserting a card into an automated teller machine, but the mechanics are different. A short animation is used to show how the card goes into the slot.

Animations can help people learn to use interactive systems quickly, and many people prefer them to explanations without animation (Shneiderman & Plaisant, 2005). Interactive tutorials can be particularly useful for learning complex interfaces. In a voting context, a tutorial would likely take more time than it was worth, and the need for examples might confuse or subtly bias some voters. One simple but effective kind of animation for providing help is the use of virtual sticky notes that appear near important parts of the interface and briefly explain their function (Shneiderman, 2002, Kang, Plaisant, & Shneiderman, 2003).

Instructional videos showing people voting could help familiarize people with unfamiliar procedures. Selker (2007) suggests showing such videos to people as they wait in line to vote. This idea has the potential to make voters more familiar with voting procedures and speed up voting.

Against. Animations, by their nature, take time. If they can convey their message faster than text alone, they may be worthwhile. If they take too long, or are not clear, they will only delay the voting process and confuse voters. It is therefore essential to carefully review and test every animation that is included in a voting interface to ensure that it is clear, concise, and gets its point across faster than text alone.

Animations can be distracting. Animations displayed on a screen while the voter was performing any action not related to the animation, such as a decorative waving flag, should be avoided. Animated characters would probably do more harm than good. Microsoft's Office Assistant, known as "Clippit," was supposed to be cute and provide help by offering suggestions, but it annoyed people and interfered with their work (Shneiderman & Plaisant, 2005).

Instructional videos showing people voting could help familiarize people with unfamiliar procedures, but must be used carefully. First, such videos would take more time than the brief animations showing a single step like inserting a card. They could also be annoying, and would also raise issues of what kind of people to show: their age, gender, and ethnicity, but perhaps even more importantly, the presence or absence of specific disabilities.

Animations or videos can cause seizures in some people with epilepsy. This is especially true when there is a flicker between 2 and 55 Hz. This is why blinking text or graphics, and any choppy, repeated animation are avoided by usability experts. These kinds of graphics can cause visual fatigue and are often annoying even to people without epilepsy (WebAIM, 2008, Shneiderman & Plaisant, 2005).

4 Do Ballot Graphics Help Voters with Cognitive Disabilities?

Historically, graphics have been used on ballots for decoration, to inform or to persuade voters. They have also been used to deceive voters or take away the secrecy of the ballot. But the reason graphics were first included on official ballots was to make voting easier for people who would have had trouble with a text-only ballot. Are graphics still necessary or useful for this purpose? In this section, we will consider a number of cognitive disabilities that can make text-based voting systems difficult to use and whether the use of graphics on the ballot could affect the voting process for people who have these disabilities.

Cognitive disabilities are the extra difficulties some people have performing certain mental tasks. These difficulties can be very specific, although they may be caused in many ways, which we describe only briefly below to illustrate the scope of this issue. From the perspective of designing for accessibility, it is important to understand the effects, and try to design interfaces to make mental tasks easier for people with each disability (WebAIM, 2008).

4.1 Sources of Cognitive Disabilities

In the US, learning disabilities affect over 7.5% of population, most commonly in the form of reading difficulties called dyslexia (Pastor & Reuben, 2002). Difficulties specific to math and writing also affect some people. People with learning disabilities have normal or above average intelligence, but their specific impairments often persist into adulthood.

Intellectual disabilities are marked by low overall intelligence and are found in about 1% - 3% of the population. It caused by a variety of genetic and environmental factors, although the specific cause is not always known (Lewis, 2007). Intellectual disabilities can inhibit social behavior in addition to cognitive skills.

Dementias are marked by progressive memory loss, confusion, and difficulty with language, but symptoms may vary greatly from one day to another. Alzheimer's disease affects four million Americans, and along with other dementias, will become more common as the population ages (Kantor, 2006).

Brain damage can be caused by injury or disease. About 1.4 million people are treated for Traumatic Brain Injuries, or TBI, annually, including skull fractures and concussions. Many more concussions go untreated. Five million Americans require daily assistance due to TBI (National Institute of Neurological Disorders and Stroke, 2008). Language deficits (called aphasia) caused by brain damage include difficulty reading and writing.

Over 780,000 strokes occur annually in the US, causing cognitive and motor deficits. Strokes can lead to general cognitive deficits, memory and language problems, and neglect disorders, in which a person disregards part of their visual field (National Institute of Neurological Disorders and Stroke, 2008).

4.2 Designing to Accommodate Cognitive Disabilities

Over the past few decades, there has been a major push in the design of devices and interfaces towards the idea that technology should be made to work for the widest possible audience. People differ in age, sex, cultural background, physical size and abilities, cognitive styles and abilities, and the technologies they use. Objects and interfaces designed with only one group in mind may be impossible or difficult to use for a different group. However, there are ways of designing technology such that it is usable for a broad audience, and many of these innovations improve the experience for all users, or at least do not make it worse. Shneiderman, who coined the term "universal usability" to describe this philosophy, makes the analogy to the curb cuts in sidewalks that were designed to help people in wheelchairs cross the street, but also help people pushing strollers (Shneiderman & Plaisant, 2004). The most important principle of universal usability is to meet the needs of the users. In this section, we will consider the needs of users with cognitive disabilities, and discuss the design choices, for voting systems and ballots, that may meet these needs.

Bohman and Anderson (2005) identify six categories of functional cognitive disabilities: language comprehension (including reading ability), memory, attention, visual comprehension, math comprehension, and problem-solving. This section addresses ways that interfaces are adapted to be as usable as possible for people with these disabilities.

Reading ability. As discussed in Section 2, graphics are sometimes used to help people with low reading ability to vote, but they are not the only method. Low reading ability refers to several distinct problems, which may overlap in some people. People with the learning disability dyslexia, or with brain damage, may have good language skills in general, but trouble reading words. People with intellectual disabilities usually have low reading ability. Reading can be difficult for people with low vision or who are not fluent in the language on the ballot. Audio interfaces and standards for legible text and plain language can help in many of these cases.

People with dyslexia often use computer-generated speech to help them with text-based web pages (Marshall, 2007). Multiple media formats are recommended by some experts as useful for people with cognitive disabilities (Jiwani, K., 2001). Using audio and text together may help users with some reading ability, as the audio and text will reinforce each other, and the user can still benefit from the visual aspects of the interface. In addition, some dyslexics need clear, simple, consistent graphic navigational icons. Flashing text, font variations, distracting sounds and animations, and textured, patterned backgrounds will cause problems (Marshall, 2007).

Plain language is a movement towards making text easy to read by choosing simple words and familiar grammatical structures. The US Government has been moving towards writing documents intended for the public in plain language. Plain language is not only intended to help people with poor language or reading skills, but also for everyone else by making the information faster to read and more clear (plainlanguage.gov). Short, unambiguous instructions can help avoid the confusion that leads to spoiled ballots (Scott, 2008). Consider the differences between the instructions "vote for one," and "one to be elected," or even "you may vote for one, less than one, but not more than one." The last two are actual instructions found on ballots in Louisiana and South Carolina, respectively (Niemi & Herrnson, 2003). The plain language guidelines described by Redish (2006) include putting instructions in chronological order, and close to the parts of the interface they describe.

Verbal comprehension. Some people have trouble with language in general, which can be worse than simply having trouble reading. For instance people with autism have trouble with non-literal language like irony, idioms, or metaphor (WebAIM, 2008), often regardless of the mode in which the message is conveyed. To accommodate this disability, experts recommend language that is simple and straightforward with explanations of any unusual terms or phrases. The plain language standards described above can meet many of these needs. Supplemental information sources such as audio, illustrations, or a good help system may help people with verbal comprehension disabilities vote independently. It is difficult to know whether graphics would help people by providing an alternative to language, or simply confuse them by adding extraneous information.

Memory and attention. Some people with TBI, Attention Deficit Disorder (ADD), or intellectual disabilities often have lower attentional control and memory abilities than other people. Minimizing the amount of information that needs to be remembered is a universal goal in interface design (Shneiderman & Plaisant, 2005), and is particularly important for people with memory or attention disabilities. It is poor design, in general, to require people to remember their earlier votes or the meanings of unfamiliar symbols in order to use an interface. The interface should be kept free of distracting elements like unnecessary text or graphics. However, icons can be used to attract attention to important parts of a ballot that might otherwise be missed (Design for Democracy, 2007).

Visual comprehension. On ballots, graphics are often used to supplement text and draw attention to important parts, and this use is recommended by some experts (Design for Democracy, 2007). Cluttered designs or overreliance on icons are bad for most users, but particularly for people with poor object recognition abilities due to brain damage. Icons that rely on wordplay or specific cultural knowledge are generally considered bad for interfaces intended to reach a broad audience (Fernandes, 1995), and could be particularly difficult for users with visual comprehension problems. Graphics should be accompanied by words that convey the same message. Clean line drawings are often more effective than photographs (Fernandes, 1995, Design for Democracy, 2007). Certain kinds of brain damage can limit a person's ability to recognize faces (Kanwisher at al., 1997). For these voters, photographs or drawings of candidates would be of no value.

Mathematics comprehension. Very little math should be necessary to vote. The biggest challenge regarding voters' math comprehension is preventing undervoting and overvoting, which are voting for too few and too many candidates in a race, respectively and this needs to be conveyed as clearly as possible to the voters. Overvoting is prevented in electronic systems. Undervoting cannot be prevented, in part because it may be the voter's intention to vote for fewer than the maximum candidates in a race. However, undervoting can be brought to the attention of the voter in either an electronic voting system or an optical scanner to allow the voter to correct accidental undervotes. Textual or graphical cues (such as an icon in a focal color, for example, yellow or a symbol that will capture users' attention) can help alert a voter (Herrnson, et al, 2008).

Problem-solving ability. Interfaces should be designed to make it clear what actions are available, and hide any irrelevant options. Part of the motivation for plain language is to take the guesswork out of understanding instructions. People who have particular difficulty with problem solving will be greatly helped by well-designed interfaces, including clear graphical cues (Serra & Muzio, 2002, Shneiderman & Plaisant, 2005, WebAIM, 2008).

Finally, voters, for the most part, prefer to vote independently rather than rely on assistance from either family or poll workers. This need for independence may lead to reluctance to ask for help, even if the voter does not know what to do (Selker, 2007). Some voters with cognitive disabilities may not think of themselves as disabled, may feel some stigma associated with their disability, or may simply not wish to bother poll workers. As a result they do not ask for help or to use assistive technologies. The research suggests that for these voters with cognitive disabilities, and for all voters, voting technologies must be designed to be universally usable and this includes usability and accessibility of the graphical elements.

5 Conclusions

Much of the discussion in this paper reflects best practice of interface design based on human factors, usability, and accessibility research. The analysis in this paper reveals the underlying complexity of the effect of graphical elements on ballots and electronic voting systems. However, there is only a small amount of research that focuses on voting systems, such as (Design for Democracy 2007) and (Selker 2007). In particular, the use of graphics on ballots has been suggested as a way to address the needs of voters with cognitive disabilities. However, specific research is needed to establish that graphics indeed will support these voters. Research does show that basic universal usability concepts and plain language address many of the cognitive issues and is helpful to all voters.

6 Future Research

There are two basic questions about the usability and accessibility of graphics on ballots. First, do graphics on the ballot affect the usability of voting systems or influence voting patterns? Second, do graphics on the ballot provide better accessibility for voters with cognitive disabilities?

6.1 Usability Research

Usability is most often studied with careful observation by the researcher one-on-one with the user interacting system. To understand how the design of graphical elements affects voting systems for the majority of users, however, requires a different approach (Hernnson, et al. 2008). This typically involves simulated elections and large numbers of participants. The participants go through the election process as if voting.

The goal here is not to compare systems, but features of systems with careful experimental design. We would like to know whether a graphical feature affects the accuracy or speed of voting and whether it affects voters' decisions. This approach could be used to investigate potential problems with graphics on the ballot such as poorly reproduced photos or candidates' appearances.

6.2 Accessibility Research

Do graphics make ballots more or less accessible for people with cognitive disabilities? The link between the disability and the technology to alleviate it is not as obvious as audio systems for the blind or input devices for those with dexterity problems. A further complication is that many people with what we are here calling cognitive disabilities do not consider themselves disabled, and vote using standard voting technology as opposed to special accessible systems. People with more severe cognitive disabilities may not vote often or are used to having people help them vote, including marking their ballots for them.

Research and best practices have shown that, in general, the best way to make interfaces accessible to people with cognitive disabilities is to make them as clear and simple as possible. Many of the technologies that help people with other kinds of disabilities to vote, such as audio, external control devices, and adjustable text, will help people with cognitive disabilities as well. But, is it possible that graphically-based systems will help those who cannot use text? This would be a case in which graphics could be the difference between being able to vote and not. Experiments could be designed to explore the effectiveness of party logos, candidate photos, and informational graphics. Participants with a wide variety of cognitive disabilities could be used to test various implementations of graphics on voting systems.

References

1. Argersinger, P.H.: New Perspectives on Election Fraud in the Gilded Age. Political Science Quarterly 100(4) (1985)
2. Baker, P.M.A., Roy, R.G.B., Moon, N.W.: Getting Out the Vote: Assessing Technological, Social and Process Barriers to (e)Voting for People with Disabilities. In: The Twenty-Seventh Annual APPAM Research Conference, Washington, DC (2005)
3. Ballew, C.C., Todorov, A.: Predicting political elections from rapid and unreflective face judgments. Proceedings of the National Academy of Sciences 104(46), 17948–17953 (2007)
4. BBC News. Brazil's vote – fast but fiddly. BBC News (October 7, 2002), http://news.bbc.co.uk/2/hi/americas/2300051.stm (retrieved July 18, 2008)
5. Darcy, R., Schneider, A.: Confusing Ballots, Roll-Off, and the Black Vote. The Western Political Quarterly 42(3), 347–364 (1989)
6. Design for Democracy. Effective Designs for the Administration of Federal Elections (2007), http://www.aiga.org/resources/content/4/2/8/3/documents/EAC_Effective_Election_Design.pdf (retrieved July 25, 2008)
7. Dubner, S.J., Levitt, S.D.: Why Vote? The New York Times Magazine, (November 6, 2005), http://www.nytimes.com/2005/11/06/magazine/06freak.html (retrieved July 24, 2008)
8. Elections New Zealand (2008) (web site), http://www.elections.org.nz/
9. Evans, E.C.: A History of the Australian Ballot System in the United States. The University of Chicago Press, Chicago (1917)

10. Fernandes, T.: Global Interface Design: a Guide to Designing International User Interfaces. Academic Press Inc., Boston (1995)
11. Goodrich, M.: 19th Century Ballots from California (2004),
    http://www.votingtechnologyproject.org/ballots/huntington/
    MainPage.htm (retrieved June 23, 2008)
12. Heller, S.: To the Letter Born. Campaign Stops: Strong Opinions on the 2008 Campaign. The New York Times (April 2, 2008),
    http://campaignstops.blogs.nytimes.com/2008/
    04/02/to-the-letter-born/ (retrieved June 24, 2008)
13. Heller, S.: McCain's Optimum Look. Campaign Stops: Strong Opinions on the 2008 Campaign. The New York Times (April 21, 2008),
    http://campaignstops.blogs.nytimes.com/2008/04/21/
    mccains-optimum-look/ (retrieved June 24, 2008)
14. Herrnson, P.S., Niemi, R.G.: Beyond the Butterfly Ballot: The Complexity of U. S. Ballots. Perspectives on Politics 1, 317–326 (2003)
15. Herrnson, P.S., Niemi, R.G., Hanmer, M.J., Bederson, B.B., Conrad, F.C., Traugott, M.W.: Voting Technology: The Not-So-Simple Act of Casting a Ballot. Brookings Institution Press, Washington (2008)
16. Jiwani, K.: Designing for users with Cognitive Disabilities (2001),
    http://www.otal.umd.edu/uupractice/cognition/
    (retrieved July 24, 2008)
17. Kang, H., Plaisant, C., Shneiderman, B.: New approaches to help users get started with visual interfaces: multi-layered interfaces and integrated initial guidance. In: Proceedings of the 2003 annual conference on Digital government research. ACM, Boston (2003)
18. Kantor, D.: Alzheimer's disease and Dementia. Medline Plus Medical Encyclopedia (2006),
    http://www.nlm.nih.gov/medlineplus/ency/article/000760.htm
    and http://www.nlm.nih.gov/medlineplus/ency/article/000739.htm
    (retrieved July 21, 2008)
19. Kanwisher, N., McDermott, J., Chun, M.M.: The Fusiform Face Area: A Module in Human Extrastriate Cortex Specialized for Face Perception. The Journal of Neuroscience 17(11), 4302–4311 (1997)
20. Kroeger, A.: Film of Zimbabwe 'vote-rigging.' BBC News (July 5, 2008),
    http://news.bbc.co.uk/2/hi/africa/7491077.stm (retrieved July 18, 2008)
21. Lewis, R.A.: Mental retardation. Medline Plus Medical Encyclopedia (2007),
    http://www.nlm.nih.gov/medlineplus/ency/article/001523.htm
    (retrieved July 8, 2008)
22. Marshall, A.: Web Design for Dyslexic Users. Downloaded (2007) (July 23, 2008),
    http://www.dyslexia.com/info/webdesign.htm
23. National Institute of Mental Health. The Numbers Count: Mental Disorders in America (2008), http://www.nimh.nih.gov/health/publications/
    the-numbers-count-mental-disorders-in-america.shtml
    (retrieved July 21, 2008)
24. National Institute of Neurological Disorders and Stroke. Stroke: Hope Through Research (NIH Publication No. 99-2222),
    http://www.ninds.nih.gov/disorders/tbi/detail_tbi.htm (retrieved July 21, 2008)

25. National Institute of Neurological Disorders and Stroke. Traumatic Brain Injury: Hope Through Research (NIH Publication No. 02-2478), http://www.ninds.nih.gov/disorders/tbi/detail_tbi.htm (retrieved July 21, 2008)
26. Nielsen, J.: Designing Web Usability. New Riders Publishing, Indianapolis (2000)
27. Norman, D.A.: The Psychology of Everyday Things. Basic Books, New York (1988)
28. Oregon Secretary of State. Voters' pamphlet. Volume 2 – candidates (2004), http://www.sos.state.or.us/elections/nov22004/guide/cover.html (retrieved July 25, 2008)
29. Oregon Secretary of State. Voters' Pamphlets distributed Across Oregon (Press Releaease) (October 12, 2006), http://www.sos.state.or.us/executive/pressreleases/2006/1012.html (retrieved July 25, 2008)
30. Overheardinnewyork.com. You're Kidding Yourself if You Think Those Things Don't Matter. Message posted anonymously to (July 1, 2008), http://www.overheardinnewyork.com/archives/015249.html
31. Pastor, P.N., Reuben, C.A.: Attention deficit disorder and learning disability: Unites States, 1997-98. Vital and Health Statistics 10, 206 (2002)
32. Redish, J.: Guidelines for Writing Clear Instructions and Messages for Voters and Poll Workers (2006), http://vote.nist.gov/032906PlainLanguageRpt.pdf (retrieved July 23, 2008)
33. Reynolds, A., Steenbergen, M.: How the world votes: The political consequences of ballot design, innovation, and manipulation. Electoral Studies 25, 570–589 (2006)
34. Schur, L., Shields, T., Kruse, D., Schriner, K.: Enabling Democracy: Disability and Voter Turnout. Political Research Quarterly 55(1), 167–190 (2002)
35. Scott, J.S.: Plain Language: Adding Simplicity to Voting (2008), http://www.upassoc.org/civiclife/voting/documents/plain_language_eac_roundtable.pdf (retrieved July 22, 2008)
36. Selker: The Technology of Access: Allowing People of Age to Vote for Themselves. McGeorge Law Review 39(4), 1113–1137 (2007)
37. Serra, M., Muzio, J.: The IT Support for Acquired Brain Injury Patients – the Design and Evaluation of a New Software Package. In: Proceedings of the 35th Annual Hawaii International Conference on Systems Sciences (2002)
38. Shneiderman, B.: Promoting universal usability with multi-layer interface design. In: ACM SIGCAPH Computers and the Physically Handicapped, pp. 73–74 (2002)
39. Shneiderman, B., Plaisant, C.: Designing the user interface: strategies for effective human-computer interaction, 4th edn. Pearson Education, Boston (2005)
40. Smith, B.: RNC fights use of elephant logo. Politico (July 17, 2008), http://www.politico.com/news/stories/0708/11834.html (retrieved July 17, 2008)
41. Smithsonian National Museum of American History. Vote: the Machinery of Democracy (2004), http://americanhistory.si.edu/vote/index.html (retrieved June 23, 2008)
42. Tanielian, T.L., Jaycox, L.: Invisible wounds of war: psychological and cognitive injuries, their consequences, and services to assist recovery. RAND Corporation, Santa Monica, CA (2008)
43. Todorov, A., Mandisodza, A.N., Goren, A., Hall, C.C.: Inferences of Competence from Faces Predict Election Outcomes. Science 308, 1623–1626 (2005)

44. WebAIM. Cognitive Disabilities (2008),
    http://www.webaim.org/articles/cognitive/ (retrieved July 8, 2008)
45. Ware, C.: Information visualization: Perception for Design. Morgan Kaufmann, San Francisco (2004)
46. Galitz, W.: The Essential Guide to User Interface Design: An Introduction to GUI Design Principles and Techniques. John Wiley and Sons, Chichester (2007)
47. Willis, J., Todorov, A.: First Impressions: Making Up Your Mind After a 100-Ms Exposure to a Face. Psychological Science 17(7), 592–598 (2006)

Appendix: Figures A through E of the Ballots

Fig. A. Blanket ballot, featuring detailed party symbols.
http://americanhistory.si.edu/vote/reform.html

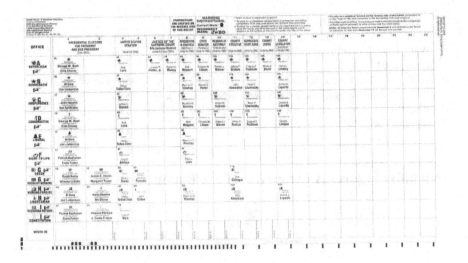

Fig. B. A Broome County, New York absentee ballot from 2000. The eagle and star represent the Republican and Democratic Parties.
http://vote.nist.gov/ballots_n/NY_broome20001107absent.pdf

Fig. C. Guinea-Bissau ballot paper
http://aceproject.org/regions-en/gi/GW ACE Electoral Knowledge Network
1998-2006 © ACE Electoral Knowledge Network

Fig. D. A sample ballot from the Republic of South Africa's 1994 elections. The name of the party, a party symbol, the initials of the party, and a picture of the presidential candidate are included. All pictures are in full color. Note that the names of the candidates, including the winner, Nelson Mandela, are not included.

The actual ballot was very similar but included stickers featuring late additions to the ballot.
http://aceproject.org/south_africa_3_lg.jpg/image_view_fullscreen
ACE Electoral Knowledge Network1998-2006 © ACE Electoral Knowledge Network

Fig. E. A paper ballot from the controversial 2008 run-off election in Zimbabwe. The ballot features the names of the candidates and their parties, as well as black-and-white party symbols and photographs. Tsvangirai withdrew from the run-off due to voter intimidation, but remained on the ballot. The photo is from AFP, and was the third picture in this BBC web gallery: http://news.bbc.co.uk/2/hi/in_pictures/7476935.stm

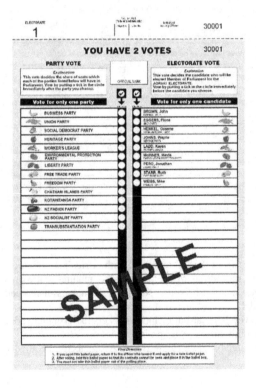

Fig. F. A sample ballot from New Zealand

Assessing Voters' Attitudes towards Electronic Voting in Latin America: Evidence from Colombia's 2007 E-Voting Pilot

R. Michael Alvarez[1], Gabriel Katz[1,*], Ricardo Llamosa[2], and Hugo E. Martinez[2]

[1] California Institute of Technology, DHSS, DHSS 228-77, Pasadena, CA 91125, USA
gabriel@hss.caltech.edu
[2] CIDLIS - Universidad Industrial de Santander

Abstract. Electronic voting could increase citizens' electoral participation and trust in countries characterized by fragile democratic institutions and public discredit of the political system such as those in Latin America. This paper examines attitudes towards e-voting among participants in a large scale pilot project conducted in Colombia in 2007, focusing on the perceived reliability and usability of different automated voting technologies. Using a multivariate probit model, we determine the effect of socio-demographic, geographic and technical factors on users' evaluations of electronic voting *vis a vis* the traditional paper ballot system. Our results show that users find e-voting not only easier than the current voting system, but also substantially more reliable. While voters' opinions on usability are driven by technical issues, their trust in the new technologies is strongly affected by individual characteristics. We conclude that e-voting entails a promising opportunity to empower voters and increase confidence in elections in Colombia.

Keywords: e-voting pilot, Latin America, multivariate probit, reliability, usability, trust in government, voter confidence.

1 Introduction

Most social science research analyzing the interaction between citizens and automated voting systems has focused on the accuracy of different e-voting technologies and, in particular, on the so-called residual vote [2], [3], [4].[1] However, the growing trend towards electronic voting in developing democracies [24] underscores the need to broaden the analysis to encompass core issues such as the potential role of electronic voting in increasing voters' confidence in the electoral process and in strengthening political participation [18], [25]. In the

---

* Corresponding author.
[1] Residual votes are ballots that cannot be counted in a specific election. There may be multiple reasons for residual votes, such as spoiled or unmarked ballots, ballots in which the voter marked more names than allowed, etc.

P.Y.A. Ryan and B. Schoenmakers (Eds.): VOTE-ID 2009, LNCS 5767, pp. 75–91, 2009.

case of Latin America, where e-voting technologies have been increasingly used at national, state and local elections since their introduction in Brazil in the mid 1990s, it has been argued that electronic voting could help increase the efficacy and transparency of electoral processes [5], [6], supporting free and fair elections and enhancing the legitimacy of elected authorities in a context characterized by citizens' low degree of trust in democratic and political institutions [20], [32]. Moreover, given the relatively high levels of (complete and functional) illiteracy and the complexity of the manual voting systems prevalent in the continent, the introduction of e-voting devices with user friendly features could lower the information and cognitive barriers to electoral participation, contributing to the *de facto* enfranchisement of important segments of the electorate that face considerable problems at the moment of exercising their right to vote [21].

For electronic voting to fulfill this fundamental role in developing countries, a prerequisite is that citizens can easily use and trust e-voting technologies. Besides obvious complex technological considerations, a voting system is ultimately 'only as good as the public believes it to be' [23]. In this sense, [5] have distinguished between voters' trust in electronic voting systems and the 'trustworthiness' of the system itself, and [25] have shown that voters' perceptions about the security and usability of e-voting technologies is not only - not even necessarily - related to the actual technical properties of the devices, but also influenced by personal and contextual factors. Moreover, previous research has shown that voters might prefer electronic voting systems over traditional paper-based methods even though the former might not perform better than the latter in terms of efficiency or effectiveness, and could be potentially more vulnerable [14], [19].[2] More generally, the information systems literature has recognized that, in order to be successfully adopted and trusted, technology-based transactions must be perceived as useful, easy to use and secure [11], [13]. Neglecting these issues when considering the introduction of electronic voting systems might result in technology becoming a barrier, rather than a tool for increasing citizens' participation and trust in elections, with potentially undesirable and dangerous implications for the perceived legitimacy of the democratic process [18], [26], [28].

The lack of empirical evidence and systematic analysis of past e-voting experiences in Latin America has prevented so far an in-depth study of voters' assessments of electronic voting technologies along these dimensions.[3] The few academic articles evaluating the use of electronic voting in the region have almost exclusively focused on the case of Brazil, with virtually no research on any

---

[2] See [14] for a definition of efficiency and effectiveness in the context of evaluating alternative voting technologies.

[3] By now, electronic voting has been used in official elections in Argentina, Brazil, Mexico, Panama, Puerto Rico and Venezuela, while other countries (Colombia, Paraguay, Peru) have conducted pilot tests to determine the feasibility and convenience of its implementation. All of these experiences have been 'supervised e-voting' elections, rather than 'remote' or 'telematic' e-voting.

of the other elections or pilot tests.[4] Even in the case of Brazil, however, most analyses are mainly theoretical or descriptive [5], [27], [28].

This paper addresses these shortcoming and adds to the existing literature on electronic voting in Latin America, using data from an e-voting pilot conducted in Colombia in October 2007. The data collected during the Colombian pilot allows us to assess voters' opinions towards automated voting in comparison to the current system using paper ballots and to apply formal statistical methods to examine the effect of individual and aggregate factors on voters' evaluations of electronic voting. In addition, since different voting technologies were tested in the pilot, we can examine the sensitivity of respondents' opinions about e-voting to the prototypes used. As noted by several researchers, the characteristics of specific devices can have differential effects on the voting behavior of particular groups of citizens and on their general attitudes towards electronic voting [9], [18], [31]. Taking these differences into account is particularly relevant in Latin America, given the sociodemographic characteristics of the electorate and the relatively large number of parties competing for office, which imposes higher cognitive demands on voters and increases the potential influence of design effects on electoral behavior [8]. Our focus lies on the analysis of voters' opinions about the usability and reliability of electronic voting systems and their potential policy implications, rather than on comparing the actual performance of automated voting *vis a vis* traditional methods. In view of the importance of voting as a central democratic institution and the heated debates surrounding the implementation of e-voting in Latin America [27], [28], our research can provide valuable insights about the convenience and implications of adopting electronic voting systems and their potential to enhance the quality of electoral processes in less developed democracies.

The remainder of the paper is organized as follows. The next section describes the main characteristics of Colombia's 2007 e-voting pilot. Section 3 presents and comments the results from a multivariate statistical model aimed at estimating the effect of different socio-demographic and technological factors on voters' evaluation of electronic voting. Finally, Section 4 summarizes the main empirical findings and discusses their implications in the light of the foreseeable move towards the adoption of new voting technologies in Latin America.

2   The 2007 Colombia E-Voting Pilot

In 2004, a modification in Colombian electoral law opened the possibility of adopting an automated voting system in the country and regulated its implementation.[5] In order to explore the feasibility of introducing e-voting in official

---

[4] While [8] analyze the 2005 Buenos Aires e-voting pilot, they do not focus on evaluations of electronic voting systems from the voters' perspective or on comparing automated voting with the traditional manual system.

[5] Law 892 of July 7, 2004.

elections, a large scale voting pilot was conducted in the country in 2007.[6] The explicit purpose of the pilot was to test different voting technologies in order to evaluate their functional features and to analyze users' attitudes towards electronic voting, particularly in relation to the traditional paper ballots. The comparison with the current electoral system in place in Colombia is particularly relevant given our research purpose. Besides examining if Colombian voters perceive electronic voting to be easier to use or more convenient than the manual system in place, as has been the focus of most studies in this area, we are also interested in analyzing whether e-voting can have any effect on voters' trust in the electoral process. As in many countries in the Latin America, public trust in elections and electoral authorities is very low in Colombia: in 2005, an opinion poll by the Universidad de los Andes showed that the National Electoral Authority ranked at the bottom of Colombian institutions in terms of citizens' confidence. Only 53.2% of respondents in the study declared to trust elections, while the level of confidence in the electoral authority was even lower (48.6%) [33].

The pilot was scheduled for October 27, 2007, the day before municipal elections were held throughout the country, in order to capitalize on the nationwide 'political climate' to encourage participation in the experiment. The organization and supervision of the pilot was in charge of Colombia's Electoral Authority and the Center for Software Research and Development from the Universidad Industrial de Santander, and a team of political scientists from the US assisted as academic consultants. The field study was conducted in nine locations across three cities: the country's capital, Bogotá, with a population of almost 7,000,000; Pereira, with more than 400,000 inhabitants; and San Andrés, with a population of 70,000. In order to select the cities for the study, the countries' urban centers were divided in three strata according to their population (large, medium and small) and, within each stratum, the chosen cities were selected taking into account their infrastructure and logistical facilities, as well as the representativeness of their populations.[7] In each city, voting booths were installed in three shopping malls selected due to their their geographical location, guaranteeing a large and diverse pool of potential subjects. The location of the testing sites, as well as the organization of in-site training sessions for those interested in taking part in the pilot, was publicized by the Colombian Electoral Authority in the weeks prior to the field experiment.

Participation in the pilot was voluntary, and subjects were not given any incentive to participate. Citizens in each of the testing locations were invited to take part in a mock election in which they had to choose one candidate for

---

[6] Electronic voting machines had been previously used, along with the traditional paper ballots, in a few polling stations during the 1992 national elections, as well as in a dozen local elections throughout the country. None of these e-voting pilots, though, had focused on analyzing voters' attitudes towards electronic voting.

[7] Cities with more than 1,000,000 inhabitants were included in the first category. Urban centers with populations ranging between 200,000 and 1,000,000 were classified as 'medium-sized', and those with less than 200,000 inhabitants were included in the last category.

Table 1. Characteristics of the participants in Colombia's e-voting pilot

Socio-demographic variables (%)		Bogota	Pereira	San Andres	Total
Age	18-30	37.8	26.4	34.1	32.9
	31-50	45.1	44.9	52.2	46.5
	>50	17.1	28.7	13.7	20.6
Education	Primary or less	2.8	5.6	4.8	4.2
	Secondary	32.4	35.6	54.6	38.1
	University	64.8	58.8	40.5	57.7
Gender	Female	39.5	38.0	51.0	41.3
	Male	60.5	62.0	49.0	58.7
Total number of participants		1,171	843	280	2,294

president and one for the senate. In case of acceptance, they were randomly assigned to one of the available voting machines and received the instructions and a 5-minute training needed to operate it. The only eligibility requirement was to be older than 18 years of age and being able to provide a valid form of identification ('cédula de identidad'); registration and inscription procedures were analogous as those used in official elections. A total of 2,294 participants took part in the test. After casting a vote, participants were asked to provide basic socio-demographic information - age, education, gender - and to complete a survey containing seven questions dealing with usability issues of the devices tested, as well as with their general perceptions about electronic voting compared to the procedure based on paper ballots. Table 1 provides summary data about the socio-demographic characteristics of the participants in the pilot.

Four different voting devices supplied by private vendors were tested in the pilot (Figure 1). Two machines for each of the e-voting systems were installed in each of the testing locations, totaling 24 machines in each city and 72 in the pilot. All the prototypes were equipped with headphones and keypads for visually-impaired voters to privately interact with the terminal.

The first three prototypes were touch-screen direct recording electronic (DRE) machines. After inserting a smart card into the reader attached to the terminals, participants were presented with the name, number and logo of seven parties running candidates for office in the presidential and the senate race, as well as with the names of the candidates running for President (4) and for the Senate (58 in total), sorted according to the party number and the candidates' personal code.[8] Voters could scroll and select their candidates - one for each race - by tapping onto the screen. Before registering the vote, users were asked to confirm

---

[8] As in most Latin American countries, each party in Colombia is assigned a different list number when registering the candidates running for a specific election. Candidates and parties advertise this number during the campaign, together with the party and candidate's name.

their choices at the end of the process. Only at this review stage could they stop, change or cancel the vote. After the confirmation, the vote could not be changed and the information was digitally stored in the machine. Overvotes - e.g., ballots selecting more than one candidate for the presidential or senate race - were not admitted by any of these prototypes; the voter was notified of the mistake and requested to correct it in order to proceed with the vote. After casting their vote, participants returned the smart cards to the poll workers, who reprogrammed it for the next user. There were two primary differences between these DRE devices. First, unlike *Prototype 1*, both *Prototypes 2* and *3* had voter-verifiable audit trails, the former only on screen, the latter also a paper trail that had to be deposited by the user in a box after the vote. Also, under *Prototype 1*, the participant had to select the order in which she wanted to vote - i.e., in the presidential or senate election - priot to casting a ballot, using an electronic card connected to the voting machine. In contrast, voters using *Prototypes 2* and *3* could move through the screen to switch between the two races.

The last prototype, *Prototype 4*, was an optical scan (OS) device. The staff supervising the test provided each participant with a paper ballot including all the relevant information (party name, logo, and number, and the complete list of candidates for each race). Voters marked their preferences for the presidential and senate race with a special pencil on the paper ballot and introduced it into the scanner. The only possibility of changing the vote once the ballot was introduced into the scanner was if the voter had cast an invalid vote or left the ballot blank. In both cases, the voter was notified of the potential mistake, and had the option of correcting it or casting the vote anyway. In the case of a spoiled ballot, correcting the mistake required the user to approach the staff supervising the pilot, request a new ballot and start the process over again. This prototype was not equipped with a smart card reader.

It is worth mentioning that, while the evaluation by the organizers of the field experiment was largely positive, this first large scale experience with electronic voting in Colombia also revealed the importance of organizational and logistic aspects that need to be taken into account for future testing and implementation of e-voting technologies in the country. The process of delivering and installing the voting machines simultaneously in nine voting sites, the organization of help desks and the training of the support staff and the participants in the pilot proved to be difficult tasks, requiring considerable planning and coordination between the private vendors, the academic supervisors and the electoral authority. The voting sessions highlighted the need for more extensive training of both the participants and the election authorities, as well general informative sessions about the characteristics of the system, before it can be used in official elections. Also, although choosing shopping malls as testing locations provided convenient facilities and infrastructure for the field experiment and ensured a large influx of potential subjects, it probably affected the composition of the sample. In fact, a large majority of the participants in the test had very high education levels compared to the average Colombian population. This, together with the fact that participation was voluntary, limits the possibility of generalizing the results presented

Fig. 1. The figure plots the different voting devices tested in the 2007 Colombia's e-voting pilot: *Prototype 1* (upper left), *Prototype 2*(upper right), *Prototype 3* (lower left) and *Prototype 4* (lower right)

in this paper to the overall voting population and underscores the need to conduct further tests in alternative locations and with a more heterogeneous subject pool. However, given that participants in each experimental site were randomly distributed across prototypes, there was no systematic relationship between voters' personal characteristics in each location and the prototype assignment, and thus these problems do not invalidate the internal (i.e., in-sample) validity of our results.[9] Moreover, our randomized research design mitigates some concerns that have plagued previous studies in this area, such as vote tampering, differential turnout rates, and self-selection into different voting technologies [17], [29].[10]

3   Participants' Assessments of Electronic Voting and Their Determinants

We used the survey data collected during the pilot to analyze voters' opinions about e-voting and their evaluations of electronic voting *vis a vis* the traditional

---

[9] Balance checks based on [16] indicate no significant differences in the distribution of relevant individual characteristics across prototypes.

[10] Ideally, each voter would have been assigned to each of the four prototypes tested in random order, and then asked to compare the performance of the different voting devices. However, such designs are extremely rare in field experiments due to cost and time constraints. Field experiments, on the other hand, allow for a more realistic and representative environment than laboratory experiments [26].

paper-based system used in Colombia. Participants' responses to the survey questions allow us to examine their level of acceptance and confidence in electronic voting, the influence of their personal characteristics on these assessments, and the sensitivity of their responses to the different technologies tested. In line with the above arguments regarding the main determinants of the perceived trustworthiness of voting systems, we focus on two main aspects: usability of the different voting technologies and confidence in the system. Specifically, we examine participants' response to four questions comparing e-voting with the traditional voting procedure, each of them admitting only a 'yes' or 'no' answer:

– Usability
    1. Is electronic voting easier than the traditional voting procedure?
    2. Is correcting mistakes made easier using the electronic voting machines?
– Reliability
    1. Is e-voting more reliable than the traditional voting procedure?
    2. Am I more confident that my votes will be counted?

The first two questions aimed at measuring 'perceived ease of use', i.e., 'the degree to which a person believes that using a particular system would be free from effort' [12]. Earlier research underscored the role of perceived ease of use as a key factor for the successful adoption of technological innovations [30]. The other two questions concerned users' trust in the system: voters should not only be able to vote, but must be assured that their votes will be counted and attributed correctly [25], [29]. Furthermore, for electronic voting to contribute to increase or restore citizens' confidence in the electoral process in Latin America, it is important that the new technology fares well in this respect compared to the paper-ballot system currently in place.

Table 2 reports the percentage of positive answers to each of these four questions, discriminated by personal (age, education, gender) and geographic (city) variables. A striking result emerging from the table is the high proportion of positive answers for each of the survey questions, which in all cases is over 85 percent for the whole sample. Overall, more than 70% of the participants in the pilot answered positively to the four questions. This is a highly unusual rate of success when compared to other pilot tests in developed democracies, particularly with respect to users' trust in the computer-based voting technologies [7], [18], [34]. Interestingly, while participants could actually compare whether casting a vote was easier using the e-voting devices than with the paper ballots, there was in principle no objective measure that could indicate them whether their votes were more likely to be counted under the new system. In other words, while participants' responses to the usability questions are supported by the performance of the e-voting machines, the high proportion of positive answers to the two reliability questions cannot be explained by characteristics of the devices tested or of the electronic voting system, but are entirely based on voters' perceptions.

Another important result from Table 2 concerns the difference in the response patterns across categories of the socio-demographic and geographic variables.

Table 2. Percentage of positive responses to the four survey questions

Individual and geographic variables		E-voting is easier	Correcting mistakes is easier	E-voting is more reliable	Votes will be counted
Age	18-30	92.8	90.9	79.7	82.8
	31-50	95.7	90.5	87.0	89.7
	>50	94.6	89.9	92.9	90.5
Education	Primary or less	93.6	87.2	95.7	94.7
	Secondary	96.2	92.8	90.2	90.1
	University	93.4	89.2	82.1	85.3
Gender	Female	94.7	90.6	86.1	87.5
	Male	94.3	90.5	85.6	87.6
City	Bogota	94.7	89.0	84.7	86.7
	Pereira	94.9	93.2	87.0	89.7
	San Andres	93.4	89.0	85.6	85.7
Whole sample		94.5	90.5	85.8	87.6

The data on the two usability questions shows little variation across subsamples. The proportion of participants who found casting a vote easier under the new system is very high and similar across individual characteristics and in the three cities in which the study was conducted, and while the percentage of respondents stating that correcting mistakes is easier with the voting machines is slightly lower, the distribution is again quite similar across age, education, gender, and city. While some authors (e.g., [6]) implied that the 'digital divide' could affect the ability of older and less educated voters to use the new voting technologies satisfactorily, we find no significant differences in the responses to the two usability questions by age or education levels. In contrast, age and education do affect users' trust in the security of electronic voting. Younger and more educated users were much less likely to rely on automated voting *versus* the traditional procedure than participants over 50 or those with less than secondary education, and they were also considerably less confident that their votes would be counted under the new system. Differences in the proportion of positive responses to the two reliability questions between lowest and highest categories of age and education range between 7.7 and 13.6 percentage points, and are all strongly statistically significant.[11] A possible explanation for these differences lies in the correlation between age and education, on the one hand, and familiarity with technology, on the other. Younger and more educated people have probably higher levels of computer skills and experience and thus can be more critical about security issues than people who lack the knowledge to detect potential threats to computer security and verifiability. Even for the more

---

[11] The p-values of the tests for equal probabilities [1] between between young/old and more educated/less educated participants in each of the two reliability questions are all smaller than 0.02.

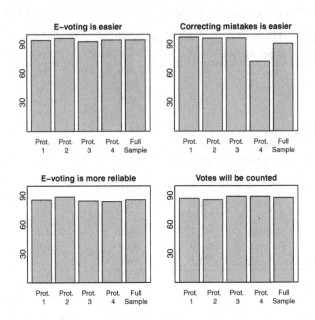

Fig. 2. Percentage of positive answers to each of the four survey questions across prototype vendors

critical users, though, the percentage of positive responses to the two reliability questions is never lower than 79%, a fact probably related to the very low degree of public confidence in elections and in the electoral system in the country [33].

Figure 2 complements the information provided in Table 2, plotting the proportion of positive responses to each of the four questions analyzed, discriminated by prototype. There is a strong consensus among participants using the four devices that e-voting is simpler than the paper-ballot system, and there are also almost no differences in the large proportions of affirmative answers to the two reliability questions across prototypes. The absence or availability of voter verifiable audit trails does not seem to influence voters' confidence in the process or their beliefs about the likelihood that their votes will be counted. The hypothesis of independence between the responses to each of these three questions and the prototype used cannot be rejected at the 0.05 level [1]. However, the figure reveals that respondents found that the optical scan device (*Prototype 4*) presented considerable difficulties at the moment of correcting their vote. While 96.5% of the participants using the three DRE machines (*Prototypes 1-3*) believed that correcting a mistake was easier than using a paper ballot, only 72% of respondents using the OS prototype agreed with this statement. This result is hardly surprising since *Prototype 4* is the one that more closely resembles the paper ballot system in this regard and, as described in Section 2, correcting a mistake is considerably more difficult than under the three DRE devices.

In order to jointly determine the effect of the different prototypes tested and of the socio-demographic and geographic variables on participants' responses, we fit a multivariate probit model *via* Simulated Maximum Likelihood [10]. The multivariate probit specification generalizes the binary probit model to estimate several correlated binary outcomes, accounting for the fact that unobservable individual characteristics beyond those included in the model might induce correlations across the responses to the different survey questions. The independent variables of interest are linearly combined into underlying latent variables that are related to the observable binary ('yes', 'no') responses through a threshold specification, with a correlated Gaussian distribution assumed for the latent variables [12]. This allows for flexible modeling of the correlation structure and direct interpretation of the regression coefficients, and enables us to 'smooth' the binary responses, determining the effect of the regressors on the probability of providing positive answers to each or all of the survey questions analyzed.[12] In our application, we include the following regressors: Age, coded as two dichotomous variables, *31-50* and *>50*; a dummy variable for those with *primary education or less*; an indicator for *Female*; two indicator variables for geographical location, *Pereira* and *San Andres*; and prototypes tested, with *Prototype 1* used as baseline.[13]

The parameter estimates from the multivariate probit model are reported in Table 3. The upper part of the table reports the estimates for the coefficients of the regressors, while the estimated correlation coefficients between the four survey questions are presented at the bottom. The p-value of the Wald-statistic for the test of joint significance ($312.48 \sim \chi^2_{35}$) is indistinguishable from 0, indicating that we can reject the hypothesis that the variables included in the model have no joint explanatory power on participants' responses. Also, a Wald test for the hypothesis of independence between the responses to the different survey questions can be rejected at the usual confidence levels ($Pr(\chi^2_6 > 321.73) \approx 0$).

The results from the multivariate model tend to confirm the main substantive findings from our descriptive analysis. Regarding the usability questions, the most evident result is the strong negative effect of *Prototype 4* on the probability of stating that correcting mistakes is easier than with the paper ballots. There are no significant differences between the three DRE devices in this regard, although participants using *Prototype 2* find e-voting relatively easier than those using *Prototype 1* after controlling for the socio-demographic and geographic factors. As mentioned in Section 2, while the voting process under *Prototype 2* could be entirely completed by navigating through the screen, *Prototype 1* required the use of an additional control panel located outside the voting booth. Among the individual variables, only *31-50* has a significant effect on the perceived ease of use of the e-voting devices. Personal characteristics - age and education - are however key determinants of voters' trust in the e-voting technologies. Older voters express a higher degree of confidence in electronic voting compared to the paper-based procedure, and are more likely to believe that their

---

[12] A detailed review of the multivariate probit model and of different approaches to estimation can be found in [10] and [12], among others.

[13] We also implemented several alternative specifications, yielding essentially identical results as those reported below.

votes will be counted than participants under 30. In particular, users' over 50 have a strong trust in e-voting. Also, less educated participants are more likely to answer affirmatively to the two reliability questions than those with higher education, after controlling for the remaining variables. There are no statistically significant differences in users' opinions about the probability that their votes will be counted across prototypes, although participants using *Prototype 2* are relatively more confident in e-voting compared to the traditional manual procedure than those using *Prototype 1*. This could be related to the fact that *Prototype 2* prints a voter-verifiable audit trail on screen, allowing users to check that their vote actually reflects their intent. However, while *Prototype 3* also issues a voter-verified paper ballot, there are no significant differences in voters' opinions about the reliability of prototypes *1* and *3*.

The estimated correlation coefficients shown at the bottom of Table 3 indicate a positive and statistically significant relationship between responses to the different questions. As expected, the correlations are stronger within groups of questions than between them. In particular, voters who believe that e-voting is more reliable than the manual procedure are also very likely to be more confident that their votes will be counted under the new system. However, the estimates also indicate that participants who saw electronic voting as a convenient way to cast their votes were also more likely to trust in e-voting *vis a vis* the paper-based system. This suggests that implementing an e-voting system that is perceived by voters to be both reliable and easy to use could have a strong positive effect on public confidence in the electoral process in Colombia.

Based on the estimates reported in Table 3, Figure 3 plots the effect of a change in each of the relevant variables on the average probability of providing a positive answer to each and to all of the four questions analyzed, while holding all the remaining variables at their actual sample values.[14] This allows us to isolate the impact of each predictor on respondents' opinions on usability and reliability. The two plots in the upper panel of the figure compare the probabilities of positive responses for the two extreme categories of participants in terms of age and education, clearly illustrating that individual characteristics have a strong effect on the perceived reliability of electronic voting. Other things equal, the probability that participants aged 50 or older believe that e-voting is more reliable than the paper-based system is on average 12.6 percentage points higher than for those under 30, and they are also 7 percentage points more likely to trust that their votes will be counted than younger respondents. In the same direction, the expected probability of providing a positive answer to these two reliability questions among participants with less than secondary education is 0.94. For those with University education, the average likelihoods are 0.86 and 0.87, respectively. In contrast, the average differences between older/younger and less educated/more educated respondents regarding their views on usability issues are all lower than 4 percentage points. Again, as seen in the lower panel of Figure 3, differences in this respect are mainly due to technical factors: *ceteris*

---

[14] Since the estimates for the coefficients of *Female* are never significant, we do not examine the effect of gender in this analysis.

Table 3. Multivariate Probit Estimates

Variable	E-voting is easier	Correcting mistakes is easier	E-voting is more reliable	Votes will be counted
Age: 31-50	0.27***	-0.14	0.29***	0.31***
	(0.10)	(0.10)	(0.07)	(0.08)
Age: >50	0.16	-0.19	0.62***	0.31***
	(0.13)	(0.12)	(0.11)	(0.20)
Education: primary or less	-0.10	-0.25	0.52**	0.40*
	(0.22)	(0.18)	(0.24)	(0.22)
Female	0.07	-0.01	0.04	0.04
	(0.09)	(0.09)	(0.07)	(0.07)
Pereira	-0.01	0.32***	0.07	0.12
	(0.10)	(0.10)	(0.08)	(0.08)
San Andres	-0.14	0.06	0.06	-0.08
	(0.12)	(0.11)	(0.09)	(0.09)
Prototype 2	0.23*	-0.14	0.16*	-0.06
	(0.13)	(0.15)	(0.10)	(0.10)
Prototype 3	-0.08	-0.13	-0.08	0.09
	(0.12)	(0.15)	(0.09)	(0.10)
Prototype 4	0.08	-1.30***	-0.08	0.10
	(0.13)	(0.12)	(0.09)	(0.10)

Correlations	E-voting is easier	Correcting mistakes is easier	E-voting is more reliable	Votes will be counted
E-voting is easier				
Correcting mistakes is easier	0.32***			
	(0.06)			
E-voting is more reliable	0.15***	0.22***		
	(0.05)	(0.05)		
Votes will be counted	0.18***	0.19***	0.65***	
	(0.05)	(0.05)	(0.03)	

Standard errors in parenthesis. Significance levels: *** 0.01, ** 0.05, * 0.1.

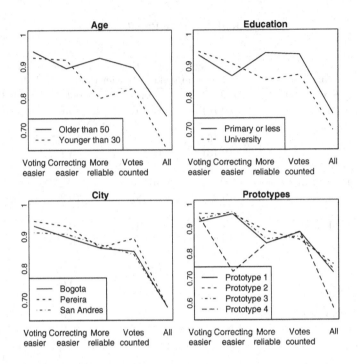

Fig. 3. Effect of the independent variables on the probability of a positive response to each and to all of the four survey questions analyzed

paribus, the expected proportion of 'yes' answers to the second usability question is more than 20 percentage points lower for the optical scan device (*Prototype 4*) than for each of the three digital recording electronic (DRE) designs.

4 Concluding Remarks

As noted by [25], electronic voting is likely to lead to changes in how citizens maintain confidence in the integrity of elections. In countries where there is widespread disbelief in the freeness and fairness of elections and where the complexity of voting procedures can actually prevent important segments of the electorate from exercising their right to vote, the introduction of e-voting systems poses both a difficult challenge and an interesting opportunity [19]. While the final result of this equation will largely depend on technical developments, as well as on factors such as citizens' familiarity with information technologies in general, the reputation and legitimacy of the electoral authorities and the quality of election administration [5], [29], a fundamental prerequisite for the successful implementation of computer-based voting is that citizens are able to use the systems with ease and trust the overall process [18].

The analysis of the data from the e-voting pilot conducted in Colombia in October 2007 shows an almost unanimous perception that electronic voting is not only simpler than the paper-based procedure currently in force, but also considerably more reliable. The proportion of respondents who declare to trust electronic voting is unusually high when compared to other international experiences, and is probably related to the comparatively low degree of public confidence in elections in many countries in Latin America. While users' opinions about the usability of e-voting devices is strongly related to technical and operative features of the machines and is sensitive to the different prototypes tested, their perceptions about the verifiability of the process are heavily influenced by personal characteristics such as age or education. Our results in this respect are in line with [25], in the sense that people will likely use black box technologies if they believe they are secure, and indicate that improving the usability and the perceived security of e-voting technologies could have a positive impact on public confidence in the electoral process in Colombia.

More generally, contrary to arguments characterizing the introduction of e-voting in Latin America as a purely supply-driven process, our results for Colombia indicate that there seems to be a demand for alternatives to traditional electoral procedures among the citizens, especially from older and less educated voters. Despite the limitations of the analysis noted above, the evidence presented in this paper suggests that, rather than being conceived as an 'expensive toy' [28], the adoption of automated voting systems could provide an opportunity to address some of the genuine electoral needs and interests of the citizenry in less developed democracies.

References

1. Agresti, A.: Categorical Data Analysis. John Wiley and Sons, New York (2002)
2. Alvarez, R.M., Hall, T.E.: Point, Click and Vote: The Future of Internet Voting. Brookings Institution Press, Washington (2004)
3. Alvarez, R.M., Hall, T.E.: Electronic Elections: The Perils and Promises of Digital Democracy. Princeton University Press, Princeton (2008)
4. Ansolabehere, S., Stewart, C.: Residual Votes Attributable to Technology. Journal of Politics 67, 365–389 (2005)
5. Avgerou, C., Ganzaroli, A., Poulymenakou, A., Reinhard, N.: ICT and citizens' trust in government: lessons from electronic voting in Brazil. In: Paper presented at the 9th International Conference on Social implications of Computers in Developing countries, Sao Paulo (2007)
6. Barrat, J.: A preliminary question: Is e-voting actually useful for our democratic institutions? What do we need it for? In: Electronic Voting 2006, pp. 51–60. Gesellschaft für Informatik, Bonn (2006)
7. Braun, N., Brandli, D.: Swiss E-Voting Pilot Projects: Evaluation, Situation Analysis and How to Proceed. In: Electronic Voting 2006, pp. 51–60. Gesellschaft für Informatik, Bonn (2006)
8. Calvo, E., Escolar, M., Pomares, J.S.: Ballot Design and Split Ticket Voting in Multiparty Systems: experimental evidence on information effects and vote choice. Electoral Studies 28, 218–231 (2009)
9. Card, D., Moretti, E.: Does Voting Technology Affect Election Outcomes? Touchscreen Voting and the 2004 Presidential Election. Review of Economics and Statistics 89, 660–673 (2007)

10. Cappellari, L., Jenkins, S.P.: Multivariate probit regression using simulated maximum likelihood. The Stata Journal 3, 278–294 (2003)
11. Carter, L., Belanger, F.: The utilization of e-government services: citizen trust, innovation and acceptance factors. Information Systems Journal 15, 5–25 (2005)
12. Chib, S., Greenberg, E.: Analysis of multivariate probit models. Biometrika 85, 347–361 (1998)
13. Davis, F.D.: Perceived Usefulness, Perceived ease of Use, and User acceptance of Information Technology. MIS Quarterly 13, 319–340 (1989)
14. Everett, S.P., Greene, K.K., Byrne, M.D., Wallach, D.S., Derr, K., Sandler, D., Torous, T.: Electronic Voting Machines versus Traditional Methods: Improved Preference, Similar Performance. In: CHI Proceedings - Measuring, Business and Voting, Florence, Italy (2008)
15. Gelman, A., Hill, J.: Data Analysis Using Regression and Multilevel/Hierarchical Models. Cambridge University Press, New York (2007)
16. Hansen, B.B., Bowers, J.: Covariate Balance in Simple,Stratified and Clustered Comparative Studies. Statistical Science 23, 219–236 (2008)
17. Herron, M., Wand, J.N.: Assessing partisan bias in voting technology: The case of the 2004 New Hampshire recount. Electoral Studies 26, 247–261 (2007)
18. Herrnson, P.S., Niemi, R.G., Hanmer, M.J., Bederson, B.B., Conrad, F.C.: Voting Technology: The Not-So-Simple Act of Casting a Ballot. Brookings Institution Press, Washington (2008)
19. Kohno, T., Stubblefield, A., Rubin, A.D., Wallach, D.S.: Analysis of an Electronic Voting System. In: IEEE Symposium on Security and Privacy, Oakland, California (2004)
20. Latinbarometro: Una década de mediciones. Corporación Latinbarómetro, Santiago de Chile (2004)
21. Limongi, F.: Reformas Institucionais, Participacao, Competicao e Inclusao Politica. USP, Sao Paulo (2006)
22. List, L.A.: Field Experiments: A Bridge between Lab and Naturally Occurring Data. Advances in Economic Analysis and Policy 6(2) (2006), Article 8
23. McGaley, M., Gibson, J.P.: Electronic Voting: A Safety Critical System (2003)
24. Milkota, K.: E-democracy conference: a summary of findings. EVE conference, Paris (2002)
25. Oostveen, A.M., van den Besselaar, P.: Security as belief: User perceptions of the security of electronic voting systems. In: Prosser, A., Krimmer, R. (eds.) Electronic Voting in Europe: Technology, Law, Politics and Society. Lecture Notes in Informatics, vol. P-47, pp. 88–97. Gesellschaft für Informatik, Bonn (2004)
26. Oostveen, A.M., van den Besselaar, P.: Trust, Identity and the Effects of Voting Technologies on Voting Behavior. Social Science Computer Review 23, 304–311 (2005)
27. Rezende, P.A.: Electronic Voting Systems - Is Brazil ahead of its time? First Workshop on Voter-Verifiable Election Systems Denver (2003)
28. Rodrigues-Filho, J., Alexander, C.J., Batista, L.C.: E-Voting in Brazil, - The Risks to Democracy. In: Electronic Voting 2006, pp. 85–94. Gesellschaft für Informatik, Bonn (2006)
29. Stein, R., Vonnahme, G., Byrne, M., Wallach, D.S.: Voting Technology, Election Administration and Voter Performance. Election Law Journal 7, 123–135 (2008)
30. Tornatzky, L.G., Klein, R.J.: Innovation characteristics and Innovation adoption-implementation: a meta-analysis of findings. IEEE Transactions on Engineering Management 29, 28–45 (1982)

31. Tomz, M., Van Houweling, R.P.: How Does Voting Equipment Affect the Racial Gap in Voided Ballots? American Journal of Political Science 47, 46–60 (2003)
32. UNDP: Democracy in Latin America: Towards a citizens' democracy. United Nations Development Programme, New York (2004)
33. Universidad de los Andes: Colombia. Giro hacia la derecha? Technical Report, Observatorio para la Democracia. Universidad de los Andes, Bogota (2005)
34. van den Besselaar, P., Oostveen, A.M., De Cindio, F., Ferrazzi, D.: Experiments with e-voting technology: experiences and lessons. In: Cunningham, P., et al. (eds.) Building the Knowledge Economy: Issues, Applications, Cases Studies. IOS Press, Amsterdam (2003)

Developing a Legal Framework for Remote Electronic Voting

Axel Schmidt, Dennis Heinson, Lucie Langer, Zoi Opitz-Talidou,
Philipp Richter, Melanie Volkamer, and Johannes Buchmann

Technische Universität Darmstadt
Center for Advanced Security Research Darmstadt (CASED)
Universität Kassel
{axel,langer,buchmann}@cdc.informatik.tu-darmstadt.de,
{dennis.heinson,prichter}@uni-kassel.de,
zoi.opitz-talidou@noerr.com, volkamer@cased.de
http://www.cased.de

Abstract. This paper describes how to legally regulate remote electronic elections. Electronic voting systems have to respect the constitutional election principles. For technological solutions, this translates into security requirements that have to be fulfilled by the operational environment in which the voting takes place. Therefore [26] introduced the concept of providing the technical and organizational implementation of a remote electronic election by a qualified trustworthy third party. This paper adds legal regulation to support this concept. The legal framework addresses the secure operation of remote electronic voting services as well as their accreditation and supervision by an official authority.

Keywords: E-Voting, Voting Service Provider, Legal regulation, Trust concept.

1 Introduction

This paper describes how to legally regulate remote electronic elections within the German legal environment. Our work introduces results of a project developing a legal framework for non-parliamentary remote electronic elections in Germany. Possible application scenarios include the election of the works council in a company or the chairmanship of an association. So far, electronic voting has only been regulated for federal parliamentary elections, and does not address remote voting, but merely electronic voting with machines at polling stations. These have been increasingly used since 1999, especially for the election of the German Bundestag (Federal Diet). Their usage is regulated in the German Federal Electoral Act (Bundeswahlgesetz, [11]) and the German Federal Voting Machines Ordinance (Bundeswahlgeräteverordnung, [16]). Subsequently, in early March 2009, the German Federal Constitutional Court rendered judgment on the use of voting machines. The decision had been precedented by the deployment and use of voting machines in the parliamentary elections for the German Bundestag

P.Y.A. Ryan and B. Schoenmakers (Eds.): VOTE-ID 2009, LNCS 5767, pp. 92–105, 2009.

in 2005. The court ruled statute, ordinance and using the particular type of voting machine for political elections unconstitutional. It held that the technology that was used does not comply with the constitutional principle of "the public nature of elections" ([10], [9]). This principle requires that voters be able to examine all essential steps of the voting and counting procedure in a reliable way without any specialist knowledge. Applied to e-voting in general, the holding primarily makes the security objective of verifiability mandatory, including *individual verifiability* (every voter can verify that her vote was accounted for correctly) and *universal verifiability* (anyone is able to verify the correctness of the voting and tallying process) (cf. [31], [27] or [23]).

Current remote electronic voting protocols use different approaches to provide verifiability. However, the verification functionality required by the judgment is not defined in detail. Moreover most protocols indeed require special knowledge of the voter in order to verify the election process. Consequently it is an open question to what extent current remote electronic voting protocols are able to observe the principle of the public nature of elections as required by the judgment.

However, applying the reasoning of [3], the statements of the judgment do not prohibit remote electronic voting in non-political elections. The principle of the public nature of elections does not apply to all types of elections per se: The principle is not part of the expressly enumerated voting principles. The court derives it from German Constitutional Articles 38, 20.1 and 20.2 [4]. Its scope and limitations are therefore also developed by the judiciary. The present judgment as well as former judgments declared the principle as an integral part to a functioning democracy. Popular sovereignty demands that the public can effectively express its political opinion. This requires trust in the process by which its representatives are chosen. The voters need to be certain that their ballot carries its desired effect in transmitting their sovereignty to their representatives. It is thus necessary that the electoral process is performed "under the public eye" so that the sovereign may keep trust in his/her political participation. This however can only be assured by a right to immediate monitoring of the process. The counter-implication of the above is that the principle of the public nature of election does not have to be observed under all circumstances if an election does not transfer sovereignty from the public to the legislator. This is the case for most non-political elections (cf. [3]).

Consequently, remote electronic voting systems may be implemented in accordance with the judgment in the following election scenarios: Non-political elections are not subject to the judgment's holding. As explained above, such elections generally do not need to observe the principle of the public nature of election. Hence, remote electronic voting here could be implemented as additional voting channel equal to the regular channel of voting at a polling station. However, in some non-parliamentary scenarios, other legal regulation specifically requires the principle of the public nature of elections. For example, elections of the works council in a company are required to observe this principle by the German Works Constitution Act (Betriebsverfassungsgesetz, [20]). Still, in such scenarios remote electronic voting may be implemented as an additional means of voting, where it can replace or support absentee voting. Here, the lack of voting transparency (public nature of elections) is legally acceptable. According to legal scholarship and prior decisions, the several election principles must be balanced among each others. Limited compliance with one principle can be justified by benefits for others. Absentee voting benefits universal suffrage because it allows convenient access to the voting system from remote locations. Remote electronic voting can do the same by enabling the voter to vote from every place that has network access, including home or office. Therefore more people could exercise their right to vote, for example people who otherwise would not be able to go to a polling station. Hence, in our paper we restrict to non-political elections and do not consider remote electronic voting as a replacement for voting at polling stations. Consequently the holding of the judgment on the public nature of elections do not apply to the scenarios we consider in our legal framework.

There are different ways of implementing remote electronic voting. Several companies provide software solutions that require direct implementation by the election host (the institution holding the election). Examples are the Scytl system or the Polyas system from Micromata ([29], [33]). As shown in [26] in this scenario the voting protocols still need many technical and organizational security requirements to be fulfilled by the operational environment in which the election takes place. For example, the protocols often require trustworthy components or a Public Key Infrastructure and they rely on secure communication channels. General requirements like availability of the voting system or assistance to voters have to be satisfied. Satisfying all of these requirements is a complex and expensive task for the election host and hereby reduces the potential benefits of electronic voting. To solve this problem, [26] introduced the concept of outsourcing the technical and organizational implementation of electronic elections to a professional and qualified trusted third party, the "Voting Service Provider" (VSP). The VSP performs the electronic election technically on behalf of the election host. The VSP provides the secure hardware and software, the expert knowledge and the skilled personnel to satisfy the technical and organizational requirements for secure electronic elections.

The idea of outsourcing the implementation of an electronic election to a VSP introduces a third party to the election scenario. It is therefore of prime importance to make the VSP a trustworthy party. A suitable instrument to do so is legal regulation.

In a project funded by the German government, an interdisciplinary circle of experts in e-voting and technical law has started developing a legal framework for regulation of remote electronic voting services. The concept of regulating VSPs allows for easy evaluation and supervision of the voting system as well as its operation by the operational environment. The framework consists of a parliamentary statute and a corresponding ordinance, to be passed by executive order. The statute is intended to contain legal requirements for non-political remote electronic elections and regulate the operation of VSPs. The ordinance is supposed to provide more specific details, especially on the evaluation and accreditation of VSPs. This paper presents and discusses results of these efforts.

The goal is to provide a detailed overview of approaches and means to ensure legal conformity as a basis for secure, reliable and trustworthy electronic voting.

In Section 2 we provide details on projects and research related to our work. We present first results of our legal framework in Section 3. In Section 4, we discuss open issues and future work. In Section 5 we consider possible applications of the legal framework. We conclude the paper in Section 6.

2   Background

The legal framework presented in this paper is being developed by jurists specialized in technical law as well as computer scientist working in the field of e-voting. This joint work is a result of the "voteremote" project funded by the German Federal Ministry of Economics and Technology. The goal of the voteremote project was to enable secure and practical remote electronic voting. The concept of the Voting Service Provider and its legal regulation implements this goal (cf. [26], [25]). The intention of the legal framework is to provide a solution to ensure trustworthiness of remote electronic voting services. It enables the party responsible for an election to use remote electronic voting as an alternative to absentee voting or presence voting. Also, it professionalizes the implementation of remote electronic elections by providing a legal foundation for VSPs and their evaluation and accreditation. Finally, the framework states technical and organizational requirements which have to be fulfilled in order to satisfy the basic election principles of a universal, direct, free, equal, and secret election.

No legal framework for remote electronic elections or VSPs exists in Germany presently. However the operation of Certification Authorities (CAs) and the use of electronic signatures are legally regulated. The concept of a CA being a trusted third party executing security critical tasks is similar to the VSP. A CA is an essential part of a Public Key Infrastructure. It issues and manages cryptographic keys and certificates for customers to enable cryptographically secured authentication, signature and encryption tasks. Therefore the CA uses secure hardware and software and has to care for secure processes and organization as well as qualified personnel. Due to the similarity this concept served as a rolemodel for the VSP. The legal regulation for electronic signatures and CAs in Germany comprises the German Signature Act [18] and the corresponding Signature Ordinance [17] which have been examined in detail as orientation for the legal framework for electronic elections and VSPs. In more detail, the German Signature Act states requirements for electronic signatures and regulates the operation, accreditation and supervision of CAs. Therefore an independent authority is appointed, the German Federal Network Agency. It is responsible for supervision and accreditation of CAs regarding their legal compliance. If a CA applies for accreditation the responsible authority evaluates all technical and organizational security measures of the CA for compliance with the requirements of the legal regulation. For the purpose of evaluation the act requires CAs to provide a detailed document (called "security concept") containing necessary information about the deployed security measures. The ordinance provides details on the content of the mentioned security concept. It must contain a description of all necessary technical, organizational and constructional security measures and their suitability as well as a description of processes, deployed products, the reliability of the personnel and remaining risks. Additionally, the ordinance provides concrete guidelines on how to evaluate products for qualified electronic signatures. The ordinance prescribes to evaluate products following the Common Criteria for Information Technology Security Evaluation [6] or the Information Technology Security Evaluation Criteria (ITSEC) [22]. This comprehensive regulation enables trustworthy, secure and legally compliant operation of CAs.

3   Regulatory Framework

This section provides a detailed overview of the proposed legal framework. The general approach is to define organizational and technical requirements for remote electronic voting services that assure compliance with constitutional and other legal requirements while providing a trustworthy environment for voting and incentives for VSPs to participate. Our legal framework consists of a statute and a corresponding ordinance. This separation is necessary, because legal regulations made by statutes are intended to be valid long-term and apply to many scenarios. Passing a statute is a complex process and thus changes to the final statute are to be avoided. Consequently, statutes are restricted to general rules and regulations. We solve this by introducing a separate ordinance to be passed by executive order. It contains more concrete technical details, so the regulation may be adapted to new scenarios and techniques more easily. The ordinance keeps the statute free from details and allows quick reaction to technical changes. It provides details, technical and organizational requirements and provisions to concretize the regulation given in the statute. For example, it includes the specific requirements for accreditation, the evaluation and certification procedure, details on briefing or requirements for performing the operation of remote electronic elections. Regulatory procedure splits in accreditation and supervision. Accreditation brings proof of initial compliance with the rules and regulations set forth in the framework. Supervision makes sure they are continually adhered to.

3.1   The Statute

Purpose, Scope and Terminology. Purpose of our statutory approach is is to create a legal framework for certified trustworthy remote electronic voting services. The framework is not limited to specific types of elections. It regulates by focusing on the service of providing remote electronic elections for different non-political types of elections. A "remote electronic election" is an electronic election in which the voter is able to cast his/her vote using a networked terminal device. A "VSP" is everyone providing remote electronic voting services for business, not necessarily accredited. The act does not preclude non-accredited VSPs from offering similar services. This assures conformity with Article 12 of the German Constitution [4]. Consequently, the accreditation procedure is fully voluntary. However, there are several reasons and incentives to become accredited: Other laws may prescribe accreditation for a specific type of election. Also, employing a certified VSP can facilitate and professionalize remote electronic elections. This can create market demand for certified VSPs. The act leaves rights and duties of the party hosting the election untouched.

Accreditation. The accreditation requirement is one element that promotes trust in the election procedure. It assures evaluation and certification of compliance with basic election principles, technical/organizational security and data protection. Generally, accreditation means that a VSP has provided reliable proof of verified trustworthiness of its services. For this, a VSP has to apply for an official certificate of trustworthy remote electronic voting services. An administrative authority will be responsible for accrediting VSPs. This authority may employ private services to perform the accreditation process, thereby reducing administrative effort. Accredited VSPs will be issued a certificate by the responsible authority. They may then carry the title "Accredited VSP" to indicate their compliance with the framework and thereby their trustworthiness. To continually ensure this, a repeat accreditation process is mandatory. We suggest every three years or earlier in case of severe security relevant changes to technology or organization. If a VSP does not fulfill the obligations imposed by the statute or the corresponding ordinance or if an accreditation requirement is no longer fulfilled, the responsible authority will revoke the accreditation.

Accreditation Requirements. Accreditation requires the reliability and specialist qualification necessary for the operation of a VSP, particularly regarding the personnel. A VSP is reliable if it guarantees observation of the legal provisions regarding its operation. It has the necessary specialist qualification if its personnel have the knowledge, experience and skills necessary for this activity. A VSP will only be accredited if it fulfills the obligations concerning the security objectives, the technical and organizational security requirements, the operation of a remote electronic election as well as briefing and documentation (as defined by the corresponding ordinance, see Section 3.2) in a way that ensures secure and reliable remote electronic voting services. Additionally, accreditation requires the VSP to operate in accordance with the legal provisions on data protection, especially the provisions of the German Federal and State Data Protection Acts and the German Teleservices Act [19].

Proof of Requirements for Accreditation. The reliability of personnel is proven by an up to date certificate of good conduct according to the Federal Central Criminal Register Act (Bundeszentralregistergesetz, [8]). The specialist qualification necessary for particular tasks during operation is proven by means of respective certificates on special education and advanced training. The security concept (cf. Section 3.2) must be evaluated and certified with respect to its suitability and practical implementation by the responsible authority. The evaluation includes software, hardware as well as technical and organizational security of the VSP. In addition, fulfillment of the data protection provisions must be certified by an official authority, which does not necessarily have to be the same as the accrediting and supervising authority.

Legal Obligations of the VSP

Election Principles. A key component to achieve trust in the voting process is for a remote electronic election to comply with the basic election principles to an extent defined by the requirements of the particular type of non-parliamentary election. The remote electronic voting service must be permanently available during the voting period, ensuring all voters have a chance to cast their vote (universal suffrage). The VSP must ensure secret voting without any interference or manipulation. No connection between voter and vote may be established (secret ballot). At the same time, it also has to ensure identification and authentication of the voters. All electronic voting documents, including cast votes must be protected from loss or manipulation (equal suffrage). Alteration of voting documents must be recognizable; their integrity must be verifiable (principle of the public nature of elections).

Performing a Remote Electronic Election. The accredited VSP must use a register of persons entitled to vote and persons with the right to stand for election from the party responsible for the election (election host) into the remote electronic voting service. The reliable identification of eligible voters and candidates presupposes correct registers. The host is responsible to create and deliver such registers to the VSP. The host generally remains responsible for the voting process while the VSP is responsible only for the technical and organizational implementation. Therefore the accredited VSP has to enable the host to initiate, to suspend and to terminate the election and to initiate the counting of votes at its will. All voting options must be displayed to the voters. No preference for a particular option may be suggested from the way of presentation. The VSP has to enable voters to abort the voting procedure, to correct their vote any number of times before the final cast and to verify the correct storage of the vote. They must also be able to cast an invalid vote intentionally. Voters must not be able to show their voting decision to others using the voting system. After completion of the election, the accredited VSP must ensure a correct counting of votes verifiable at any time.

Briefing Obligation. It is the responsibility of the accredited VSP to brief voters and host on remaining security risks and necessary measures they have to take for secure usage of the remote electronic voting service. For example, the VSP must inform about risks resulting from malicious software like viruses and how to protect the terminal devices used for voting against this threat. However the VSP is still responsible to ensure that an insecure terminal cannot jeopardize more than the voting decision cast at this particular terminal. For the briefing of the voters, the VSP must inform every voter with textual instructions. The voter must confirm having taken notice of these instructions as a prerequisite for participating in the election.

Documentation Obligation. The accredited VSP must document the measures taken to assure compliance with statute and ordinance in a way that both documentation and its integrity can be verified at any time, for example using qualified signatures and time stamps. The documentation must be archived for later inspection. Immediately after completion of the election, the accredited VSP must provide the documentation to the election host. The ordinance specifies details on the extent of documentation.

Supervision

Responsible Authority. To ensure legal compliance and a standardized security level of remote electronic voting services, the operation of VSPs is controlled by a federal authority. Its responsibilities include accreditation and supervision of the VSPs.

Measures of Supervision. The responsible authority may employ private subsidiaries for performing the supervision. To ensure the observation of this statute and the ordinance, it is authorized to enforce measures towards VSPs as well as the evaluation and certification subsidiaries it employs. The responsible authority must prohibit a VSP or an evaluation or certification subsidiary from conducting business temporarily, partially or entirely, if the prerequisites for accreditation or recognition are no longer fulfilled, unsuitable products are used or obligations are violated. The responsible authority must provide names, addresses and other contact data of accredited VSPs to the public.

3.2   The Ordinance

The Security Concept. Its security concept is the basis for the evaluation of a VSP. The VSP has to explain all measures taken to assure compliance with regulations. Thus, the security concept must contain the following descriptions: all necessary technical, constructional and organizational security measures and their suitability, the technical products used, a the organization of setup and process, compliance with the election principles, with data protection statutes and of measures for ensuring and maintaining operation, especially in case of emergencies, the procedures for evaluating and ensuring the reliability of the deployed personnel and an estimation and validation of remaining security risks. To sum up, the security concept includes all security relevant aspects of the VSP. Software and hardware are addressed as well as measures concerning organization and personnel. We provide recommendations on suitable evaluation methods to be used by the responsible authority in Section 4.

Requirements for Performing Remote Electronic Elections. It must be ensured that every person eligible to vote is enabled to cast her vote during the voting period without undue interruption or being prevented from voting. Therefore a high rate of service availability is necessary. Practical experience shows that such availability can be achieved by implementing technical measures like backup and redundancy systems and high bandwidth network connections. Upon interruptions, the voting system must ensure a secure restart sustaining the legal election principles and saving the votes already cast and all necessary data present before interruption. The voting system must transmit, receive and store identification data of the voters and votes protected from unauthorized disclosure. The voting system must be able to detect unauthorized modification, erasure and addition of identification data of the voters, votes, protocol data and further relevant data. Immediately ahead of the voting procedure, the VSP has to provide means for the party responsible for the election to verify that the ballot box does not contain any votes and that all other parts of the voting system are in their predefined initial state. The VSP has to accomplish identification and authentication of the voter by use of at least two independent security measures. The VSP must display the whole content of the electronic ballot in a reasonable and discernible manner. The vote count must be initiated publicly on the premises of the election host and the result must be published. Additionally, an accredited VSP must document all essential actions during the election and protect the record from unauthorized access. This documentation includes data, events and actions from the particular voting process. In particular, anonymous ballot data must be stored in way that makes recounting possible. Access to the recorded data is to be allowed as far as it supports recounts but must be restricted if the particular data would violate the secrecy of the votes or any other security objective of the election.

Extent of Documentation. All documentation regarding the remote electronic election has to be archived outside the voting system and protected against manipulation by means of qualified signatures. The electronic votes must be stored in a way enabling recount any number of times by means of arbitrary tallying software to provide transparency and verifiability of the tallying procedure.

4   Discussion

This section discusses some of the open issues of our regulatory framework and makes recommendations on how to resolve them. The evaluation and accreditation procedure introduced by the framework is of great importance for the trustworthiness of remote electronic elections and VSPs. In order to be accredited, we require a VSP to provide a security concept which serves as foundation for the evaluation performed by an official authority (cf. Section 3.1). The procedure comprises evaluation of both the voting system software and the operational environment. For the responsible authority, well approved evaluation methods exist for most aspects of the security concept. Therefore, existing certifications of adequate quality can replace further evaluation to avoid double effort. However, the decision remains with the responsible authority. We recommend the following evaluation methods. The voting system software is intended to be evaluated according to the "Common Criteria for Information Technology Security Evaluation" [6], which is an internationally approved evaluation standard. We recommend the Common Criteria Protection Profile "Basic set of security requirements for Online Voting Products" as the basis for evaluation, which was released in 2008 by the German Federal Office for Information Security (BSI, [13]). This Protection Profile is intended to be a foundation for all upcoming Protection Profiles for online voting systems and products. Pursuant to the Protection Profile we recommend an evaluation assurance level (EAL) of at minimum EAL 2+ for voting systems in order to comply with the regulatory framework. In accordance with [7] the required evaluation level could be increased to EAL 4+ depending on the intended application scenario. The core of the system could even be evaluated according to the highest level EAL 7 if necessary. For the evaluation of the operational environment of the VSP we recommend the following methods. Evaluation of personnel can be based on certificate of good conduct according to the Federal Central Criminal Register Act [8]. Technical, organizational and constructional measures can be evaluated according to IT-Grundschutz/ISO 27001 [14]. The evaluation of data protection measures could be conducted by the approved Independent Centre for Privacy Protection Schleswig-Holstein (ICPP, Unabhängiges Landeszentrum für Datenschutz Schleswig-Holstein, [21]), a cooperation of specialized evaluation authorities which conduct data protection audits.

Another important issue is the selection of the authority that will be responsible for accreditation and supervision of VSPs. In the context of the German Signature Law, the respective responsible authority for supervision and accreditation of CAs is the Federal Network Agency (Bundesnetzagentur, [15]). For evaluation and certification purposes the Federal Network Agency authorizes third parties, for example the Federal Office for Information Security (BSI, [12]) and the TÜVIT [34]. Their qualification and experience in supervision and evaluation of CAs suggests employing them for the supervision and evaluation of VSPs as well. However, depending on the election scenario, great care must be taken that the independence of these authorities does not come in doubt. Otherwise, the goal of trustworthiness may be compromised. The authority could be seen as governmental intervention where it would be inappropriate. Nonetheless, we consider an official authority a reasonable approach to create trust in VSPs for non-political elections. Because here, the authority is very unlikely to have interest in the outcome of the elections, there is also not much reason for collusion. If independence is seen as crucial, it could be enhanced by assigning different authorities for different types of elections. Another idea is for political elections to deploy several supervising authorities thereby sharing the control. This is an open question and subject for further research.

Another open issue is to explore whether our regulatory framework could be extended so VSPs could be used in parliamentary (i.e. political) elections. As stated above, the requirements by the principle of the public nature of elections are not binding for the concept of a VSP in non-political elections. If VSPs were ever to be used in parliamentary elections, strict requirements would have to be fulfilled. How could this be achieved? The principle of the public nature of elections requires the voting process and its result to be verifiable by the voter.

Every voter must be able to perform the verification without any special knowledge. Satisfying both aspects at the same time is a technical challenge. Recent e-voting protocols support different verifiability techniques like voter-verifiable receipts or a bulletin board (see for example the protocols of Baudron et al. [2], the Civitas scheme from Clarkson et al. [5], the Helios scheme from Ben Adida [1], Juels and Catalano [24], Lee and Kim [27], the "Pret a voter" scheme from Ryan [28] or Neff's scheme [30]). Some protocols therefore rely on trustworthy components, so the verification partially depends on the voter trusting the correct functionality of the voting system. Rivest and Wack therefore defined the term of *software independence*: "A voting system is software-independent if an undetected change or error in its software cannot cause an undetectable change or error in an election outcome." [32]. Some protocols claim to provide verifiability without the need to trust the voting system, for example Neff's scheme [30]. Most voting systems with such sophisticated verifiability properties however use complex methods, for example special receipts which require special technical knowledge of the voter. The holding by the Constitutional Court would not permit this. Therefore a combination of technical and organizational approaches may be able to jointly satisfy what the principle of the public nature of elections requires. The court explicitly allowed for this option - as long as it leaves a means for individual verification of correct voting procedure. A solution could be an easy-to-understand voter-verifiable voting protocol. This could be implemented as open-source software, because the demand for verifiability of the system code would outweigh the business interest of the developer in keeping the code proprietary. The voting system should be embedded in a secure and trustworthy operational environment, which certified VSPs could create. The voting system software and hardware is to be evaluated and certified. All essential steps of the voting process must be documented. The documentation must be publicly accessible for verification purposes as long as its disclosure does not violate the basic election principles or provisions regarding data protection. Votes are to be stored outside the voting system for recount purposes by means of arbitrary counting software. A lack of comprehensive verifiability in the voting system might not be replaceable by evaluation and certification. But a combined approach of technical and organizational measures can reduce the problem significantly.

5   Application and Implementation

Entities may choose to employ accredited VSPs in various ways. Corporations may, for example, prescribe in its bylaws that if remote electronic elections are performed, accredited VSPs are to be assigned. As a matter of corporate compliance, this may prevent liability to shareholders or other parties for lack of security should the results of an election come in doubt. Similarly, a public body may include the use of VSPs in its ordinances. The respective entity should then contact one of the accredited VSPs to enter in a remote voting services contract.

For the presented approach to be implemented, the statute has to be written out in full and then pass the legislative procedure. Legislative competence lies with the German Bundestag, Art. 74 I Nr. 11 GG, [4]. A federal regulation is necessary pursuant to Art. 72 II GG, [4], since non-parliamentary elections often claim validity nationwide. Also, their similar performance nationwide asks for federal regulation.

6   Conclusion

This paper presents an approach to a legal regulation of remote electronic election service providers (VSPs) in non-political elections. It considered the requirements for electronic elections resulting from the judgment of the German federal constitutional court on the use of electronic voting machines. By suggesting legal regulation that addresses independent supervision as well as evaluation and accreditation we introduced a comprehensive trust concept for VSPs that can serve as a foundation for providing secure, trustworthy and legally compliant remote electronic elections.

References

1. Adida, B.: Helios: Web-based Open-Audit Voting. In: Proceedings of the Seventeenth Usenix Security Symposium. USENIX Security (2008)
2. Baudron, O., Fouque, P.A., Pointcheval, D., Stern, J., Poupard, G.: Practical Multi-Candidate Election System. In: PODC, pp. 274–283 (2001)
3. Buchmann, J., Roßnagel, A.: Das Bundesverfassungsgericht und Telemedienwahlen. Zu den Auswirkungen des Urteils des Bundesverfassungsgerichts zu elektronischen Wahlgeräten für die Durchführung von "Internetwahlen" in nichtpolitischen Bereichen. In: Kommunikation und Recht, K&R (2009), Heft 7/8
4. Federal Constitution for the Federal Republic of Germany (Grundgesetz für die Bundesrepublik Deutschland), http://www.bundestag.de/parlament/funktion/gesetze/grundgesetz/gg.html, english translation: http://www.bundestag.de/interakt/infomat/fremdsprachiges_material/downloads/ggEn_download.pdf
5. Clarkson, M., Chong, S., Myers, A.: Civitas: Toward a Secure Voting System. In: IEEE Symposium on Security and Privacy, pp. 354–368. IEEE, Los Alamitos (2008)
6. The Common Criteria Portal, http://www.commoncriteriaportal.org/
7. Grimm, R., Volkamer, M.: Development of a Formal IT Security Model for Remote Electronic Voting Systems. In: Electronic Voting 2008 - EVOTE 2008. LNI, vol. 131, pp. 185–196. Gesellschaft für Informatik, Bonn (2008)
8. German Federal Central Criminal Register Act (Bundeszentralregistergesetz), http://www.gesetze-im-internet.de/bzrg/index.html
9. German Federal Constitutional Court (Bundesverfassungsgericht): Use of voting computers in 2005 Bundestag election unconstitutional. Press release no. 19/2009 (March 3, 2009) http://www.bundesverfassungsgericht.de/pressemitteilungen/bvg09-019en.html
10. German Federal Constitutional Court (Bundesverfassungsgericht): Judgment (March 3, 2009), 2 BvC 3/07 and 2 BvC 4/07 (2009), http://www.bundesverfassungsgericht.de/entscheidungen/cs20090303_2bvc000307.html

11. German Federal Electoral Act (Bundeswahlgesetz),
    http://www.gesetze-im-internet.de/bwahlg/index.html
12. German Federal Office for Information Security (BSI),
    http://www.bsi.de/english/index.htm
13. German Federal Office for Information Security (BSI): Common Criteria Protection Profile for Basic set of security requirements for Online Voting Products (Common Criteria Schutzprofil für Basissatz von Sicherheitsanforderungen an Online-Wahlprodukte),
    http://www.bsi.de/zertifiz/zert/reporte/pp0037b.pdf, english translation:
    http://www.bsi.de/zertifiz/zert/reporte/pp0037b_engl.pdf
14. German Federal Office for Information Security (BSI), IT-Grundschutz Catalogues,
    http://www.bsi.de/english/gshb/download/index.htm
15. German Federal Network Agency (Bundesnetzagentur), http://www.bundesnetzagentur.de/enid/8c75681be0bdb7b0dd939bd54f8d6826,0/xn.html
16. German Federal Voting Machines Ordinance (Bundeswahlgeräteverordnung),
    http://www.gesetze-im-internet.de/bwahlgv/index.html
17. German Ordinance on Electronic Signatures (Signaturverordnung, SigV),
    http://bundesrecht.juris.de/sigv_2001/index.html, english translation:
    http://www.bundesnetzagentur.de/media/archive/3613.pdf
18. German Signatures Law (Signaturgesetz, SigG),
    http://bundesrecht.juris.de/sigg_2001/index.html, english translation:
    http://www.bundesnetzagentur.de/media/archive/3612.pdf
19. German Teleservices Act (Telemediengesetz),
    http://www.gesetze-im-internet.de/tmg/
20. German Works Constitution Act (Betriebsverfassungsgesetz),
    http://www.gesetze-im-internet.de/betrvg/
21. Independent Centre for Privacy Protection Schleswig-Holstein (ICPP) (Unabhängiges Landeszentrum für Datenschutz Schleswig-Holstein),
    https://www.datenschutzzentrum.de/faq/guetesiegel_engl.htm
22. Information Technology Security Evaluation Criteria (ITSEC),
    http://www.bsi.bund.de/zertifiz/itkrit/itsec-en.pdf
23. Joaquim, R., Zuquete, A., Ferreira, P.: REVS – A Robust Electronic Voting System. In: Proceedings of IADIS International Conference e-Society 2003, Lisbon, pp. 95–103 (2003)
24. Juels, A., Catalano, D., Jakobsson, M.: Coercion-Resistant Electronic Elections. In: WPES 2005, Proceedings of the 2005 ACM workshop on Privacy in the electronic society, pp. 61–70. ACM, New York (2005)
25. Langer, L., Schmidt, A.: Onlinewahlen mit Wahldiensteanbieter - das Verbundprojekt voteremote. In: Proceedings of EDem 2008 E-Democracy Conference, pp. 281–290. OCG, Austria (2008)
26. Langer, L., Schmidt, A., Buchmann, J.: Secure and Practical Online Elections via Voting Service Provider. In: ICEG 4th International Conference on e-Government 2008, pp. 255–262. RMIT University, Melbourne (2008)
27. Lee, B., Kim, K.: Receipt-Free Electronic Voting Scheme with a Tamper-Resistant Randomizer. In: Lee, P.J., Lim, C.H. (eds.) ICISC 2002. LNCS, vol. 2587, pp. 389–406. Springer, Heidelberg (2003)
28. Lundin, D., Ryan, P.: Human readable paper verification of Pret a Voter. Technical Report 1071, School of Computing Science. Newcastle University (2008)

29. Micromata GmbH: Polyas voting system,
    http://www.micromata.de/en/produkte/polyas.jsp
30. Neff, A.: Practical high certainty intent verification for encrypted votes,
    http://www.votehere.com/old/vhti/documentation/vsv-2.0.3638.pdf
31. Riera, A.: An Introduction to Electronic Voting Schemes. Technical Report PIRDI
    9-98, University of Barcelona (1998), http://pirdi.uab.es/document/pirdi9.ps
32. Rivest, R., Wack, J.: On the Notion of "Software Independence" in Voting Systems
    (2006), http://vote.nist.gov/SI-in-voting.pdf
33. Scytl, http://www.scytl.com/
34. TÜVIT, http://www.tuvit.de/english/Home.asp

VeryVote: A Voter Verifiable Code Voting System[*]

Rui Joaquim[1], Carlos Ribeiro[2], and Paulo Ferreira[2]

[1] ISEL, Polytechnic Institute of Lisbon
Rua Conselheiro Emídio Navarro 1, 1959-007 Lisboa, Portugal
rjoaquim@cc.isel.ipl.pt
[2] INESC-ID, Intituto Superior Técnico
Rua Alves Redol 9 - 6 andar, 1000-029 Lisboa, Portugal
carlos.ribeiro@ist.utl.pt, paulo.ferreira@inesc-id.pt

Abstract. Code voting is a technique used to address the secure platform problem of remote voting. A code voting system consists in secretly sending, e.g. by mail, code sheets to voters that map their choices to entry codes in their ballot. While voting, the voter uses the code sheet to know what code to enter in order to vote for a particular candidate. In effect, the voter does the vote encryption and, since no malicious software on the PC has access to the code sheet it is not able to change the voter's intention. However, without compromising the voter's privacy, the vote codes are not enough to prove that the vote is recorded and counted as cast by the election server.

We present a voter verifiable code voting solution which, without revealing the voter's vote, allows the voter to verify, at the end of the election, that her vote was cast and counted as intended by just performing the match of a few small strings. Moreover, w.r.t. a general code voting system, our solution comes with only a minor change in the voting interaction.

Keywords: Code voting, Internet voting, election integrity.

1   Introduction

The secure platform problem [1] of remote voting, i.e. the use of unreliable/not trustworthy client platforms such as the voter's computer and the Internet infrastructure connecting it to the election server, is one of the major problems that prevents the spread of electronic remote elections, e.g. Internet Voting.

Code voting [2,3] is a technique that addresses the secure platform problem establishing a secure connection between the voter and the election server by means of codes printed in a code sheet previously and anonymously delivered to the voter. As explained in Sec. 2.1, this general approach only confirms that the

---

[*] This work was supported by the Portuguese Foundation for Science and Technology grants SFRH/BD/47786/2008 and PTDC/EIA/65588/2006.

P.Y.A. Ryan and B. Schoenmakers (Eds.): VOTE-ID 2009, LNCS 5767, pp. 106–121, 2009.

election server receives the right vote code. It does not prove that the candidate selected by the vote code really receives the voter's vote.

However, to guarantee the election integrity a fully (end-to-end) verifiable election system is needed. Therefore, we need to verify that the votes are cast-as-intended and counted-as-cast [4]. Cast-as-intended means that the recorded vote represents the voter's intention, and counted-as-cast means that tally correctly reflects the sum of the recorded votes. In a general code voting system we have none of these properties.

VeryVote addresses the secure platform problem in an end-to-end verifiable way. We achieve this end-to-end verifiability by adapting the MarkPledge cryptographic receipts technique [5] to a general code voting system. In the process of making a code voting system end-to-end verifiable we have compromised some of the voter's privacy to the election server, as described in Sec. 6.3. On the other hand, we provide verification mechanisms that allow an universal verification of the tally and also a simple voter verification that her vote was recorded as cast, while still protecting the voter's privacy from the general public. Additionally, our solution also simplifies the code sheet creation and distribution processes.

In the next section we present the related work, followed by and overview of VeryVote on Sec. 3. Then, in Sec. 4 we present the building blocks of our vote protocol and on Sec. 5 we describe the vote protocol. Finally, we evaluate VeryVote in Sec. 6 and conclude in Sec. 7.

2   Related Work

In this section we first present an overview of code voting systems. Then, we present the MarkPledge technique that we have adapted in order to provide the cast-as-intended and counted-as-cast properties to a generic code voting protocol.

2.1   Code Voting Systems

The first code voting implementation we are aware of was proposed in 2001 by Chaum [2], the SureVote system. Since then the code voting approach was used in the UK on some pilots of Internet, SMS and telephone voting [6,7]. In [8,9,10] you can find an analysis and some solution proposals to the vote selling problematic in a general code voting system. Oppliger and Schwenk present in [11] a proposal to improve the user friendliness of code voting by using CAPTCHAs. A different approach was used in [12], where the code sheets are generated by the voter with the help of a secure token, which in the voting phase translates the vote code to an encrypted vote in order to provide a verifiable vote tally. On the other hand, this last approach requires trust in the secure token, which can undetectably manipulate the voter's vote.

Generally, a code voting system addresses the insecure platform problem of remote voting by means of a vote protocol based on a code sheet. This approach consists in secretly sending, e.g. by mail, code sheets to voters that map their choices to entry codes in their ballot. While voting, the voter uses the code sheet to know what code to enter in order to vote for a particular candidate. In response, the election server sends back to the voter a confirmation code, which is associated with the vote code in the voter's code sheet. If the confirmation code is right the voter knows that her vote code has reached the election server. However, a correct confirmation code does not imply the use of the voter's selection by the election server when computing the election tally.

2.2   MarkPledge Cryptographic Receipts

The goal of the Andrew Neff's MarkPledge cryptographic receipts [5] is to prove that a particular vote encryption is an encryption of a vote for the selected candidate. The proof is based on a special form of vote encryption, formally described in [5]. For sake of simplicity we present here a more informal description based on [13, 4].

The MarkPledge technique starts by a special encoding of each candidate in the ballot. A vote is formed by a sequence of numbers, one for each voting option. Each number is a special encoding of a 0 or a 1: 1 for the selected candidate and 0 for every other candidate. In consequence of this special vote encoding it is possible to encrypt the vote and then verify the encryption without disclosing the encrypted vote.

Follows a more detailed explanation of the encoding, encryption and verification of a MarkPledge vote.

Special Bit Encoding and Encryption – The encrypted vote is formed by a special bit encryption for each candidate, which we denote $BitEnc$. For the selected candidate it is encrypted a 1, $BitEnc(1)$, and for all other candidates it is encrypted a 0, $BitEnc(0)$.

Consider α as the security parameter that defines the soundness of the MarkPledge technique as $1 - \frac{1}{2^\alpha}$. Then, the $BitEnc$ of a bit b, $BitEnc(b)$, is an α-length sequence of Ballot Mark Pairs (BMPs). Each BMP is composed of two independent El Gamal ciphertexts ($BMP = [l_i, r_i]$). Each ciphertext that forms a BMP is either an encryption of a 1 ($Enc(1)$) or a 0 ($Enc(0)$).[1] The $BitEnc(b)$ is defined as follows:

- If $b = 1$, then all BMPs are of the form $[Enc(0), Enc(0)]$ or $[Enc(1), Enc(1)]$.
- If $b = 0$, then all BMPs are of the form $[Enc(0), Enc(1)]$ or $[Enc(1), Enc(0)]$.

A vote verification is based on the proof that the particular $BitEnc(b)$ of the selected candidate is a $BitEnc(1)$. Due to the special type of encryption used it is possible to prove in zero knowledge and with soundness $1 - \frac{1}{2^\alpha}$ that a particular encryption $c = BitEnc(1)$. We describe a variation to the original verification scheme [13, 5], as it is more suitable for our CodeVoting adaptation goals. The

---

[1] Recall that in normal El Gamal encryption [14] the value 0 is not part of the plaintext domain. Therefore, what we really have are two values v_0, v_1, chosen from the plaintext domain, which respectively represent value 0 and value 1.

verification process of this variation is based on a random challenge (*chal*) to *BitEnc(b)*. Follows the details of the verification steps between a Prover $\mathcal{P}$ and a Verifier $\mathcal{V}$:

1. $\mathcal{V}$ sends *commit(chal)* to $\mathcal{P}$, e.g. hash(*chal*).
   At this point it is necessary to commit to *chal* in order to prevent an easy vote selling/coercion attack. On the other hand, it is necessary to keep the *chal* secret to prevent the construction of a fake *BitEnc(1)*.
2. $\mathcal{P}$ sends $c = BitEnc(b)$ and a bit string (ChosenString) to $\mathcal{V}$, where bit i of ChosenString corresponds to the bit encrypted within both elements of BMP_i. Therefore, ChosenString is α bits long. Recall that only a *BitEnc(1)* is composed of BMPs encoding two ones or two zeros.
3. $\mathcal{V}$ sends an α bits long random challenge (*chal*) to $\mathcal{P}$, which must match *commit(chal)*.
4. For each bit i of *chal*, $\mathcal{P}$ reveals the randomness[2] used for BMP_i element l_i if $chal_i = 0$, or for element r_i if $chal_i = 1$. This reveals *OpenBitEnc(b)*, an α-length bit string that results from the concatenation of the decrypted bits, one for each BMP within c.
5. $\mathcal{V}$ checks that this string matches ChosenString.

The soundness of this protocol derives from the randomness of *chal*, which ensures that, if $b = 0$, then $\mathcal{P}$ must guess the single α-length bit string that will be revealed by *chal*.

The proof is zero knowledge since $\mathcal{V}$ "cannot" use the results to prove to a third party that $c = BitEnc(1)$. $\mathcal{V}$ can only reveal one (already chosen) element of each BMP, i.e. she cannot open the *BitEnc* for any other value of *chal*. Therefore, $\mathcal{V}$ has only a success chance of $\frac{1}{2^\alpha}$ in an attempt to prove to a third party that $c = BitEnc(1)$, i.e. the third party must choose exactly the same challenge chosen by $\mathcal{V}$.

Vote Encryption and Verification – The main idea of the vote encryption and verification steps is quite simple: i) the Voting Machine (*VM*) creates an encrypted ballot composed of a *BitEnc(0)* for all candidates except for the chosen one, which will have a *BitEnc(1)*, and ii) the voter runs the verification protocol that will prove that there is a *BitEnc(1)* associated to the chosen candidate.

We assume that the ballot is well formed, i.e. it contains only one *BitEnc(1)*. There are techniques to verify that the ballot is well formed but they are outside the scope of this paper (e.g. Neff in [5] suggests the use of techniques presented in [15, 16]).

The voter interaction protocol is thus:

1. Alice, our voter, enters her candidate choice (*j*) and the *commit(chal)*.

---

[2] Revealing the randomness allows for the ElGamal encryption reconstruction of the BMP element, and thus for the verification of the encrypted value.

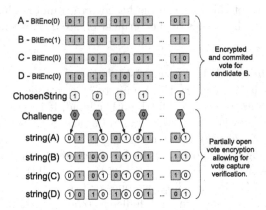

Fig. 1. MarkPledge vote encryption and verification. The vote encryption represents a vote for candidate B ($BitEnc(1)$). The values inside the circles form the $strings(i)$ and correspond to the bits of the $OpenBitEncs(b_i)$, which are revealed accordingly with the value of the challenge.

2. The VM outputs the encrypted vote and displays the ChosenString, which matches the encrypted string for $c_j = BitEnc_j(b_j)$, the bit encryption corresponding to Alice choice j. (c.f. lines B - BitEnc(1) and ChosenString in Fig. 1).

3. Alice enters $chal$, which must match $commit(chal)$.

4. The VM completes the proof that $b_j = 1$, and uses the same $chal$ to simulate the same proof for all others b_i, i.e. it uses $chal$ to create a $OpenBitEnc(b_i)$ for each $i \neq j$.

   As a result of this operation the VM outputs a vote receipt containing a text string for each index/candidate ($string(i)$). The $string(i)$ represent an encoding of the α-length bit string that results from the $OpenBitEnc(b_i)$ (in our example we use the original binary encoding).

5. Alice verifies that the ChosenString appears next to her candidate of choice, i.e. it matches $string_{(j)}$. Additionally, Alice must verify that the text strings present in the receipt match the encrypted vote, i.e. they match the corresponding $OpenBitEncs$. However this process can be leveraged using a third party organization that verifies the correctness of the vote encryption [13].

Note that, the receipt does not reveal which of $string_{(i)}$ was the real ChosenString displayed by the VM to Alice. Alice also cannot convincingly prove which string is the real one.

It is also important to emphasize that the MarkPledge verification technique only works if Alice does not reveal her $chal$ prior to the VM commitment to the encrypted vote. If VM knows the $chal$ in advance it can freely manipulate Alice's vote. This vulnerability can be exploited by message reordering and social engineering attacks [4].

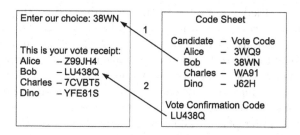

Fig. 2. In step (1) the voter uses the vote code $38WN$ to vote for the candidate Bob. Then, in step (2) the voter gets a MarkPledge receipt for her vote, therefore the vote confirmation code (the *ChosenString* of *BitEnc*(1)) appears next to the candidate Bob.

3   VeryVote Overview

As explained in Sec.2.1, the simple verification that the election server (ES) replies with the right reply code is no proof that the ES will use the corresponding candidate when performing the election tally. The reply code only serves to prove that the right vote code has reached the ES and nothing else.

VeryVote uses a generic code voting interaction between the voter and the ES. However, it also produces an encrypted vote (and a cryptographic vote receipt) based on the received vote code. The vote encryption allows the publication of the link between the encrypted votes and the voters who casted them.

The publication of the encrypted vote/voter association allows voters to verify their votes using the cryptographic receipts produced by the ES. Additionally, a cryptographic vote tallying protocol can be used to provide proofs that the tally is computed correctly. The cryptographic vote encryption and tally verification makes VeryVote end-to-end verifiable.

To provide the end-to-end verifiable property and to allow the correction of any detected error, it is necessary for the ES to know who is casting the votes, c.f. 6.2. Therefore, the code sheet generation and delivery process can be significantly simplified. Which means that, in opposition to a traditional code voting system, in VeryVote the code sheet delivery is not anonymous, although it needs to be secret, i.e. only known to the ES and the voter. Therefore, the ES creates the code sheets, seals them, e.g. puts them inside a sealed envelop and/or adds a scratch surface to the code sheet, and then sends the code sheets to each voter, e.g. by mail. This procedure allows the ES to easily associate each code sheet to a particular voter on election day.

The code sheet produced by the ES contains a vote code for each candidate and one confirmation code that works similarly to the reply code in a traditional code voting system. However, at the voting phase, the voter besides receiving just the reply code, receives a MarkPledge cryptographic vote receipt with the confirmation code associated with the selected candidate, cf. Fig. 2.

After the election end, there is a claiming period where a voter can verify that her vote was recorded as casted. The check performed by the voter is simply a match of her MarkPledge receipt with the one published by the ES. Nevertheless, the political parties and other third party organizations must verify the correctness of the published receipts, c.f. Sec.2.2. By using this two step verification of the MarkPledge technique it is possible to split the verification process between the voter and some other organization. The voter performs the simple verification step, leaving the more complex part of the verification to organizations with much more resources than an average voter.

During the claiming period, and if any error is detected in the verification process, a voter should be allowed to invalidate her vote. We also suggest to allow the revoking of the Internet vote at the voter's wishes to mitigate two problems with the VeryVote system: first, since VeryVote is an Internet voting system the voter may not have the desired privacy while voting, and therefore may have been exposed to some kind of coercion/vote selling; and second, the voter may not have completely understood the voting process and therefore may have doubts about the casted vote. Therefore, we argue that a secondary voting channel should be available.[3] The invalidation of the Internet vote is simple because the encrypted votes are not anonymous.

After the claiming stage, any vote that was not invalidated is included in the tally process, which is also cryptographically verifiable. Therefore, anyone can assert on the validity of the tally.

4   Protocol Building Blocks

We use some well known constructions as building blocks of our vote protocol. Therefore, and before entering into the details of our vote protocol, we present a short description of the building blocks used.

Threshold encryption scheme – We need a threshold encryption scheme to enable a vote and tally verification without compromising the voters' privacy. In a threshold encryption scheme the secret key s is shared among several authorities, the trustees T. To recover a message encrypted with the public key it is required the cooperation of t (a configurable threshold) trustees.

Our protocol specification relies on the El Gamal encryption scheme [14]. More precisely, a variant described by Cramer et al. [16].

Mix Net – To provide an anonymous and verifiable tally we propose the use of a mix net [18]. Namely, we propose the use of a verifiable re-encryption mix net such as the one proposed by Neff in [19].

BitEnc Implementation – As in the original MarkPledge scheme [5], we use the $BitEnc$ construction based on El Gamal encryption (cf. section 2.2).

---

[3] A possible solution to allow the voter to cast a new vote is the one used in Estonia [17], where on election day any voter who casts a paper ballot automatically revokes the Internet vote.

Public Bulletin Board – To enable public verification of the election's integrity all non private data should be public, for which we use the usual public bulletin board construction [13, 16]. All data in the bulletin board is authenticated by means of digital signatures.

Shared Random Number Generation Protocol – In our protocol we need a random number generation by a set of trustees $\mathcal{T}$. We propose the use of a simple two round protocol to generate the shared random number:

1. In the first step each trustee t_i of $\mathcal{T}$ secretly generates a random number r_{t_i} and commits to it by publishing a signed hash of the random number.
2. After the commitment of all trustees, each trustee reveals its random number. Then, all trustees verify the correctness of the commitments published in the first step. If all commitments are correct, the shared random number is computed by applying a bitwise exclusive or to all the random numbers r_{t_i} generated by the trustees.

5   Vote Protocol

In this section we specify the vote protocol. Here we explain in detail how to securely generate a MarkPledge cryptographic vote receipt on top of a traditional code voting solution.

5.1   Protocol Notation

$\mathcal{V}, \mathcal{V}_{id}$ - respectively the voter and the voter's identifier.

CS - code sheet containing a vote code (vc) for each candidate and a vote confirmation code (vcc) used to verify the MarkPledge receipt.

ES - election server. After the election end it works like a public bulletin board publishing the encrypted votes, the final results, and all the verification data.

APP - vote client application running at the voter's PC.

$\mathcal{T}$ - the trustees. The trustees can be representatives of political parties and/or representatives of independent organizations.

E_{sk} - election threshold shared private key.

E_{pk} - election threshold generated public key.

$\{M\}_A$ - digital signature of message M with the private key of entity A. More precisely, digital signature on the result of an hash function to message M.

$A \rightarrow B : M$ - message M sent from entity A to entity B.

$A \rightarrow B \rightarrow C : M$ - message M sent from entity A to entity C using the capabilities of entity B.

$BitEnc(b)_{E_{pk}}$ - the $BitEnc$ construction for bit b using the election public key.

MP_{Venc} - MarkPledge vote encryption composed by a $BitEnc(1)_{E_{pk}}$ for the voter's chosen candidate and $BitEnc(0)_{E_{pk}}$ encryptions for all other candidates.

$chal$ - challenge which determines the elements of $BitEnc(b)_{E_{pk}}$ to be open.

$O(MP_{Venc}, chal)$ - open MarkPledge vote encryption accordingly with the $chal$, i.e. the MarkPledge receipt.

$SO(MP_{Venc}, chal)$ - the strings associated with each candidate that results from opening MP_{Venc}, i.e. the strings that represent the $OpenBitEncs$.

5.2   Election Setup

Some time before the election day the ES creates the code sheets, seals them, e.g. using a special type of envelop or a scratch surface on the code sheet, and sends them to each voter, e.g. by mail. The seal and delivery process must ensure that the code sheet remains secret to anyone but the ES and the voter.

Also some time before the election day, the trustees T generate the threshold election key pair. The key pair should be generated in a way that only the cooperation of t trustees is able to decrypt a message encrypted with the election public key.

The ES then uses the election public key to generate all the $BitEncs(b)_{E_{pk}}$ that will form the MarkPledge vote encryptions for all voters. Then, the ES publishes all the generated $BitEncs(b)_{E_{pk}}$ and commits to them by means of a digital signature. Being n the number of candidates, the ES generates for each voter $(n-1)$ $BitEnc(0)_{E_{pk}}$ and one $BitEnc(1)_{E_{pk}}$. The $BitEnc(1)_{E_{pk}}$ must correspond to the vcc of the voter's CS. Only the ES knows which $BitEnc(b)_{E_{pk}}$ is the $BitEnc(1)_{E_{pk}}$.

Our protocol is independent of the authentication method used. Therefore, we assume that sometime before the election day the voters receive their voting credentials, e.g. a username/password or an electronic voter ID card able to authenticate the voter.

Just before the election start, and after the ES commitment to all the $BitEncs(b)_{E_{pk}}$, the trustees create a shared random election value $srev$ using the shared random number generation protocol. The $srev$ will be used during the election to facilitate the creation of a random and unpredictable challenge to the MarkPledge vote encryption. Therefore, it is crucial for the vote protocol security that the $srev$ creation occurs only after the publication of the ES commitment to the $BitEncs(b)$.

5.3   Vote Procedure

The vote procedure starts when the V opens the APP. Then, the following takes place:

1. $V \rightarrow APP \rightarrow ES : V_{id}$ The V authenticates herself to the ES. For simplicity, we only show a message containing V_{id}. However, in practice a message containing a username/password would be exchanged or, in the case of strong authentication by means of digital signatures, a strong mutual authentication protocol should be used, e.g. the X.509 three-pass authentication.
2. $V \rightarrow APP \rightarrow ES : vc_f$ After a successful authentication, the voter votes by looking into her CS and typing the vote code associated with her favorite candidate vc_f, which is then sent by the APP to the ES.

3. $ES \rightarrow APP : O(MP_{Venc}, chal), \{O(MP_{Venc}, chal)\}_{ES}$ After receiving the vote code selected by the voter vc_f, the ES prepares a MarkPledge encryption (MP_{Venc}) and the corresponding receipt ($O(MP_{Venc}, chal)$):

(a) The ES builds a MP_{Venc} with the previously committed $BitEncs(b)_{E_{pk}}$. The MP_{Venc} is composed by the committed $BitEnc(1)_{E_{pk}}$ for the selected candidate and a random selection of the committed $BitEncs(0)_{E_{pk}}$ for each other candidate.

(b) To prove the correction of the vote encryption to the voter, the ES then generates a random challenge to the MP_{Venc}. The challenge $chal$ is simply the hash of the concatenation of the MP_{Venc} with the $srev$. Since the $srev$ value was not known to the ES at the time of the CS creation and distribution, this process of challenge generation results in a kind of Fiat-Shamir heuristic [20] making possible a non interactive proof of the MP_{Venc} correction.

(c) Finally, the ES creates the MarkPledge receipt $O(MP_{Venc}, chal)$ by opening the MP_{Venc} accordingly with the generated $chal$.

The MarkPledge signed receipt is then sent to the APP.

4. $APP \rightarrow V : SO(MP_{Venc}, chal)$ The APP then verifies the signature and the correctness of the $O(MP_{Venc}, chal)$. If the verification is successful it presents to the voter a vote receipt composed of the strings ($OpenBitEncs$ encodings) that result from $O(MP_{Venc}, chal)$. The voter then performs a first receipt check and confirms that the vcc appears associated with the selected candidate in the $SO(MP_{Venc}, chal)$, cf. Fig. 2.

The vote receipt can also be printed in order to facilitate a second, and stronger, verification at the claiming stage.

5. (optional) $APP \rightarrow ES : \{O(MP_{Venc}, chal)\}_V$ If a strong authentication mechanism is used to authenticate the voters, e.g. a digital signature performed by an electronic voter ID card, then a last message validating the vote is sent to the ES. This message consists in a signature on the MarkPledge receipt.

5.4 Claiming Stage

When the election ends there is a small time period, that we call the claiming stage, where a voter can check and revoke her vote.

Right after the election end the ES publishes all the generated $O(MP_{Venc}, chal)$, the $SO(MP_{Venc}, chal)$ and the identification of the voter who "owns" that vote. At this point anyone can verify the correctness of the $O(MP_{Venc}, chal)$ by checking: i) the $BitEncs(b)$ used in its construction, ii) the correctness of the value of $chal$, and iii) the correctness of the $SO(MP_{Venc}, chal)$. Since this validation process is somewhat complex we only assume that the political parties and/or independent organizations perform this validation. Additionally, these third party organizations should also verify that all the MP_{Venc} are well-formed, c.f. sec. 2.2.

If the $SO(MP_{Venc}, chal)$ is validated by a third party the voter only has to check that the receipt matches the one published in her name. A match means that with a $(1 - \frac{1}{2^{\alpha}})$ probability the encrypted vote represents the voter choice.

5.5   Tallying the Votes

Publishing the election's tally is straightforward because the ES knows the exact contents of each vote; however, to prove the correctness of the tally it is necessary to perform some additional steps.

After the claiming stage all votes that were not revoked by the voters are considered valid for the tally. Then, the validated votes go through a verifiable mix-net protocol [21, 19]. At the end of the anonymization process, the trustees decrypt and publish the votes in a shared and verifiable way [16]. The published vote decryption allows the political parties and other interested entities to verify the correctness of the vote decryption. With the validated vote decryption everyone can use the clear votes to perform/validate the tally.

Note that the mixing and decryption of the votes can not be performed over the $BitEnc(b)$ constructions of the encrypted vote. The reason why is the following: if the individual elements of the $BitEnc(b)$ construction were decrypted, even after mixing, it would be trivial to correlate a decrypted vote with the corresponding encrypted vote, therefore loosing all vote anonymity. To solve this problem an additional standard El Gamal bit encryption for each $BitEnc(b)$ must be added to the MP_{Venc} [22]. It is then proved that the each single standart bit encryption corresponds to the bit encrypted within the corresponding $BitEnc$ construction. Finally, the mixing and decryption processes take as input these new bit encryptions instead of the $BitEnc$ constructions, therefore protecting the voter's privacy. These new bit encryptions do not change the voter interaction in any way. The validation of the new bit encryptions is part of validation of the MP_{Venc} well-formedness.

Note that, the reason we use a threshold shared election key pair instead of one generated by the ES is that if the records of the CS creation are destroyed jointly with the information of which $BitEncs(b)$ are $BitEncs(1)$ the votes become secret even to the ES. The destruction of such data can be assured by physical procedures under the supervision of the political parties. Therefore, at that stage the privacy of the voters is in the hands of who has the election key, and that is the reason why we suggest the use of a threshold election key shared among several trustees. Nevertheless, we must point out that if such measures take place it is also necessary to prevent subliminal channels in the randomness used by the ES, i.e. kleptograhic attacks [23]. If there is simple a key pair generated by the ES the tally procedure is as previously, only now the vote decryption step is done by the ES instead of being done by the trustees.

6   Evaluation

In this section we show that VeryVote, besides addressing the uncontrolled client platform problem of Internet voting, also gives strong overall election integrity guarantees, while still protecting the voter's privacy. We start by presenting the assumptions used in our evaluation followed by the election integrity evaluation. Finally, we present an analysis on the privacy guarantees of VeryVote.

6.1 Assumptions

We assume the following:

- The codes in the code sheets are randomly generated by the ES and secretly delivered to the voters, i.e. only the voter and the ES know the codes in the voter's code sheet.
- No more than $t-1$ of the trustees are dishonest.
- The cryptographic primitives and constructions used are secure and verifiable: El Gamal threshold encryption, mix net and $BitEnc$ constructions; digital signatures and hash functions.
- The vote codes and the vote confirmation code are composed of respectively 4 and 6 alphanumeric symbols. We assume the use of 62 symbols, all uppercase and lowercase letters and digits, which gives 62^4 (roughly 14.7 millions) possible values for the vote codes and 62^6 (roughly 56.8 thousand millions) possible values for the vote confirmation code.
- The voter has in her possession the printed vote receipt.
- The political parties and/or independent organizations verify the data published by the ES.
- At the claiming stage the voter verifies her vote with the printed receipt.
- When the election ends the records of the CS creation and the information of which $BitEncs(b)$ are $BitEncs(1)$ are physically destroyed or in alternative we assume that the ES is trustworthy in what concerns the voters' privacy.

6.2 Election Integrity

Election Integrity at the Uncontrolled Client Platform – In VeryVote the APP running at the uncontrolled client platform has only a negligible chance to manipulate the voter's vote, i.e. it would need to guess a valid vote code different from the one used by the voter. In an election with n candidates the chances of that happening are $(n-1)/62^4$. Only in this case the APP can change the voters vote and produce a fake vote receipt that fools momentarily the voter, i.e. the voter will easily detect the vote manipulation while verifying her vote receipt at the claiming stage.

In order to prevent a simple denial of service attack by the APP, a voter should be able to submit several vote codes at least until she submits one valid vote code (the vote update issue will be discussed later in privacy analysis). Therefore, measures should be taken to prevent the APP from trying a significant amount of vote codes guesses, such as the introduction of a delay or requiring the solution of a CAPTCHA in each try.

Nevertheless, even if the APP guesses a valid vote code the voter would catch the misbehavior at the claiming stage, while confirming her vote receipt with the ES published data.

Election Integrity at the Vote Record and Tallying Processes – Since we assume the use of secure and verifiable constructions for the threshold encryption and mix nets, we automatically have the integrity verifications of the tallying process. What we have new in VeryVote is the possibility to verify that the vote is recorded as cast. Therefore, we only present here an analysis on the integrity of the vote record process.

Because the ES publishes all encrypted votes along with the vote receipts and the association with the voter who "cast" it, it is trivial for the voter to detect a receipt different from the one she has. Therefore, the only way the ES can pass such verification is to give the voter a "tampered" vote receipt, i.e. a vote receipt that shows the right association between the vcc and the candidate selected by the voter but which in fact encrypts a vote for a different candidate.

Since the ES commits to the $BitEncs(b)$ that form the vote before the generation of the $srev$, there is no possibility to known in advance what the challenge will be. Therefore, the only possibility to construct a tampered receipt is to try all the combinations possible for the $BitEncs(b)$ positions in the receipt, and hope that luck provides the correct challenge to the vote encryption.

However, if the committed $BitEnc(1)$ corresponds to the confirmation code on the voter's code sheet, then in a tampered receipt there will be the same value (the confirmation code) associated to two distinct candidates. To prevent that from happening such type of receipts should be considered invalid, which prevents the attack. In the case of accidental creation of an invalid receipt the ES must create another one using another combination of the $BitEncs(0)$.

Consequently, the only way the ES has to produce a valid tampered receipt is to commit to a $BitEnc(1)$ that is not related to the confirmation code in the voter's code sheet. However, this would not be a smart move because then the ES only has a probability of $n!/62^6$ to create a valid (tampered or not) receipt for the voter. For instance, if $n = 10$ the probability of success is less than 0.01%.

Although, it is worth noticing that because of the exponential nature of the factorial function, increasing much more the number of candidates will force the use of a very long vote confirmation code, which makes the system unusable. On the other hand, for a smaller number of candidates and the same probability of success a smaller confirmation code can be used, which makes the receipt shorter and more easily verifiable.

Another problem that could affect the election integrity verification of the vote record is someone tampering with the CS in the distribution process. In this case the voter will catch the misbehavior with a very high probability $(1 - (1/62^6))$. The voter can then revoke her vote a correct the problem.

The Advantages of Using MarkPledge Receipts – Saying that in a traditional code voting system the voter cannot verify that her vote is used in the tally is not entirely true. If each code sheet is published after the election with the corresponding selection made by the voter who used it, then the voter can verify that her vote was correctly used. Note that this publication implies the publication of the election tally because now anyone can sum up the casted votes.

Assuming that the code sheets were anonymously distributed to the voters, the verification described above is anonymous. However, now a voter cannot complain and correct her vote. Changing a vote after knowing the final results of the election is not democratic and implies that the voter must prove that a particular vote is hers.

Note also that, if both the code sheets distribution and the voting process are anonymous, there is nothing that prevents the entity that created the codes sheets to impersonate an anonymous voter and cast a vote for her. No one knows who has voted.

Using MarkPledge receipts we allow the publication of the encrypted vote along with the identity of the voter who "casted" the vote. Then, and before anyone knowns the election results, every voter can verify her vote and correct it without revealing the contents of the encrypted vote. Therefore, only validated votes will be part of the election tally. Additionally, any attempt to introduce votes for voters who did not voted can be identified or prevented if a strong voter's authentication mechanism is used.

6.3   Voter's Privacy

VeryVote makes possible the verification that the voter's intention is really used in the tally. However, to allow this verification part of the voters' privacy was lost, namely in what concerns the ES.

In VeryVote, the ES knows each voter's choice, at least before the destruction of the creation records of the code sheets and $BitEncs(b)$ by physical procedures at the end of the election. Assuming that there are no subliminal channels, what remains are the votes encrypted with a threshold encryption key shared among the trustees.

The encrypted votes are then anonymized in a verifiable way by the mix. At last the anonymized votes are decrypted by the trustees. Assuming a threshold value of t, then only the cooperation of t trustees can decrypt the anonymized votes. Consequently, if no more than $t - 1$ trustees are dishonest only the anonymized votes are decrypted and the voters' privacy is protected. No one, not even the trustees known which vote belongs to which voter.

Finally, it is important to analyze the implications of the MarkPledge receipt in the voter's privacy. In all code voting systems the code sheet together with the vote receipt (reply code or MarkPledge receipt in our case) can be considered a proof of vote. Therefore, the voter plays a big role in protecting her own privacy, i.e. a voter to protect her own privacy must keep the code sheet secret. However, in opposition to a simple reply code, the MarkPledge receipt allows for an anonymous verification of the vote, as described in Sec. 6.2.

Vote Buying and Coercion – As described in Sec. 6.3, the voter can build up a receipt if she joins the MarkPledge receipt with her code sheet. Therefore, this proof can be used to facilitate vote buying/selling or coercion.

Nevertheless, it is possible to discourage vote buying using the vote update technique [24]. VeryVote already has the vote update possibility in the claiming stage. Since a voter must not justify why she is revoking the previous casted vote, the vote revoke facility can be used as merely an opportunity to update a previous casted vote. Therefore, the attacker can only confirm the vote receipt validity after the claiming stage. This late verification automatically discourages vote buying attacks: if the attacker pays in advance it can be cheated by the voter, and if the attacker only pays after the election end, the voter can be cheated by the attacker. Therefore, the vote update possibility and the mutual distrust between the voter and the vote buyer should be enough to discourage such attacks.

The coercion problem is not so easily mitigated because it is more a psychological attack, and therefore may work independently of the voting technology used. Nonetheless, there are particular cases of coercion, e.g. family voting, that work better in uncontrolled voting environments, e.g. vote by mail and Internet voting. It is worth noticing that the possibility of vote update offered by VeryVote can in some extent minimize the coercion problem but it does not solve it.

7   Conclusions

VeryVote is a code voting sytem that addresses the secure platform problem. However, unlike other code voting systems, and due to the use of MarkPledge vote receipts, VeryVote is end-to-end verifiable. In VeryVote the submitted votes are encrypted and published in a non anonymous way. Therefore, a voter can check that her vote was correctly recorded by using her MarkPledge vote receipt. After a claiming stage where the voters can revoke and update their previously submitted vote, the valid votes enter into a verifiable vote tally process. The verification of both the correctness of the recorded votes and of the election tally process makes VeryVote end-to-end verifiable.

Nevertheless, the end-to-end verifiability also carries more responsibility to the voter. Now the voter can verify that her vote is counted as intended but she must also take an active role protecting her own privacy by keeping her code sheet secret. It is also worth noticing that in order to introduce the end-to-end verifiability we have made the voting interaction between the voter and the ES more complex, which may cause some usability problems.

As future work it would be interesting to study the usability of the system, and if it is possible to eliminate the election server as a trustworthy entity with respect to the voters' privacy.

Acknowledgments. The authors would like to thank the valuable comments of the anonymous reviewers.

References

1. Rivest, R.L.: Electronic voting. In: Syverson, P.F. (ed.) FC 2001. LNCS, vol. 2339, pp. 243–268. Springer, Heidelberg (2001)
2. Chaum, D.: Surevote. International patent WO 01/55940 A1 (2001),
   http://www.surevote.com/home.html
3. Oppliger, R.: How to address the secure platform problem for remote internet voting. In: Erasim, E., Karagiannis, D. (eds.) 5th Conference on Sicherheit in Informationssystemen (SIS 2002), pp. 153–173. vdf Hochschulverlag, Vienna (2002)

4. Karlof, C., Sastry, N., Wagner, D.: Cryptographic voting protocols: A systems prespective. In: 14th USENIX Security Symposium, pp. 33–50 (2005)
5. Neff, A.: Practical high certainty intent verification for encrypted votes (2004), http://www.votehere.com/old/vhti/documentation/vsv-2.0.3638.pdf
6. UK's Electoral Commission: Technical report on the may 2003 pilots (2003), http://www.electoralcommission.org.uk/about-us/03pilotscheme.cfm
7. UK's National Technical Authority for Information Assurance: e-voting security study (2002),
http://www.ictparliament.org/CDTunisi/ict_compendium/paesi/uk/uk54.pdf
8. Helbach, J., Schwenk, J.: Secure internet voting with code sheets. In: Alkassar, A., Volkamer, M. (eds.) VOTE-ID 2007. LNCS, vol. 4896, pp. 166–177. Springer, Heidelberg (2007)
9. Oppliger, R., Schwenk, J., Helbach, J.: Protecting code voting against vote selling. In: An Analytical Description of CHILL, the CCITT High Level Language. LNI, vol. 128, pp. 193–204. GI (2008)
10. Helbach, J., Schwenk, J., Schage, S.: Code voting with linkable group signatures. In: EVOTE 2008 (2008)
11. Oppliger, R., Schwenk, J.: Captcha-based code voting. In: EVOTE 2008 (2008)
12. Joaquim, R., Ribeiro, C.: Codevoting protection against automatic vote manipulation in an uncontrolled environment. In: Alkassar, A., Volkamer, M. (eds.) VOTE-ID 2007. LNCS, vol. 4896, pp. 178–188. Springer, Heidelberg (2007)
13. Adida, B., Neff, A.: Ballot casting assurance. In: EVT 2006, Vancouver, B.C., Canada, USENIX/ACCURATE (2006)
14. ElGamal, T.: A public-key cryptosystem and signature scheme based on discrete logarithms. IEEE Transactions on Information Theory IT-31(4), 469–472 (1985)
15. Cramer, R., Damgård, I., Schoenmakers, B.: Proofs of partial knowledge and simplified design of witness hiding protocols. In: Desmedt, Y.G. (ed.) CRYPTO 1994. LNCS, vol. 839, pp. 174–187. Springer, Heidelberg (1994)
16. Cramer, R., Gennaro, R., Schoenmakers, B.: A secure and optimally efficient multi-authority election scheme. In: Fumy, W. (ed.) EUROCRYPT 1997. LNCS, vol. 1233, pp. 103–118. Springer, Heidelberg (1997)
17. Estonian National Electoral Commitee: Internet voting in estonia (2007), http://www.vvk.ee/engindex.html
18. Chaum, D.: Untraceable electronic mail, return addresses, and digital pseudonyms. Commun. ACM 24(2), 84–88 (1981)
19. Neff, C.A.: Verifiable mixing (shuffling) of elgamal pairs (2004)
20. Fiat, A., Shamir, A.: How to prove yourself: Practical solutions to identification and signature. In: Odlyzko, A.M. (ed.) CRYPTO 1986. LNCS, vol. 263, pp. 186–194. Springer, Heidelberg (1987)
21. Jakobsson, M., Juels, A., Rivest, R.: Making mix nets robust for electronic voting by randomized partial checking. In: 2002 USENIX Security Symposium, San Francisco, CA, USA, pp. 339–353 (2002)
22. Adida, B.: Advances in Cryptographic Voting Systems, PhD thesis. MIT (2006)
23. Gogolewski, M., Klonowski, M., Kubiak, P., Kutyłowski, M., Lauks, A., Zagórski, F.: Kleptographic attacks on e-election schemes with receipts. In: Müller, G. (ed.) ETRICS 2006. LNCS, vol. 3995, pp. 494–508. Springer, Heidelberg (2006)
24. Volkamer, M., Grimm, R.: Multiple casts in online voting: Analyzing chances. In: Robert Krimmer, R. (ed.) Electronic Voting 2006, Castle Hofen, Bregenz, Austria, GI. LNI, vol. P-86, pp. 97–106 (2006)

Minimum Disclosure Counting for the Alternative Vote

Roland Wen and Richard Buckland

School of Computer Science and Engineering
The University of New South Wales
Sydney 2052, Australia
{rolandw,richardb}@cse.unsw.edu.au

Abstract. Although there is a substantial body of work on preventing bribery and coercion of voters in cryptographic election schemes for plurality electoral systems, there are few attempts to construct such schemes for preferential electoral systems. The problem is preferential systems are prone to bribery and coercion via subtle signature attacks during the counting. We introduce a minimum disclosure counting scheme for the alternative vote preferential system. Minimum disclosure provides protection from signature attacks by revealing only the winning candidate.

Keywords: Preferential voting, alternative vote, instant runoff voting, online elections, counting schemes.

1 Introduction

Most cryptographic election schemes in the literature are designed for plurality (first past the post) electoral systems, where each voter chooses a single candidate and the winner is the candidate who receives the most votes. But using these schemes for preferential electoral systems exposes voters to potential bribery and coercion through signature attacks. We introduce a preferential counting scheme that protects voters from such attacks.

Preferential electoral systems are widespread in Australia. Indeed, all Australian parliamentary elections at national and state levels use preferential systems. In most cases elections for the lower house use the alternative vote and elections for the upper house use the single transferable vote. The single transferable vote is a generalisation of the alternative vote for electing multiple candidates rather than a single candidate. These preferential systems are also common in Ireland and Malta, and they are sometimes used for local government elections in parts of New Zealand, the UK, and the USA. In this paper we only consider the alternative vote.

The aim of preferential electoral systems is to give voters greater scope in expressing their choices. The distinguishing feature of these systems is that voters *rank* candidates in order of preference. The alternative vote is one of the more complex instances of preferential systems because the counting procedure has many rounds of counting. In each round a candidate is excluded and the votes

P.Y.A. Ryan and B. Schoenmakers (Eds.): VOTE-ID 2009, LNCS 5767, pp. 122–140, 2009.

for this candidate are transferred to the *remaining* (not yet excluded) candidates according to the preferences given on the ballots for that candidate. We elaborate below on the mechanics of the counting procedure.

1.1 The Alternative Vote

The alternative vote, also known as preferential voting or instant runoff voting, is a majoritarian system for filling a single vacancy. To be elected, a candidate must receive a *majority* (more than half) of the votes.

Each ballot contains a sequence of preference votes. A voter fills out a ballot by ranking every candidate in consecutive numerical order starting from 1 for the first preference. A common variant is optional preferences, where voters assign a minimum of one preference but need not assign all preferences.

The counting takes place in recursive rounds. Each round is a 'last' past the post election. The election authorities tally the votes considering only the most preferred remaining candidate in each ballot. Then they exclude the candidate with the lowest round tally and transfer each vote for that candidate to the next preferred remaining candidate on the corresponding ballot. The next round is in effect a sub-election for the remaining candidates. The process recursively repeats until a single candidate remains. The authorities announce this candidate as the winner.

Notice that it is possible to stop the counting as soon as a candidate obtains a majority. The counting algorithm we described performs a complete distribution of the votes. For a given number of candidates, this algorithm has a constant number of counting rounds.

In the event that multiple candidates have the lowest tally in a round, there are a variety of tie-breaking rules used in practice to determine the last candidate, for instance randomly or by comparing tallies from previous rounds. All such rules eventually resort to breaking ties randomly or arbitrarily when a 'true' tie occurs. In this paper we simply resolve all ties randomly and in future work we describe more elaborate techniques for other common methods.

1.2 The Signature Attack

The information-rich nature of the ballots in preferential systems introduces the possibility of a signature attack, commonly referred to as the Italian attack due to its infamous use in Italian elections [3]. A signature attack potentially compromises voter anonymity during the counting and is an effective technique for bribing and coercing voters. Any election is open to this attack when the number of possible voting options is relatively large compared to the number of voters. Preferential elections are particularly vulnerable because the number of possible preference permutations is factorial in the number of candidates.

To 'sign' a preferential ballot, a voter can for example allocate the first preference to a particular candidate and use the ordering of the remaining preferences as a covert channel that contains a signature. Even for a relatively modest number of candidates and a large voting population, such a signature is highly likely to be unique. For any prescribed first preference candidate, an election with C candidates has $(C-1)!$ possible covert signatures. The national upper house election in Australia has about 80 candidates, and so there are 79! possible signatures. Even if every atom in the universe voted in this election, there would still be a negligible probability that any randomly chosen signature would also be cast by another voter.

A covert signature of this form is revealed when the ballots are exposed during the counting, and it links the voter to the vote. In traditional paper elections, only election authorities and independent scrutineers appointed by the candidates can observe the ballots. We can only hope they are trustworthy. Alarmingly in Australia, recent moves to improve the transparency of elections have inadvertently made it trivial to perform signature attacks. In order to allow independent scrutiny in elections that use electronic counting, a ruling under Freedom of Information legislation [26] has led election authorities to publish every ballot electronically!

Subtle variations of the signature attack may still be feasible with only partial knowledge of the votes. An adversary can embed uncommon sequences of preferences in the signatures. Then the adversary can glean any available information about these contrived sequences to narrow down the set of *possible signatures*. For example if a candidate's tally remains the same across two rounds, then that candidate cannot be the next preference in any of the votes for the candidate excluded in the first of those rounds. In this way even when the adversary cannot identify exact signatures in the votes cast, it is still possible to determine that particular signatures are not present. This possibility may well be sufficient to allow coercion.

Election authorities frequently publish partial counting data such as the final placing of each candidate and all the round tallies for each candidate. But even releasing seemingly innocuous aggregate counting data has risks. Given the subtlety of signature attacks, it is not always immediately obvious whether disclosing particular information can have detrimental consequences.

Naturally much depends on the eventual distribution of the votes cast. Nevertheless an adversary can make some educated guesses, especially when there are few major candidates and many minor candidates. Several types of signature attacks on partial information are currently known [25]. But determining precisely what information is useful for mounting signature attacks and how effective are such attacks remains an open problem. Therefore revealing any information apart from the identity of the winning candidate can potentially expose voters to signature attacks.

Consequently, to eliminate the possibility of covert channels and intentional or accidental information leakage, the precautionary principle suggests that a conservative approach to secure counting is prudent. Ideally the counting process should be entirely secret and reveal only the winning candidate. The challenge for preferential systems lies in counting the votes in a secret yet universally verifiable manner.

1.3   Contributions

We introduce an alternative vote counting scheme that reveals only the identity of the winning candidate. We call this level of privacy minimum disclosure. This is the same notion of privacy used in Hevia and Kiwi's yes/no election scheme [12]. Minimum disclosure provides the strongest possible protection against attacks on counting information. In particular it prevents signature attacks on preferential systems.

Our scheme also satisfies the usual security requirements of correctness, universal verifiability, and robustness against corrupt authorities. The scheme can be used as an independent counting procedure or in conjunction with an existing online voting scheme.

The idea behind our counting scheme is to perform the counting on encrypted ballots. Each ballot is a list of encrypted preference votes in descending order of preference and each preference vote is for a distinct candidate.

The counting scheme uses a hide and seek paradigm to manipulate lists of ciphertexts without revealing anything about the order of a list. This approach repeatedly applies a three-step process.

1. Execute a distributed operation to conceal the ordering of the ciphertexts.
2. Execute another distributed operation to identify ciphertexts with certain properties.
3. Perform open operations, such as homomorphic addition, on the identified ciphertexts.

The distributed operations are cryptographic protocols that require the collaboration of multiple authorities. As such the main drawback of the scheme is the amount of work for the authorities. The extensive use of multiparty computation techniques is an inevitable trade-off in achieving both minimum disclosure and robustness, especially for electoral systems with elaborate counting algorithms, such as the alternative vote. In an election with A authorities, C candidates and V voters, the total computational and communication complexities for our scheme are $O(AC^2V)$.

1.4   Organisation

Section 2 discusses existing online voting schemes and preferential counting schemes. Section 3 defines the security model and Section 4 covers the necessary cryptographic building blocks. Section 5 describes the details of the minimum disclosure counting scheme and Section 6 proposes an optimised tallying protocol. Section 7 analyses the security and complexity of the scheme. Section 8 explains how to combine the counting scheme with common online voting schemes.

2   Related Work

In the general literature on cryptographic elections, preventing bribery and coercion centres on the requirements of receipt-freeness and coercion-resistance. Informally, receipt-freeness [2] means that voters who cast valid votes cannot be bribed or coerced into proving how they voted because it is not possible for them to prove how they voted. Coercion-resistance [15] is the stronger requirement that voters cannot even prove whether they abstained, or cast invalid or random votes.

Receipt-free and coercion-resistant voting schemes focus on protecting voters from bribery and coercion during the voting itself. But they rarely consider the details of the counting. During the counting these schemes generally rely on statistical uncertainty in the votes to prevent voters from being identified by their votes. Every possible voting option must be likely to receive some votes from honest voters. For simple plurality elections, this is generally a reasonable assumption. But for preferential elections, it is not. This compromises receipt-freeness and coercion-resistance.

Contemporary online voting schemes have two main approaches to counting votes: public counting and private counting. Both methods reveal covert signatures and also absent signatures.

Voting schemes that perform public counting [15,17,19,20] implement only the voting stage of an election. Voters submit encrypted votes as their ballots. Then the authorities anonymise the ballots (generally through mix-nets) before decrypting them. To calculate the election result, any party can openly perform a known counting algorithm on the publicly revealed plaintext votes.

Conversely, voting schemes that perform private counting [1,2,13] implement both the voting and counting stages of a plurality election. Voters submit votes that are encrypted with an additively homomorphic cryptosystem. To calculate the election result, the authorities use the homomorphic property to combine all the encrypted votes into an encrypted tally for each possible voting option. Then they decrypt only these tallies. This approach maintains the privacy of individual votes because it publishes only the tallies. But as there are tallies for every voting option, it still reveals the same information about the votes as public counting. To calculate the result in a preferential election, any party can still openly perform the appropriate counting algorithm on the publicly revealed tallies.

To counter such signature attacks, Goh and Golle [7] propose an alternative vote counting scheme that only discloses the round tallies for each candidate. But there still remains some scope for signature attacks that exploit the round tallies to cull the set of possible signatures. Keller and Kilian [16] also propose a scheme with the same level of privacy.

Heather [11] describes a counting scheme for the more complex single transferable vote. In addition to revealing the candidates' round tallies, the transfer method also leaks partial sequences of preferences for previously excluded candidates. This extra information facilitates more effective signature attacks by significantly narrowing down the set of possible signatures.

Teague et al. [25] propose a single transferable vote counting scheme that achieves greater secrecy than the above schemes. When applied to the alternative vote, it conceals the round tallies and reveals only the order in which the candidates are excluded. But the scheme relies on the trustworthiness of a single authority who can learn the plaintext contents of all the ballots.

3 Security Model

3.1 Participants and Adversary Model

The only participants in the counting scheme are the authorities who perform the counting. All communication is public and via an authenticated bulletin board. The security model is for a static, active adversary who can corrupt up to a threshold of the authorities.

3.2 Security Requirements

A secure counting scheme must satisfy the following requirements.

Minimum Disclosure. Apart from the identity of the winning candidate, no party or adversary gains any additional information about the candidates or the ballots than what was known before the counting commenced. The transcript of the counting is computationally indistinguishable from the transcript of the counting for any fake input list of the same number of valid votes that elects the same winning candidate. Revealing only the winning candidate prevents potential signature attacks including those that exploit partial counting information.

Correctness. All input votes are correctly counted and no other votes are counted.

Universal Verifiability. Any observer can confirm that the counting is correct.

Robustness. The counting tolerates the corrupt or faulty behaviour of any group of authorities up to a threshold.

Notice counting schemes do not consider requirements that only relate to voters during the preceding voting stage, for instance individual verifiability, robustness with respect to corrupt voters, and ensuring ballots are only cast by authentic voters. In some cases an additional integration procedure between the voting and counting may be necessary to transform the submitted ballots into a valid form for the counting.

3.3 Why So Secretive?

In current elections the authorities typically publish certain counting information for statistical purposes, and that published data alone is often sufficient for mounting signature attacks. So on the surface it might appear that in practice minimum disclosure is an unnecessarily strong requirement for online elections. However any more relaxed approach to secrecy in counting schemes can be problematic.

The amount and types of published data varies widely from election to election. But regardless of what information the authorities decide to reveal, a counting scheme must not leak any partial information that aggravates signature attacks. In other words any leaked information must be insignificant.

The problem is there is currently no method to determine if specific partial information leakage is indeed insignificant. For example suppose a counting scheme leaks the identity of the excluded candidate in each round. Such information on its own would seem insignificant. Now suppose that the authorities decide to publish all the round tallies without identifying the candidates. Again such information would seem reasonably insignificant. But by combining these two types of partial information, an adversary can make strong correlations between all the tallies and candidates. This can substantially improve the chance of mounting successful signature attacks. Although this is a rather contrived example, it illustrates the difficulty in analysing the risk of partial information leakage. In fact the risk depends on context-specific factors such as the number of voters, the number of candidates and the a posteriori distribution of preference permutations.

In the absence of precise definitions of what partial information is sensitive, a cryptographic counting scheme should provide the strongest possible level of secrecy in order to suit any alternative vote election. Then if necessary the authorities can explicitly weaken the scheme to reveal exactly the desired counting data but nothing more. This approach mitigates the risk of additional unforeseen attacks.

4   Cryptographic Preliminaries

The minimum disclosure counting scheme relies on several distributed cryptographic protocols that provide privacy, universal verifiability and robustness. Rather than depending on specific instances of these protocols, we simply model them as ideal primitives. We state typical costs of the protocols in terms of a security parameter k.

4.1   Additively Homomorphic Threshold Cryptosystem

An additively homomorphic cryptosystem is a public-key cryptosystem that enables any party to efficiently compute an encryption of the sum of two messages given only the encryptions of the individual messages. For concreteness we describe the scheme using the Paillier cryptosystem [21], which is semantically secure under the Decisional Composite Residuosity Assumption. The public key is (g, n), where $n = pq$ is an RSA modulus and $g = n + 1$. All plaintext operations are modulo n and all ciphertext operations are modulo n^2. For simplicity we omit the modular reduction in the notation.

A message $m \in \mathbb{Z}_n$ is encrypted by randomly generating $r \in \mathbb{Z}_n^*$ and computing the ciphertext

$$[\![m]\!] = g^m r^n \in \mathbb{Z}_{n^2}^* \ .$$

The Paillier cryptosystem has two homomorphic properties.

Addition. For plaintexts $m_1, m_2 \in \mathbb{Z}_n$,

$$\llbracket m_1 \rrbracket \boxplus \llbracket m_2 \rrbracket = (g^{m_1} r_1^n) \times (g^{m_2} r_2^n)$$
$$= g^{m_1 + m_2} (r_1 r_2)^n$$
$$= \llbracket m_1 + m_2 \rrbracket .$$

Multiplication by a constant. For a plaintext $m \in \mathbb{Z}_n$ and constant $c \in \mathbb{Z}_n$,

$$c \boxdot \llbracket m \rrbracket = (g^m r^n)^c$$
$$= g^{cm} (r^c)^n$$
$$= \llbracket cm \rrbracket .$$

In the threshold version of Paillier [4,6], each authority has a share of the private key. A quorum of authorities must collaborate to decrypt any ciphertext. The decryption process is universally verifiable and reveals no additional information to any coalition of authorities smaller than the quorum.

To decrypt a ciphertext share and prove correctness, each authority performs $O(k)$ modular multiplications and broadcasts $O(k)$ bits. Publicly verifying and combining the shares of the A authorities costs $O(Ak)$.

4.2   Plaintext Equality and Inequality Tests

Plaintext equality and inequality tests compare the plaintexts of given ciphertexts without revealing the plaintexts. Given a pair of encrypted messages $\llbracket m_1 \rrbracket$ and $\llbracket m_2 \rrbracket$, a plaintext equality test [14] determines whether $m_1 = m_2$, and a plaintext inequality test [22,24] determines whether $m_1 > m_2$. In both cases the only public output is the boolean result of the test.

As for decryption in a threshold cryptosystem, the protocols to perform these tests are distributed operations that require the collaboration of a quorum of authorities, each of whom has a secret share of the private key. In fact the last step of these protocols requires a threshold decryption to reveal the result. The tests are universally verifiable and reveal no additional information to any coalition of authorities smaller than the quorum.

Plaintext equality tests have the same complexity as threshold decryptions. Plaintext inequality tests are more expensive, with the dominant additional cost being a bit extraction step described below. The total complexity for A authorities is $O(Alk)$ multiplications when the plaintexts are in a known range $[0, 2^l)$. In the counting scheme inequality tests are only used to compare encrypted tallies, and for V voters each tally is at most $l = \lceil \log_2 V \rceil$ bits.

4.3   Secure Bit Extraction

A bit extraction protocol [24] converts an encrypted message into separate encryptions of the individual bits of the message. Given an encrypted message $\llbracket m \rrbracket$, where $0 \leq m < 2^l$ and the binary representation is $m = m_0, \ldots, m_{l-1}$, the output is $\llbracket m_0 \rrbracket, \ldots, \llbracket m_{l-1} \rrbracket$. The bit extraction is a universally verifiable threshold protocol and reveals no additional information to any coalition of authorities smaller than the quorum.

In the bit extraction protocol each authority privately performs $O(lk)$ multiplications including proofs of correctness. Publicly verifying and combining the individual results of the A authorities costs $O(Alk)$.

4.4   Verifiable Mix-Nets and Rotators

A verifiable re-encryption mix-net [8,10,18] is a series of servers that each randomly mix (by permuting and re-encrypting) a list of messages. In the case that each message is a tuple of ciphertexts rather than a single ciphertext, such as with preferential ballots, the mix-net re-encrypts every ciphertext in the tuple individually and preserves the structure of the tuple.

A verifiable rotator cascade [5] is similar to a mix-net. The difference is that each server randomly rotates (by cyclically shifting and re-encrypting) a list of messages. Rotation is particularly useful when it is necessary to preserve the relative ordering of the messages. Although it is possible to construct rotators using mix-nets [23], a direct implementation is more efficient.

Both mix-nets and rotator cascades conceal the correspondence between input and output messages as long as at least one server is honest. The mixing and rotating are both universally verifiable. For l ciphertexts, re-encrypting and proving correctness typically costs $O(lk)$ multiplications for each server. Publicly verifying the entire protocol when there are A servers costs $O(Alk)$.

5   The Minimum Disclosure Counting Scheme

The minimum disclosure counting scheme implements secure counting for alternative vote elections. It commences after the voting has finished and the authorities have performed all necessary ballot processing including the removal of invalid ballots.

We describe the counting scheme as a series of high-level protocols. Multiple authorities collaborate to execute the protocols. They post the result of every operation on an authenticated bulletin board with full revision tracking.

Each step in the protocol execution is either a distributed operation that requires a quorum of authorities to collaborate or a completely open operation that *any party* can compute from posted messages. The distributed operations are the distributed protocols described in Section 4, as well as operations constructed from those protocols. All other operations are open operations. A single arbitrary authority posts the results of the open operations but each authority individually performs the operations and verifies the correctness of the posted results.

Some of the open steps require a known encryption of a known plaintext message. In such cases, rather than probabilistically encrypting the plaintext with a secret randomness value, the authority *deterministically* encrypts the plaintext with a known randomness value of 1 and subsequent operations are used to add any necessary secret randomness.

Note in the following protocol descriptions we sometimes abuse notation to have $[\![x]\!]$ refer to a variable that contains an encryption of x.

5.1   Data Structures and Auxiliary Protocols

The counting stores the following encrypted information in list-based data structures:

Candidates   A list of encrypted remaining (non-excluded) candidates in random order.

Ballot   A list of encrypted preference votes. Each preference vote is for a remaining candidate, and the list ordering represents a voter's preferences for the candidates in descending order.

Ballots   A list of *Ballot* objects each of which corresponds to a valid vote cast by a voter.

Counters   A dictionary of encrypted candidate-tally mappings each of the form $([\![c]\!], [\![t]\!])$, where the key c is a candidate and t is the tally for c in the current round. We represent the dictionary as a list of encrypted pairs.

In addition to the count, tally and exclude protocols specified in the following subsections, several auxiliary protocols are used to manipulate the encrypted data:

pet $([\![m_1]\!], [\![m_2]\!])$ Perform a plaintext equality test on the input ciphertexts.

pit $([\![m_1]\!], [\![m_2]\!])$ Perform a plaintext inequality test on the input ciphertexts.

mix $(\textbf{\textit{List}})$ Randomly permute and re-encrypt a list of messages. Each message can be a single ciphertext or a pair of ciphertexts.

rotate $(\textbf{\textit{List}})$ Randomly cyclically shift and re-encrypt a list of messages. Each message can be a single ciphertext or a pair of ciphertexts.

append $(\textbf{\textit{List}}, m)$ Append the message m to *List*. The message can be a single ciphertext or a pair of ciphertexts.

remove $(\textbf{\textit{List}}, [\![m]\!])$ Remove all ciphertexts matching $[\![m]\!]$ from *List*. In the counting scheme only one element will be removed by this protocol. We implement the remove protocol by executing pet $([\![m]\!], [\![item]\!])$ for each $[\![item]\!] \in \textbf{\textit{List}}$. If *List* is a dictionary, then remove the mapping corresponding to the key m. In this case we use pet to compare $[\![m]\!]$ with the encrypted keys in *List*.

These protocols reveal no information about their encrypted inputs apart from the returned values, except that the remove protocol also reveals the *position* of the removed item in the list. In this case prior mix or rotate operations ensure the revealed position is random.

5.2   Count Protocol

The count protocol (Protocol 1) is the top-level protocol for calculating the election result. It invokes several sub-protocols to count the ballots. The inputs are the lists **Candidates** and **Ballots**. The output is the identity of the winning candidate.

```
 1:  count(Candidates, Ballots)
 2:      if Candidates has 1 remaining candidate [[c]]
 3:          decrypt([[c]]) and post c
 4:      else
 5:          Counters ← tally(Candidates, Ballots)
 6:          Counters ← mix(Counters)
 7:          [[c_ex]] ← min(Counters)
 8:          Ballots ← exclude(Ballots, [[c_ex]])
 9:          Candidates ← remove(Candidates, [[c_ex]])
10:          count(Candidates, Ballots)
```

Protocol 1: Counting for the alternative vote

Before the counting commences the authorities create the list **Candidates**. To do this they deterministically encrypt each valid candidate and then mix the ciphertexts. Additionally each ballot in **Ballots** must contain an encrypted preference vote for each valid candidate. In Section 8 we discuss how to ensure the input ballots are valid.

The count protocol is a recursive procedure that performs a complete distribution of the votes, continuing until there is only one remaining candidate. Each recursive step corresponds to a round of counting that invokes the tally protocol to privately calculate the round tally and then the exclude protocol to privately exclude a candidate.

The excluded candidate c_{ex} is the candidate with the minimum round tally. The min protocol locates $[[c_{ex}]]$ in **Counters** by executing pit $([[t_i]], [[t_j]])$ for pairs of candidate-tally mappings $([[c_i]], [[t_i]]), ([[c_j]], [[t_j]]) \in$ **Counters**. Tracking the counter with the current minimum tally and updating the minimum counter according to the result of pit requires $(C-1)$ invocations of pit for C counters. As min reveals a partial ordering of the counters, a preceding mix operation is necessary to ensure the revealed ordering is random. The min protocol resolves ties randomly and avoids revealing whether any ties occur.

5.3   Tally Protocol

The tally protocol (Protocol 2) calculates the round tally for each remaining candidate without revealing the tallies, the candidates, or the contents of the ballots. The inputs are the lists **Candidates** and **Ballots**. The output is the list **Counters**, which contains the round tally for each remaining candidate.

The protocol starts by initialising **Counters**. Each encrypted key is an exact copy of an encrypted candidate $[[c]] \in$ **Candidates**, and each encrypted tally is

```
1: tally(Candidates, Ballots)
2:     Counters ← {}
3:     for each [[c]] ∈ Candidates
4:         [[t]] ← [[0]]
5:         Counters ← append(Counters, ([[c]], [[t]]))
6:     for each Ballot ∈ Ballots
7:         Counters ← mix(Counters)
8:         [[v]] ← the highest preference vote in Ballot
9:         ([[c]], [[t]]) ← lookup(Counters, [[v]])
10:        [[t]] ← [[t]] ⊞ [[1]]
11:    return Counters
```

Protocol 2: Calculating the round tallies

the deterministic encryption of the initial tally 0. Subsequent mixing introduces secret randomness into all the ciphertexts.

The protocol iteratively calculates the tallies using the highest preference vote (the head of the list) in each ballot. For each ballot the protocol locates the correct counter and then increments it by homomorphically adding the deterministic encryption of 1. The lookup protocol locates the matching counter $([[c]], [[t]]) \in$ **Counters** by executing pet $([[v]], [[c]])$ for each $([[c]], [[t]]) \in$ **Counters**. Since lookup reveals the position of the incremented counter, a prior mix operation is necessary to ensure the revealed position is random.

5.4   Exclude Protocol

The exclude protocol (Protocol 3) deletes the excluded candidate from each ballot without revealing the identity of the excluded candidate, or the contents of any ballot. The inputs are the list **Ballots** and the encrypted excluded candidate $[[c_{ex}]]$. The output is the updated list **Ballots**.

```
1: exclude(Ballots, [[c_ex]])
2:     for each Ballot ∈ Ballots
3:         Ballot ← append(Ballot, [[m]])
4:         Ballot ← rotate(Ballot)
5:         Ballot ← remove(Ballot, [[c_ex]])
6:         Ballot ← rotate(Ballot)
7:         Ballot ← remove(Ballot, [[m]])
8:         Ballot ← restore(Ballot)
9:     return Ballots
```

Protocol 3: Deleting the excluded candidate from each ballot

For each **Ballot** the protocol executes remove to delete the encrypted preference vote $[[v]]$ with $v = c_{ex}$. However, as the remove protocol leaks the position of the removed item, it is necessary to conceal the position of $[\![v]\!]$. Hence the exclude protocol first executes a rotate operation. Then although the randomly shifted position of $[\![v]\!]$ is known at the instant of deletion, there is no correlation with its original position in the ballot.

At this point exclude must undo the rotation to return the ballot to its original ordering. To permit this, prior to the original rotate the protocol appends a deterministically encrypted marker $[\![m]\!]$ (where m is a publicly known and invalid preference) to the end of the ballot. Then afterwards it executes remove to delete $[\![m]\!]$. This also reveals the end of the ballot and the restore operation simply shifts the list of preferences back to its original ordering. Note the rotate before the marker is removed conceals the relative positions of $[\![v]\!]$ and $[\![m]\!]$.

5.5   Optional Preferences Variant

A common variation in preferential systems is that voters are only required to assign one preference, and the remaining preferences are optional. The minimum disclosure counting scheme can also accommodate this situation. In this case we still require that ballots contain an encrypted preference vote for each valid candidate. Every ballot simply contains an additional encrypted null candidate $[\![\perp]\!]$ as a terminator after the last desired preference. The voter, or possibly the voting application, enters the remaining preferences in arbitrary order after $[\![\perp]\!]$.

The only change needed in the counting scheme is in the count protocol. The list **Candidates** now contains $[\![\perp]\!]$ and the recursion terminates when there are two remaining candidates (the winner and $\perp$). To conceal exhausted ballots the tally protocol treats the null candidate the same as any other candidate. But the counting must disregard the null candidate's tally in order to avoid excluding the null candidate. Hence immediately before executing min, the count protocol must perform an additional remove($\textbf{\textit{Counters}}, [\![\perp]\!]$) step.

6   Optimised Tally Protocol

We can optimise the tally protocol by using a radix M representation to encode each candidate as in Baudron et al.'s voting scheme [1]. Let C be the number of candidates, V be the number of voters, $L = \lceil \log_2 V \rceil$ and $M = 2^L$. Then we encode the ith candidate as $c_i = M^{i-1}$ for $i \in \{1, \dots, C\}$.

The optimised tally protocol (Protocol 4) homomorphically adds the highest preference vote in each ballot to compute a single encryption of the sum $s = \sum_{i=1}^{C} t_i c_i$, where t_i is the tally for c_i. Under the radix $M = 2^L$ encoding, s is an integer of length CL bits where the ith block of L bits corresponds to the bit representation of t_i.

The protocol uses an extract operation (see Section 4.3) to convert $[\![s]\!]$ into an encrypted bit representation ($[\![b_0]\!], \dots, [\![b_{CL-1}]\!]$). The protocol reconstructs each encrypted tally $[\![t_i]\!]$ from its bit representation and forms the encrypted candidate-tally pairs as in the original tally protocol. The only difference is that **AllCounters** contains a counter for each valid candidate including previously

```
1:  tally(Candidates, Ballots)
2:      [[s]] ← [[0]]
3:      for each Ballot ∈ Ballots
4:          [[v]] ← the highest preference vote in Ballot
5:          [[s]] ← [[s]] ⊞ [[v]]
6:      ([[b_0]], ..., [[b_{CL-1}]]) ← extract([[s]], CL)
7:      AllCounters ← {}
8:      for each i ∈ {1, ..., C}
9:          [[t_i]] ← [[0]]
10:         for each j ∈ {0, ..., L - 1}
11:             [[t_i]] ← [[t_i]] ⊞ (2^j ⊡ [[b_{(i-1)L+j}]])
12:         AllCounters ← append(AllCounters, ([[c_i]], [[t_i]]))
13:     AllCounters ← mix(AllCounters)
14:     Counters ← {}
15:     for each remaining candidate [[r]] ∈ Candidates
16:         ([[c]], [[t]]) ← lookup(AllCounters, [[r]])
17:         Counters ← append(Counters, ([[c]], [[t]]))
18:     return Counters
```

Protocol 4: Optimised tallying

excluded candidates. The final part of the protocol filters out the counters for excluded candidates to produce **Counters** for only the remaining candidates.

Note that this optimisation is only appropriate when the sum s fits in the plaintext space, that is $C \lceil \log_2 V \rceil < k$ for a k-bit length public key. Of course it is always possible to increase k but the increased work in performing operations under a larger key may not be worthwhile. In most cases there should be no problem because C tends to be reasonably small (typically less than 20) in alternative vote elections.

The optimised `tally` protocol is essentially an efficient minimum disclosure counting scheme for plurality systems. All that remains is to mix the counters then locate the counter with the maximum tally and decrypt the winning candidate. Locating the maximum counter is analogous to the `min` protocol in Section 5.2.

7   Analysis

7.1   Security

The counting scheme satisfies minimum disclosure, correctness, universal verifiability and robustness.

Minimum Disclosure. Minimum disclosure follows from the privacy properties of the underlying primitives and the application of the hide and seek paradigm. Apart from the final decryption to reveal the winning candidate, only the plaintext equality and inequality tests potentially leak any information.

The equality tests are used to construct the `remove` and `lookup` protocols (Sections 5.1 and 5.3). Both protocols reveal only the position of an encrypted message in a list of ciphertexts. The preceding `mix` or `rotate` ensures the revealed position is random.

The inequality tests are used to construct the `min` protocol (Section 5.2). This protocol reveals a partial ordering of a list of ciphertexts according to the plaintexts. The preceding `mix` ensures the revealed partial ordering is random.

Therefore all the leaked information is random and reveals nothing about the private counting state.

Correctness. The high-level description of the counting scheme doubles as a specification of a (non-cryptographic) counting algorithm for the alternative vote.

Universal Verifiability and Robustness. The authenticated bulletin board enables any party to examine and verify every step of the protocol execution. Each step is universally verifiable and robust. There are two types of steps: distributed operations and open operations.

1. A distributed operation requires the authorities to post non-interactive zero-knowledge proofs that explicitly provide verifiability and robustness. Any party can then check whether the operation is correct.
2. An open operation is a known deterministic function on previously posted messages. An arbitrary authority posts the result. Any party can verify the open operation by independently computing the function as specified in the protocol and then comparing the result to the posted result. Robustness follows as each authority can also compute the result and compare it to the posted result. In the event of inconsistencies, all the authorities post their results. The correct result is the one that is identical for the quorum of honest authorities.

7.2   Complexity

Using typical costs of the underlying cryptographic primitives, we provide estimates of the computational and communication complexity. We use modular multiplication as the unit of measure and assume that a modular exponentiation costs $O(k)$ multiplications for a security parameter k. For all the primitives used, the number of modular multiplications performed has the same asymptotic complexity as the number of bits transferred, and so the computational complexity below also refers to the communication complexity.

In an election with A authorities, C candidates and V voters, the total cost of performing or verifying the counting is $O(AC^2Vk)$. Each authority individually performs $O(C^2Vk)$ operations. Publicly verifying and combining the individual results of the authorities has an additional cost of $O(AC^2Vk)$.

The total $O(AC^2Vk)$ complexity arises from the $O(ACVk)$ cost per counting round, with $(C-1)$ rounds in total. In each round the `tally` protocol costs each authority $O(V)$ mix operations on $O(C)$ ciphertexts, $O(CV)$ plaintext equality tests, and $O(ACVk)$ verification operations, resulting in an asymptotic complexity of $O(ACVk)$. The `exclude` protocol has the same cost. The `min` protocol does not affect the complexity as it only performs $O(C)$ plaintext inequality tests, each at a cost of $O((A \log V) k)$.

Although the optimised `tally` protocol only costs $O(V + (AC \log V) k)$ due to the $O(V)$ homomorphic additions and the $O((AC \log V) k)$ extraction of $C \log V$ bits, the overall complexity remains the same because the `exclude` protocol still costs $O(ACVk)$ per round.

8   Integration with Voting Schemes

We can construct an end to end solution for cryptographic preferential elections by combining the minimum disclosure counting scheme with an existing receipt-free or coercion-resistant online voting scheme (see Section 2). A common approach in voting schemes is for the ballot to contain an encrypted vote for a single candidate. The voter provides a non-interactive zero-knowledge proof of vote validity so that anyone can verify the ballot is for a valid candidate. Adapting such a voting scheme for preferential voting requires the following modifications.

1. Each voter casts a ballot containing a list of encrypted preference votes in descending order of preference. As in the optimised `tally` protocol (Section 6) we use the radix M representation to encode candidates. The voter also provides an explicit proof of *preferential* vote validity.
2. After removing all unauthentic ballots and ballots with incorrect proofs of vote validity, the authorities use the minimum disclosure counting scheme to compute the election result.

Since a ballot must now contain an encrypted vote for each valid candidate, the proof of preferential vote validity is more complex than for a plurality scheme. First the voter must prove that each encrypted preference vote $[\![v_i]\!]$ in the ballot is for a valid candidate, for instance using Damgård and Jurik's proof [4].

Next the voter must show that each preference vote v_i is for a distinct candidate. An efficient solution is Groth's proof of vote validity for the Borda vote [9]. The proof is for a ballot that consists of a single encrypted preferential vote $[\![v]\!]$. A valid vote is of the form $v = \sum_{i=1}^{C} \pi(i) v_i$, where C is the number of candidates, π is a permutation of the rankings $1, \ldots, C$, and v_i is a preference vote for a valid candidate.

To use this proof the voter must first convert the list of encrypted preference votes $[\![v_1]\!], \ldots, [\![v_C]\!]$ into a single encrypted preferential vote $[\![v]\!]$. In addition the conversion must be universally verifiable. The homomorphic cryptosystem provides a natural solution as anyone can compute $[\![v]\!] = (1 \boxdot [\![v_1]\!]) \boxplus (2 \boxdot [\![v_2]\!]) \boxplus \ldots \boxplus (C \boxdot [\![v_C]\!])$.

Casting a ballot is efficient for the voter. The cost of creating a ballot is $O(Ck)$ and the total cost of constructing or verifying a proof of vote validity is $O((C \log C) k)$.

9   Conclusion

We introduced a minimum disclosure counting scheme for secure counting in alternative vote elections. Its main contribution is that it achieves privacy in the counting by performing operations only on ciphertexts and decrypting only the winning candidate. Hence it thwarts signature attacks for bribery and coercion. The scheme provides stronger security than both contemporary cryptographic counting schemes and traditional manual counting. It can function as a standalone counting scheme or can be combined with an online voting scheme to form a complete online election scheme.

Even if the election authorities deliberately weaken the counting scheme to reveal specific counting data, minimum disclosure in the protocol is still important in order to ensure there is no additional and unintended information leakage. This can be especially relevant when initially adopting cryptographic counting. For instance it may be desirable to use the counting scheme in parallel with manual counting and then compare the results. Since the manual count must resolve any ties using the same random choices as the counting scheme, then in this case it would be necessary to reveal some counting data such as the order of exclusions.

Worldwide, plurality electoral systems are the most common for government elections. Interestingly, preferential electoral systems are gradually becoming more widespread. New Zealand and Scotland have recently adopted preferential systems for some elections. In parts of Canada, the UK and the USA, there is currently a push to switch to preferential systems.

Historically, a barrier to the adoption of preferential systems has been the complexity of manual counting. But now computers can automate the counting. Indeed many preferential elections already use electronic counting, where election authorities manually enter votes from paper ballots into an electronic database and a computer calculates the result. In fact for some preferential systems, such as the version of the single transferable vote recently introduced for local elections in New Zealand, the counting algorithm is so complicated that manual counting is infeasible.

Electronic counting offers many advantages. However the shift towards naive electronic counting without cryptographic safeguards is an alarming trend. One serious concern is unauthorised access to the voting data. Compromising the electronic database of plaintext votes opens the door to the potential for large-scale bribery and coercion of voters through signature attacks. Another issue is the lack of verifiability. It is notoriously difficult to detect flaws in the software implementation and the hardware. Publicly releasing the complete voting data for independent verification, as required in Australia, violates the secret ballot and jeopardises effective democracy. Therefore verifiably secure cryptographic approaches to preferential counting have an important role to play in both paper and electronic elections.

Cryptographic counting for the alternative vote raises two open problems. First, what is the optimal complexity? For C candidates and V voters, the lower bound is at least $O(CV)$ from the $O(C)$ rounds and $O(V)$ distributed ballot operations per round. Intuitively the limiting factor is the exclusion of a candidate without revealing its identity or ranking in any ballot. Regardless of the ballot representation, this seems to require $O(C)$ work per ballot. Then the optimal cost would be $O(C^2V)$.

Second, is it possible to precisely define what counting information is sensitive? In the context of signature attacks it appears very difficult to develop an appropriate definition. However a weaker requirement than minimum disclosure might enable coercion-resistant schemes of lower cost.

Acknowledgements

We thank Berry Schoenmakers for suggesting the use of verifiable rotators to greatly simplify an earlier version of our scheme. We also thank Vanessa Teague for helpful discussions. We are grateful to the anonymous referees for many valuable comments.

References

1. Baudron, O., Fouque, P.A., Pointcheval, D., Stern, J., Poupard, G.: Practical multi-candidate election system. In: PODC, pp. 274–283 (2001)
2. Benaloh, J.C., Tuinstra, D.: Receipt-free secret-ballot elections (extended abstract). In: STOC, pp. 544–553 (1994)
3. Di Cosmo, R.: On Privacy and Anonymity in Electronic and Non Electronic Voting: the Ballot-As-Signature Attack (2007),
   http://www.pps.jussieu.fr/~dicosmo/E-Vote/
4. Damgård, I., Jurik, M.: A Generalisation, a Simplification and Some Applications of Paillier's Probabilistic Public-Key System. In: Kim, K. (ed.) PKC 2001. LNCS, vol. 1992, pp. 119–136. Springer, Heidelberg (2001)
5. de Hoogh, S., Schoenmakers, B., Skoric, B., Villegas, J.: Verifiable Rotation of Homomorphic Encryptions. In: Jarecki, S., Tsudik, G. (eds.) Public Key Cryptography. LNCS, vol. 5443, pp. 393–410. Springer, Heidelberg (2009)
6. Fouque, P.A., Poupard, G., Stern, J.: Sharing Decryption in the Context of Voting or Lotteries. In: Frankel, Y. (ed.) FC 2000. LNCS, vol. 1962, pp. 90–104. Springer, Heidelberg (2001)
7. Goh, E.J., Golle, P.: Event Driven Private Counters. In: S. Patrick, A., Yung, M. (eds.) FC 2005. LNCS, vol. 3570, pp. 313–327. Springer, Heidelberg (2005)
8. Groth, J.: A Verifiable Secret Shuffle of Homomorphic Encryptions. In: Desmedt, Y.G. (ed.) PKC 2003. LNCS, vol. 2567, pp. 145–160. Springer, Heidelberg (2002)
9. Groth, J.: Non-interactive Zero-Knowledge Arguments for Voting. In: Ioannidis, J., Keromytis, A.D., Yung, M. (eds.) ACNS 2005. LNCS, vol. 3531, pp. 467–482. Springer, Heidelberg (2005)
10. Groth, J., Ishai, Y.: Sub-linear Zero-Knowledge Argument for Correctness of a Shuffle. In: Smart, N.P. (ed.) EUROCRYPT 2008. LNCS, vol. 4965, pp. 379–396. Springer, Heidelberg (2008)
11. Heather, J.: Implementing STV securely in Pret a Voter. In: CSF, pp. 157–169. IEEE Computer Society, Los Alamitos (2007)

12. Hevia, A., Kiwi, M.A.: Electronic jury voting protocols. Theor. Comput. Sci. 321, 73–94 (2004)
13. Hirt, M., Sako, K.: Efficient Receipt-Free Voting Based on Homomorphic Encryption. In: Preneel, B. (ed.) EUROCRYPT 2000. LNCS, vol. 1807, pp. 539–556. Springer, Heidelberg (2000)
14. Jakobsson, M., Juels, A.: Mix and Match: Secure Function Evaluation via Ciphertexts. In: Okamoto, T. (ed.) ASIACRYPT 2000. LNCS, vol. 1976, pp. 162–177. Springer, Heidelberg (2000)
15. Juels, A., Catalano, D., Jakobsson, M.: Coercion-resistant electronic elections. In: Atluri, V., di Vimercati, S.D.C., Dingledine, R. (eds.) WPES, pp. 61–70. ACM, New York (2005)
16. Keller, J., Kilian, J.: A Linked-List Approach to Cryptographically Secure Elections Using Instant Runoff Voting. In: Pieprzyk, J. (ed.) ASIACRYPT 2008. LNCS, vol. 5350, pp. 198–215. Springer, Heidelberg (2008)
17. Lee, B., Boyd, C., Dawson, E., Kim, K., Yang, J., Yoo, S.: Providing Receipt-Freeness in Mixnet-Based Voting Protocols. In: Lim, J.-I., Lee, D.-H. (eds.) ICISC 2003. LNCS, vol. 2971, pp. 245–258. Springer, Heidelberg (2004)
18. Nguyen, L., Safavi-Naini, R., Kurosawa, K.: Verifiable shuffles: a formal model and a Paillier-based three-round construction with provable security. Int. J. Inf. Sec. 5, 241–255 (2006)
19. Niemi, V., Renvall, A.: How to Prevent Buying of Votes in Computer Elections. In: Safavi-Naini, R., Pieprzyk, J.P. (eds.) ASIACRYPT 1994. LNCS, vol. 917, pp. 164–170. Springer, Heidelberg (1995)
20. Okamoto, T.: Receipt-Free Electronic Voting Schemes for Large Scale Elections. In: Christianson, B., Crispo, B., Lomas, T.M.A., Roe, M. (eds.) Security Protocols 1997. LNCS, vol. 1361, pp. 25–35. Springer, Heidelberg (1998)
21. Paillier, P.: Public-Key Cryptosystems Based on Composite Degree Residuosity Classes. In: Stern, J. (ed.) EUROCRYPT 1999. LNCS, vol. 1592, pp. 223–238. Springer, Heidelberg (1999)
22. Parkes, D.C., Rabin, M.O., Shieber, S.M., Thorpe, C.A.: Practical secrecy-preserving, verifiably correct and trustworthy auctions. In: Fox, M.S., Spencer, B. (eds.) ICEC. ACM International Conference Proceeding Series, vol. 156, pp. 70–81. ACM, New York (2006)
23. Reiter, M.K., Wang, X.: Fragile mixing. In: Atluri, V., Pfitzmann, B., McDaniel, P.D. (eds.) ACM Conference on Computer and Communications Security, pp. 227–235. ACM, New York (2004)
24. Schoenmakers, B., Tuyls, P.: Efficient Binary Conversion for Paillier Encrypted Values. In: Vaudenay, S. (ed.) EUROCRYPT 2006. LNCS, vol. 4004, pp. 522–537. Springer, Heidelberg (2006)
25. Teague, V., Ramchen, K., Naish, L.: Coercion-Resistant Tallying for STV Voting. In: Dill, D.L., Kohno, T. (eds.) EVT, USENIX Association (2008)
26. Victorian Civil and Administrative Tribunal: van der Craats v Melbourne City Council [2000] VCAT 447 (2000), http://www.austlii.edu.au/au/cases/vic/VCAT/2000/447.html

A Design of Secure Preferential E-Voting

Kun Peng and Feng Bao

Institute for Infocomm Research, Singapore
dr.kun.peng@gmail.com

Abstract. A secure preferential e-voting scheme is designed in this paper. It is a homomorphic e-voting scheme. It is illustrated that although mix-based voting is a very simple solution to preferential e-voting it is vulnerable to a coercion attack. The coercion attack especially attacks preferential e-voting scheme only outputs the election result and does not reveal any vote, so is invulnerable to the attack. Homomorphism of the employed encryption algorithm is exploited not only to count the votes without revealing them but also to adjust the votes when a new round of counting is needed. Moreover, it achieves all the security properties usually desired in e-voting.

Keywords: preferential e-voting, coercion attack, security.

1 Introduction

Electronic voting is a very popular cryptographic application, where the voters cast their electronic votes through a digital communication network. E-voting is applicable to various elections applications. In a simple election, there are multiple candidates and the candidate obtaining more votes than any other candidate is the winner. The simple election rule has a drawback: there may be multiple candidates to support the most popular policy such that they divide the votes for the most popular policy. With this drawback, none of them can obtain more votes than another candidate, who does not support the most popular policy but is the only candidate to support the second most popular policy. For example, a candidate A finds from a poll that another candidate B has an opposite policy and is more popular and then can exploit the drawback as follows. A hires another people C, who registers as an candidate and chooses the same policy of B. Finally, C attracts some votes from B and A wins the election. As a result, the most popular policy cannot win the election and the will of most voters cannot be realized through the election, which is against the basic principle of democracy.

To overcome the drawback, a more complex rule can be employed. When there is no candidate to win more than half of the votes, the candidate with the fewest votes is deleted and the election is run again in a new round with one fewer candidate. If still no candidate can win more than half of the votes, the candidate with the fewest votes in the new round is deleted and the election is run again in one more round with one fewer candidate. This candidate-deletion-and-vote-again process is repeated again and again until one candidate wins

P.Y.A. Ryan and B. Schoenmakers (Eds.): VOTE-ID 2009, LNCS 5767, pp. 141–156, 2009.
© Springer-Verlag Berlin Heidelberg 2009

more than half of the votes and becomes the winner. This solution is called multiple-round-voting election, which is adopted in many European nations.

Obviously, multiple-round-voting election has a drawback: the election may have to be run multiple times and the voters may have to vote for multiple rounds. Firstly, it is a waste of social resources. Secondly, it may discourage the voters and reduce the voting rate. Thirdly, it cannot guarantee an election result at a firm time, so may cause political instability. The more candidates there are, the more rounds may be needed in multiple-round-voting election and the more serious this drawback may be. In the parliamentary election in Australia sometimes there are scores of candidates and thus multiple-round-voting is impractical. So preferential election is designed to solve the problem. In a preferential election, every voter must include in his vote a complete preferential order of all the candidates. So only one round of communication is needed for a voter to submit his vote. If one candidate obtains more than half of the first choices in all the votes, it is the winner. Otherwise, the candidate with the fewest first choices is deleted and the first choices of all the votes are counted again with one fewer candidate, where the votes must be adjusted such that the second choices in the votes originally naming the deleted candidate as the first choice become the first choices in the votes. If still no candidate can obtain more than half of the first choices, the candidate with the fewest first choices in the new round of counting is deleted and the votes are adjusted and counted again. This vote-adjustment-and-counting-again process is repeated again and again until one candidate wins more than half of the first choices and becomes the winner. When necessary, the vote-adjustment-and-counting-again strategy can be extended to support multiple-winner elections. Preferential election is employed in the parliamentary election in Australia.

Implementing preferential election in e-voting is an interesting question. There are two main solutions to secure electronic voting. The first one is homomorphic voting, which does not decrypt the encrypted votes separately but exploit homomorphism of the employed encryption algorithm to collectively open the encrypted votes using a small number of decryptions. Homomorphic voting schemes[1,12,6,13,15,22] employs a homomorphic encryption algorithm like Paillier encryption [19] or modified ElGamal encryption [15] and recovers the sum of the voters' selections. In homomorphic e-voting, each vote must be in a special format, so that the number of every possible selection can be correctly counted. More precisely, in homomorphic e-voting every vote contains one or more selections (each corresponding to a candidate or a possible choice) and every selection must be one of two pre-defined integers (e.g. 0 and 1), each representing support or rejection of a candidate or choice. With such special vote formats, usually the election rule is not complex in homomorphic voting. Moreover, the cost of vote validity check must be carefully evaluated and controlled as it usually employs costly zero knowledge proof operations and corresponding verification operations. The other solution is mix-based voting [9,18,11,21], which is often employed in e-voting applications with complex election rules. The basic operation in a mix is shuffling, which re-encrypts (or partially decrypts) the encrypted votes and re-orders them. Multiple shuffling operations are employed and each of them is performed by a different tallier such that the votes are untraceable if at least one tallier is honest. Finally, the repeatedly shuffled votes are decrypted to recover all the votes. Recently, a hybrid e-voting scheme combining merits of the two solutions [20] is proposed. No matter which method is employ, a secure e-voting scheme should satisfy the following security properties.

- Correctness: it is guaranteed with an overwhelmingly large probability and without any assumption or condition (e.g. trust or hard problem) that all the valid votes and only the valid votes are counted.
- Privacy: no information about any voter's choice in the election is revealed to any polynomial party when the number of colluding talliers is not over a threshold.
- Robustness: any dishonest behaviour or abnormal situation can be detected and solved without revealing any vote.
- Public verifiability: correctness of the election can be publicly verified by any voter or observer.

A common sense is that preferential e-voting should be implemented by mix-based voting as a vote in preferential election usually contains much information and is complex. However, it is recalled in Section 2 that when mix-based e-voting is applied to preferential election, there is a special coercion attack, which is difficult to prevent. As the attack exploits the decrypted votes, a countermeasure against it should conceal the votes. Namely, homomorphic e-voting is the solution to the attack. So a secure homomorphic e-voting scheme is designed in this paper to prevent the attack. To the best of our knowledge, this is the first secure e-voting scheme invulnerable to this coercion attack while the existing e-voting schemes claiming to prevent this attack [10,17,27] cannot satisfy all the security properties. In the new scheme, homomorphism of the employed encryption algorithm is exploited not only to count the votes without revealing them but also to adjust the votes before a new round of counting without revealing unnecessary information. The newly designed homomorphic preferential e-voting scheme only outputs the election result and does not reveal any vote, so is invulnerable to the coercion attack in Section 2. Moreover, it achieves all the security properties usually desired in e-voting.

2   Background: A Coercion Attack against Preferential E-Voting

Coercion attack threatens fairness of elections. In a coercion attack, a candidate tries to coerce or buy over some voters to vote for him (e.g. through violence or bribery). For success of the attack, the cheating candidate must be able to check whether a certain voter really votes for him. So in a fair election, any voter must be prevented from proving that he casts a certain vote. This security property is usually called coercion-resistance. It is especially necessary in e-voting, which always publish all the sealed votes for the sake of public verifiability. Currently, there are two countermeasures to coercion attack. One is deniable encryption [4], while the other is re-encryption with untransferable zero knowledge proof of correctness by a third party (in the form of a trusted authority or a tamper-resistent hardware) linked through untappable communication channel [14][1]. Usually, either of these two countermeasures can prevent coercion attack in most cases. However, neither of them can prevent a certain coercion attack especially against preferential e-voting. To the best of our knowledge the attack is novel and is described in this section.

A straightforward solution to preferential e-voting is mix-based e-voting as the contents of the votes are complex. In mix-based e-voting, all the votes are decrypted and published after being repeatedly shuffled. So an attack launching a coercion attack can see the contents of all the votes although they are shuffled and thus not linked to the voters. An attacker can exploits this fact to launch a coercion attack [2] as follows.

1. Suppose there are m candidates. The attacker notices (e.g. according to a poll) that three of them have very low support rates. In some cases the attacker may hire three people with very low support rates to take part in the election as candidates.
2. The attacker asks a voter to cast a special vote: the attacker is the first choice and the three candidates are the next three choices. Moreover, the attacker chooses a special order for the three candidates.
3. After all the votes are shuffled, decrypted and published, the attacker searches for the special vote he chooses for the voter. If he finds such a vote, he believes that the voter has voted as he asks. As in normal cases the probability that the three unpopular candidates are the second, the third and the fourth choices is very low, especially when they appear in the three positions in the special order, the probability that such a vote in the published election result is from the coerced voter is high.

This attack is sometimes referred to as the "Italian attack". It is especially effective when there are many candidates (e.g. in the Australian parliamentary election). More precisely, the number of possible contents of votes is $m!$. When m is a little bit large (e.g. to be 20 or 30), $m!$ is a very large number and most of the contents usually do not appear and thus can be exploited by the attack. The attacker can adjust the number of unpopular candidates chosen as indicators in his attack. The more candidates he can choose, the more precise his attack can be. Even if we give up the one-round-communication strategy and adopt multiple-round-voting election, this attack can still work in a mix-based e-voting scheme although maybe less effective. In multiple-round-voting election, the more rounds are actually used, the more effective the attack is. Our conclusion is that this attack can always work in mix-based e-voting and the only hope to prevent it is to design a secure homomorphic e-voting.

---

[1] The untappable communication channel is in the form of an internal channel like bus or USB cable when a tamper-resistent hardware is employed.

3   Preliminaries

Existing cryptographic primitives to be employed in this paper is recalled in this section. They include the encryption algorithm to seal the votes, efficient zero knowledge proof of validity of vote and a range test technique used in tallying.

A homomorphic semantically secure encryption algorithm is employed, which has an encryption algorithm $E()$ and a decryption algorithm $D()$. A message m is encrypted into a ciphertext $c = E(m, r)$ where r is randomizer used to achieve semantic security. *For simplicity, when the randomizer is not explicitly important, we express an encryption operation as $c = E(m)$.* Homomorphism of encryption requires that $D(c_1 c_2) = D(c_1) + D(c_2)$ for any ciphertexts c_1 and c_2. Typical homomorphic semantically secure encryption algorithms include Paillier encryption [19] and modified ElGamal encryption [15]. Homomorphic semantically secure encryption supports re-encryption: $RE(c)$ re-encrypts a ciphertext c into another ciphertext encrypting the same message. The private key is shared by multiple parties (talliers in e-voting schemes) such that decryption is feasible only when the number of cooperating share holders is over a threshold ([8]). The partial decryption operation by the lth share holder is denoted as $D_l()$. Suppose the message space of the encryption algorithm is Z_q and the number of voters is n. We require that $q > 2n$.

In this paper, as homomorphic e-voting is employed, it is necessary for the voters to prove validity of their votes. In homomorphic e-voting, each vote consists of some integers, each of which must be in a strict format. In elections with complex rules (e.g. preferential voting in this paper), the content of a vote is quite complex, so proof of validity of each of them may be inefficient. A simpler validity proof operation is to prove that a ciphertext encrypts a certain message, which is simple but still costs a lot as many instances of it are needed (e.g. in the preferential e-voting scheme in this paper). In [24] an efficient integrated zero knowledge proof protocol to prove that each of multiple ciphertexts encrypts a certain message in a batch is proposed. It is much more efficient than the multiple separate zero knowledge proof protocols, each proving that one ciphertext encrypts a certain message. In this paper, proof that each of $c_1, c_2, \ldots, c_\lambda$ encrypts a using the batch proof and verification technique in [24] is denoted as $ZKP(c_1, c_2, \ldots, c_\lambda \mid a)$. A more complex validity proof operation in vote validity check is to prove that a ciphertext encrypts one of several certain messages, which also occurs in many instances but is more difficult to batch as it involves OR logic. There are a few attempts to improve efficiency of multiple instances of zero knowledge proof of encryption of one out of multiple messages. Among them the most efficient is [22], in which an efficient zero knowledge proof protocol to prove that each of multiple ciphertexts encrypts one of two possible integers is proposed. It employs batch zero knowledge proof and verification to achieve high efficiency in applications like e-voting. In this paper, proof that each of $c_1, c_2, \ldots, c_\lambda$ encrypts either a or b using the batch proof and verification technique in [22] is denoted as $ZKP\text{-}OR(c_1, c_2, \ldots, c_\lambda \mid a, b)$.

In cryptographic applications, very often it is needed to check whether an encrypted message is within a certain range without revealing the message. One solution is that a party knows the message and proves that it is in the range using a zero knowledge proof protocol. However, the zero knowledge proof [3,16] is usually not very efficient. Moreover, in some applications (e.g. the e-voting scheme in this paper) the ciphertext encrypting the message is obtained through malleable operations of ciphertexts and thus nobody knows the message. In those applications, no prover is available to prove that the message is in the range.

In [23], a range test technique is proposed to test whether an encrypted message is within a certain range. The test is performed by two parties, who share the decryption key and neither of them knows the message. In the course of the test, the encrypted message is not decrypted or revealed. The range test protocol only employs a constant number of basic cryptographic primitives, so is very efficient. When necessary, it can be extended to be a multiple-party protocol by sharing the power of one party among more parties. In this paper, to test whether a message encrypted in a ciphertext c is in a range R using the range test protocol in [23] is denoted as $RT(c, R)$, which returns YES only if the message is in R.

4   Secure E-Voting Invulnerable to the Coercion Attack

The main purpose of the new e-voting scheme is to prevent the coercion attack presented in Section 2. The other coercion attacks are well known and can be prevented by either of the two existing countermeasures deniable encryption [4] and re-encryption with untransferable zero knowledge proof of correctness by a third party linked through untappable communication channel [14], so is not our focus. Due to space limit, we do not repeat the existing countermeasures to coercion attack. We just assume one of them is employed and thus he other coercion attacks are prevented.

The new e-voting scheme is a homomorphic e-voting scheme. Each vote is a $m \times m$ matrix where m is the number of candidates. If the jth candidate is a voter's i^{th} choice, the element in the ith row and in the jth column of the matrix is 1. So there is one 1 in each row and in each column. The other elements in the matrix are 0. A homomorphic semantically secure encryption algorithm recalled in Section 3 is employed to seal the votes and encrypt all their elements. In order to prevent the coercion attack presented in Section 2, homomorphism of the employed encryption algorithm is exploited to reveal as little information as possible. No vote is decrypted and no counting result is revealed. We only find out the winner, while any information unnecessary in the search for the winner is concealed. As it is a preferential election, multiple rounds of counting may be needed. In each round of counting, the number of first choices obtained by each candidate is compared with half of the number of voters where it is not revealed. If the number of first choices obtained by a candidate is larger than half of the number of voters, it is the winner. If no winner is found, one more round of counting is needed. Before a new round of counting can be performed, the votes must be adjusted such that the candidate with the fewest first choices is deleted from all the votes. The candidate to delete is determined by comparing the number of first choices obtained by each candidate and finding out the smallest number, where no number is revealed. The procedure to delete a candidate from the votes (deleting the first choices for the candidate and using the second choices to replace the deleted first choices) is a complex secure computation protocol called deleting function, which is described in Section 4.3. The deleting function does not reveal how each vote is adjusted or any other information about any vote.

4.1 Notations

For simplicity in description of our e-voting scheme, some special notations are employed. Note that they may be different with the traditional notations for operations of matrices. Also note that in many computations in this paper, an appropriate modulus is needed. As we do not limit our e-voting scheme to a certain encryption algorithm with a special parameter setting, we do not explicitly include the moduluses in our description of the computations.

– Exponentiation of the elements in a matrix

$$
M^{\times x} = \left\{ \begin{matrix} m_{1,1}^x \ m_{1,2}^x \ m_{1,3}^x \ \cdots \\ m_{2,1}^x \ m_{2,2}^x \quad \cdots \quad \cdots \\ m_{3,1}^x \quad \cdots \quad \cdots \\ \cdots \quad \cdots \quad \cdots \end{matrix} \right\} \quad \text{where } M = \left\{ \begin{matrix} m_{1,1} \ m_{1,2} \ m_{1,3} \ \cdots \\ m_{2,1} \ m_{2,2} \quad \cdots \quad \cdots \\ m_{3,1} \quad \cdots \quad \cdots \\ \cdots \quad \cdots \quad \cdots \end{matrix} \right\}
$$

– Logarithm in terms of matrix
$x = \log_{M_1} M_2$ means $M_2 = M_1^{\times x}$ where M_1 and M_2 are two matrices of the same size.

– Multiplication of the elements of two matrices

$$
M_1 \otimes M_2 = \left\{ \begin{matrix} m_{1,1} m'_{1,1} \ m_{1,2} m'_{1,2} \ m_{1,3} m'_{1,3} \ \cdots \\ m_{2,1} m'_{2,1} \ m_{2,2} m'_{2,2} \quad \cdots \quad \cdots \\ m_{3,1} m'_{3,1} \quad \cdots \quad \cdots \\ \cdots \quad \cdots \quad \cdots \end{matrix} \right\}
$$

where $M_1 = \left\{ \begin{matrix} m_{1,1} \ m_{1,2} \ m_{1,3} \ \cdots \\ m_{2,1} \ m_{2,2} \quad \cdots \quad \cdots \\ m_{3,1} \quad \cdots \quad \cdots \\ \cdots \quad \cdots \quad \cdots \end{matrix} \right\}$ and $M_2 = \left\{ \begin{matrix} m'_{1,1} \ m'_{1,2} \ m'_{1,3} \ \cdots \\ m'_{2,1} \ m'_{2,2} \quad \cdots \quad \cdots \\ m'_{3,1} \quad \cdots \quad \cdots \\ \cdots \quad \cdots \quad \cdots \end{matrix} \right\}$

– Re-encryption of a matrix

$$
RE(M) = \left\{ \begin{matrix} RE(c_{1,1}) \ RE(c_{1,2}) \ RE(c_{1,3}) \ \cdots \\ RE(c_{2,1}) \ RE(c_{2,2}) \quad \cdots \quad \cdots \\ RE(c_{3,1}) \quad \cdots \quad \cdots \\ \cdots \quad \cdots \quad \cdots \end{matrix} \right\}
$$

$$\text{where } M = \left\{ \begin{array}{l} c_{1,1} \ c_{1,2} \ c_{1,3} \ \cdots \\ c_{2,1} \ c_{2,2} \ \cdots \cdots \cdots \\ c_{3,1} \ \cdots \ \cdots \\ \cdots \ \cdots \ \cdots \end{array} \right\}$$

4.2 The New E-Voting Scheme

Suppose there are n voters and m candidates and our e-voting scheme is as follows.

1. The voters submit their votes $C_1, C_2, \ldots, C_n$ where for $k = 1, 2, \ldots, n$

$$C_k = \left\{ \begin{array}{cccc} c_{k,1,1} & c_{k,1,2} & \cdots & c_{k,1,m} \\ c_{k,2,1} & c_{k,2,2} & \cdots & c_{k,2,m} \\ & \cdots & \cdots & \\ c_{k,m,1} & c_{k,m,2} & \cdots & c_{k,m,m} \end{array} \right\}$$

and $c_{k,i,j}$ is an encryption using the employed homomorphic encryption algorithm of the kth voter's choice for the jth candidate, which indicates whether to choose him as his i^{th} preference:

   - if the kth voter wants to choose the jth candidate as his i^{th} preference then $c_{k,i,j} = E(1)$;
   - if the kth voter does not want to choose the jth candidate as his i^{th} preference then $c_{k,i,j} = E(0)$.

2. Each voter then proves validity of his vote as follows.
   (a) The kth voter publicly performs proof $ZKP\text{-}OR(c_{k,1,1}, c_{k,1,2}, \cdots, c_{k,m,m} \mid 0, 1)$ and anyone can verify it. It guarantees that any choice in his vote is either 0 or 1.
   (b) For $i = 1, 2, \ldots, m$ the kth voter publicly proves that $\prod_{j=1}^{m} c_{k,i,j}$ encrypt 1 using $ZKP(\prod_{j=1}^{m} c_{k,1,j}, \prod_{j=1}^{m} c_{k,2,j}, \ldots, \prod_{j=1}^{m} c_{k,m,j} \mid 1)$ and anyone can verify it. It guarantees that there is only one 1 in every row of his vote.
   (c) For $j = 1, 2, \ldots, m$ the kth voter publicly proves that $\prod_{i=1}^{m} c_{k,i,j}$ encrypt 1 using $ZKP(\prod_{i=1}^{m} c_{k,i,1}, \prod_{i=1}^{m} c_{k,i,2}, \ldots, \prod_{i=1}^{m} c_{k,i,m} \mid 1)$ and anyone can verify it. It guarantees that there is only one 1 in every column of his vote.

3. The talliers calculate $e_{1,j} = \prod_{k=1}^{n} c_{k,1,j}$ for $j = 1, 2, \ldots, m$.

4. The talliers perform range tests $RT(e_{1,j}/E(\lfloor n/2 \rfloor, 0), \{1, 2, \ldots, \lfloor q/2 \rfloor\})$ for $j = 1, 2, \ldots, m$ until one test returns YES or all the m tests are done. As $q > 2n$, $D(e_{1,j}) \leq n \leq \lfloor q/2 \rfloor$. So $D(e_{1,j}/E(\lfloor n/2 \rfloor)) = D(e_{1,j}) - \lfloor n/2 \rfloor \bmod q$ is in the range $\{1, 2, \ldots, \lfloor q/2 \rfloor\}$ if and only if $D(e_{1,j}) > \lfloor n/2 \rfloor$. If the tests show that any $e_{1,j}$ encrypts an integer larger than $\lfloor n/2 \rfloor$, the jth candidate (who must win more than half of the votes) is declared as the winner and the e-voting ends. Otherwise, go on to next step.

5. The talliers compare $e_{1,j}$ for $j = 1, 2, \ldots, m$ in pairs. To compare $e_{1,\mu}$ and $e_{1,\nu}$, the tallier perform a range test $RT(e_{1,\mu}/e_{1,\nu}, \{1, 2, \ldots, \lfloor q/2 \rfloor\})$, which returns YES iff $e_{1,\mu} > e_{1,\nu}$ as $q > 2n$, $D(e_{1,\mu}) \leq n$ and $D(e_{1,\nu}) \leq n$. In this way, the talliers can find the $e_{1,j}$ encrypting the smallest integer, which is supposed to be $e_{1,\alpha}$. So the αth candidate obtains the smallest number of first choices and should be removed from the election. More precisely, the choices for the deleted candidate must be deleted from the votes such that the votes can be counted again with one fewer candidate. It is easy to delete the column representing the deleted candidate from each vote, so it is performed immediately after a candidate is deleted. More precisely, the αth column of each vote matrix is deleted and the votes $C_1, C_2, \ldots, C_n$ becomes $m \times (m-1)$ matrices.

6. Deleting the row once representing the deleted candidate's position in the preferential order and now becoming an all-zero row is more difficult, so is not performed immediately after a candidate is deleted. Instead it is performed later due to two reasons. Firstly, immediately after a candidate is deleted it is unknown which row represents him in each vote. Secondly, if the deleted candidate is not the first choice in a vote it may be unnecessary to delete the row for him. So the votes are checked before they are counted again. If the first row is an all-zero row in a vote, it is deleted from the vote; if the first row is not an all-zero row in a vote, temporally it is not necessary to delete any row in the vote. This row-deleting strategy has two advantages. Firstly, the row to delete is always in a fixed position: the first row. Secondly, an all-zero row is deleted only when it becomes the first row and will otherwise be counted by mistake. Such a checking-and-deleting procedure handles each vote in the form M, a $m \times t$ matrix of ciphertexts, in which each row either encrypts t zeros or $t-1$ zeros and 1 one. If the first row encrypts $t-1$ zeros and 1 one, the deleting function does not change the content of the vote; if the first row encrypts t zeros, the deleting function moves the first row to the last row of the matrix and the other rows must be moved one row up. Note that for the sake of vote privacy and to prevent the coercion attack in Section 2, the deleting function cannot reveal any information about the votes like which vote contains an all-zero first row or which vote is changed. The deleting function is denoted as $F()$ and is employed to handle the vote: $F(C_1), F(C_2), \ldots F(C_n)$, where the implementation of the deleting function is provided in Section 4.3. After that the first rows of the votes indicate the voters' first choices without the αth candidate.

7. Go back to Step 3 with one fewer candidate.

This protocol stops when a candidate is found to obtain more than half of the first choices and declared as the winner in Step 4. A concrete example of the new e-voting scheme is given in Table 1, where there are 4 candidates and 9 voters. There are three rounds of counting in the tallying operation, where the vote matrices are reduced from 4 columns to 3 columns and finally to 2 columns. The symbol $\times$ in a vote matrix stands for a choice unnecessary to count, which may be either 1 or 0.

Table 1. A concrete example

vote	round 1	round 2	round 3
1	1 0 0 0 × × × × × × × × × × × ×	1 0 0 × × × × × × × × ×	1 0 × × × × × ×
2	1 0 0 0 × × × × × × × × × × × ×	1 0 0 × × × × × × × × ×	1 0 × × × × × ×
3	1 0 0 0 × × × × × × × × × × × ×	1 0 0 × × × × × × × × ×	1 0 × × × × × ×
4	0 1 0 0 × × × × × × × × × × × ×	0 1 0 × × × × × × × × ×	0 1 × × × × × ×
5	0 1 0 0 × × × × × × × × × × × ×	0 1 0 × × × × × × × × ×	0 1 × × × × × ×
6	0 1 0 0 × × × × × × × × × × × ×	0 1 0 × × × × × × × × ×	0 1 × × × × × ×
7	0 0 1 0 0 1 0 0 × × × × × × × ×	0 1 0 0 1 0 × × × × × ×	0 1 × × × × 0 0
8	0 0 1 0 1 0 0 0 × × × × × × × ×	0 1 0 1 0 0 × × × × × ×	1 0 × × × × 0 0
9	0 0 0 1 1 0 0 0 × × × × × × × ×	1 0 0 × × × × × × 0 0 0	1 0 × × × × 0 0
sum	{ 3 3 2 1 }	{ 4 3 2 }	{ 5 4 }

4.3 Deleting Function

When no candidate wins more than half of the first choices, the candidate with the fewest first choices must be deleted from the election and the first choices for him must be deleted from the votes. A vote to be handled by the deleting function is in the form

$$M = \left\{ \begin{array}{cccc} c_{1,1} & c_{1,2} & \cdots & c_{1,t} \\ c_{2,1} & c_{2,2} & \cdots & c_{2,t} \\ \multicolumn{4}{c}{\cdots \quad \cdots} \\ c_{m,1} & c_{m,2} & \cdots & c_{m,t} \end{array} \right\}$$

where $c_{i,j}$ are ciphertexts of the employed homomorphic encryption algorithm encrypting either 0 or 1 for $i = 1, 2, \ldots, m$ and $j = 1, 2, \ldots, t$ such that for any i

$$\sum_{j=1}^{t} D(c_{i,j}) = 1 \text{ or } 0.$$

The deleting function is denoted as $F()$ and is more concretely defined as follows

$$F(M) = \left\{ \begin{array}{l} \left\{ \begin{array}{cccc} RE(c_{1,1}) & RE(c_{1,2}) & \cdots & RE(c_{1,t}) \\ RE(c_{2,1}) & RE(c_{2,2}) & \cdots & RE(c_{2,t}) \\ \multicolumn{4}{c}{\cdots \quad \cdots} \\ RE(c_{m,1}) & RE(c_{m,2}) & \cdots & RE(c_{m,t}) \end{array} \right\} \; if \; \sum_{j=1}^{t} D(c_{1,j}) = 1 \\[3em] \left\{ \begin{array}{cccc} RE(c_{2,1}) & RE(c_{2,2}) & \cdots & RE(c_{2,t}) \\ RE(c_{3,1}) & RE(c_{3,2}) & \cdots & RE(c_{3,t}) \\ \multicolumn{4}{c}{\cdots \quad \cdots} \\ RE(c_{m,1}) & RE(c_{m,2}) & \cdots & RE(c_{m,t}) \\ RE(c_{1,1}) & RE(c_{1,2}) & \cdots & RE(c_{1,t}) \end{array} \right\} \; if \; \sum_{j=1}^{t} D(c_{1,j}) = 0 \end{array} \right.$$

Note that as the deleting function cannot reveal any information about the votes, it employs re-encryption to randomize the ciphertexts in the vote matrix. The deleting function is actually a multiple-party computation of an encrypted vote. So we can claim that there must exist some general-purpose multiple-party computation techniques (e.g. garbled evaluation circuit [5,7]) to implement it and then we do not need to provide a detailed implementation. However, this kind of claim is somehow a little irresponsible. Firstly, the existing general-purpose multiple-party computation techniques usually only output a very short result (e.g. one bit), while the deleting function must outputs a lot of ciphertexts. Secondly, a general-purpose multiple-party computation technique is often not the most efficient solution for a special function. So a concrete implementation of multiple-party computation of the deleting function by the talliers is provided. For simplicity of description, it is supposed that there are two talliers, T_1 and T_2. However, our implementation can be easily extended to employ more talliers. The concrete implementation is as follows.

1. T_1 and T_2 calculate $c_1 = \prod_{j=1}^{t} c_{1,j}$. They then calculate $c_1' = E(1,0)/c_1$. It can be publicly verified that $c_1 c_1' = E(1,0)$.
2. T_1 randomly chooses two messages m_1 and m_1' and then calculates and publishes $c = E(m_1)$ and $c' = E(m_1')$.
3. T_1 does his partial decryption of c_1/c and c_1'/c' and publishes $c_2 = D_1(c_1/c)$ and $c_2' = D_1(c_1'/c')$. T_1 publicly proves validity of his partial decryption using zero knowledge proof of equality of discrete logarithms.
4. T_2 does his partial decryption of c_2 and c_2' obtains $m_2 = D_2(c_2)$ and $m_2' = D_2(c_2')$.

Suppose $c'_{i,j}$ is the integer on the ith row and j^{th} column in M_1. Suppose Paillier encryption [19] is employed, where the multiplicative modulus is N^2 and encryption of a message θ is $g^\theta \gamma^N \bmod N^2$ where γ is a random integer in Z_N^*. So we can suppose that

$$c = g^{m_1} s^N \bmod N^2$$
$$c'_{i,j} = c_{i,j}^{m_1} r^N \bmod N^2$$

where s and r are random integers in Z_N^*. For each $c_{i,j}$ in M and $c'_{i,j}$ in M_1, T_2 has to prove that he knows secret integers m_1, s and r such that $c = g^{m_1} s^N \bmod N^2$ and $c'_{i,j} = c_{i,j}^{m_1} r^N \bmod N^2$ as follows.

1. A chooses random integers σ and τ (e.g. bit strings with enough length). He calculates and publishes

$$\phi = g^\sigma z^N \bmod N^2$$
$$\varphi = c_{i,j}^\sigma \tau^N \bmod N^2$$

2. A long enough random challenge κ is generated by a challenger or hash function.

3. A calculates and publishes

$$w = \sigma + \kappa m_1$$
$$u = z s^\kappa \bmod N^2$$
$$v = \tau r^\kappa \bmod N^2$$

Public verification:

$$g^w u^N = \phi c^\kappa \bmod N^2$$
$$c_{i,j}^w v^N = \varphi c'^{\kappa}_{i,j} \bmod N^2$$

The verification is passed iff all the two equations are correct.

Fig. 1. ZK Proof of the same exponent and re-encryption

5. T_1 calculates and publishes $M_1 = RE(M^{\times m_1})$ and proves validity of this operation using the ZK proof protocol in Figure 1.

6. T_1 calculates and publishes $M'_1 = RE(M'^{\times m'_1})$ and proves validity of this operation using the same ZK proof technique as described in Figure 1. where

$$M' = \left\{ \begin{array}{cccc} c_{2,1} & c_{2,2} & \cdots & c_{2,t} \\ c_{3,1} & c_{3,2} & \cdots & c_{3,t} \\ & \cdots & \cdots & \\ c_{m,1} & c_{m,2} & \cdots & c_{m,t} \\ c_{1,1} & c_{1,2} & \cdots & c_{1,t} \end{array} \right\}$$

7. T_2 calculates and publishes $M_2 = RE(M^{\times m_2})$ and proves validity of this operation using the same ZK proof technique as described in Figure 1.

8. T_2 calculates and publishes $M_2' = M'^{\times m_2'}$ and proves validity of this operation using the same ZK proof technique as described in Figure 1.
9. The output result is $M_1 \otimes M_2 \otimes M_1' \otimes M_2'$.

5   Analysis

Correctness of the new e-voting scheme relies on appropriate exploitation of homomorphism of the employed encryption algorithm. In the the new e-voting scheme homomorphism of the employed encryption algorithm is employed in three operations: counting, comparison of ciphertexts through range test and the deleting function to adjust the votes. Counting the votes (more precisely the first choices in the votes) is a straightforward application of homomorphism of the employed encryption algorithm: the message encrypted in the product of the n ciphertexts representing the voter's attitude towards a candidate is the sum of the n integers representing their attitude towards the candidate, namely the number of the first choices obtained by the candidate. This principle has been widely applied in many existing homomorphic e-voting schemes and its correctness has been repeatedly demonstrated, so is not repeated again here. The principle to exploit homomorphism of encryption algorithm in range test and its correctness has been explained in [25,26,23] in great details, so is not repeated here. Our analysis focuses on correctness of the deleting function, which is novel and more complex. It is proved in Theorem 1.

Theorem 1. *The deleting function described in Section 4.3 correctly adjusts a vote.*

Proof:

$$F(M) = M_1 \otimes M_2 \otimes M_1' \otimes M_2' = RE(M^{\times m_1} M^{\times m_2} M'^{\times m_1'} M'^{\times m_2'})$$
$$= RE(M^{\times(m_1+m_2)} M'^{\times(m_1'+m_2')}) = RE(M^{\times(D(c)+D_2(c_2))} M'^{\times(D(c')+D_2(c_2'))})$$
$$= RE(M^{\times(D(c)+D_2(D_1(c_1/c)))} M'^{\times(D(c')+D_2(D_1(c_1'/c')))})$$
$$= RE(M^{\times(D(c)+D(c_1/c))} M'^{\times(D(c')+D(c_1'/c'))})$$
$$= RE(M^{\times D(c_1)} M'^{\times D(c_1')}) = RE(M^{\times D(\prod_{j=1}^{t} c_{1,j})} M'^{\times D(E(1,0)/c_1)})$$
$$= RE(M^{\times \sum_{j=1}^{t} D(c_{1,j})} M'^{\times(1-D(c_1))}) = RE(M^{\times \sum_{j=1}^{t} D(c_{1,j})} M'^{\times(1-\sum_{j=1}^{t} D(c_{1,j}))})$$

So,

– when the first row of a vote matrix M is not an all-zero row,

$$\sum_{j=1}^{t} D(c_{1,j}) = 1$$

and then

$$F(M) = RE(M^{\times 1} M'^{\times 0}) = RE(M)$$

– when the first row of a vote matrix M is an all-zero row,

$$\sum_{j=1}^{t} D(c_{1,j}) = 0$$

and then

$$F(M) = RE(M^{\times 0} M'^{\times 1}) = RE(M')$$

where $M' = \begin{Bmatrix} c_{2,1} & c_{2,2} & \cdots & c_{2,t} \\ c_{3,1} & c_{3,2} & \cdots & c_{3,t} \\ & \cdots & \cdots \\ c_{m,1} & c_{m,2} & \cdots & c_{m,t} \\ c_{1,1} & c_{1,2} & \cdots & c_{1,t} \end{Bmatrix}$

□

As the employed encryption algorithm is semantically secure, the employed proof primitives are zero knowledge and no information unnecessary for determining the election result is revealed, the new e-voting scheme achieves privacy. As all the votes are proved and verified to be valid, robustness is achieved in the new e-voting scheme. All the operations can be publicly verified, so public verification is achieved in the new e-voting scheme. Note that no vote is revealed. Moreover, the number of any specific vote is not revealed. So the coercion attack in Section 2 cannot work. As either of the two existing countermeasures against other coercion attacks can be employed, the new e-voting scheme can be invulnerable against other coercion attacks.

6   Conclusion

The secure e-voting scheme proposed in this paper is invulnerable against a newly discovered coercion attack. It achieves all the usually desired security properties. In the future work, efficiency of the e-voting scheme may be improved. There are two costly operations, vote validity check and the deleting function. We notice that some choices are actually not counted. For example, in Table 1, the choices represented by × are not counted at all. So verification of vote validity may be simplified in some way such that the unnecessary verification can be avoided. Even if the whole matrix for each vote has to be proved and verified to be valid, there may be a more efficient proof and verification mechanism. We notice that each vote is actually a permutation matrix[2] and a secret matrix can be proved to be a permutation matrix in [9,11]. If the proof techniques in [9,11] can be adopted in vote validity check in the new e-voting scheme, efficiency can be improved. As for the deleting function, its strategy may be optimised and the zero knowledge proof operations in it may be batched to improve efficiency.

---

[2] In a permutation matrix, there is just one 1 in each row and just one 1 in each column, while all the other elements are 0.

References

1. Baudron, O., Fouque, P.-A., Pointcheval, D., Stern, J., Poupard, G.: Practical multi-candidate election system. In: Twentieth Annual ACM Symposium on Principles of Distributed Computing, pp. 274–283 (2001)
2. Benaloh, J., Tuinstra, D.: Receipt-free secret-ballot elections. Technical report
3. Boudot, F.: Efficient proofs that a committed number lies in an interval. In: Preneel, B. (ed.) EUROCRYPT 2000. LNCS, vol. 1807, pp. 431–444. Springer, Heidelberg (2000)
4. Canetti, R., Dwork, C., Naor, M., Ostrovsky, R.: Deniable encryption. In: Kaliski Jr., B.S. (ed.) CRYPTO 1997. LNCS, vol. 1294, pp. 90–104. Springer, Heidelberg (1997)
5. Cramer, R., Damgård, I., Nielsen, J.B.: Multiparty computation from threshold homomorphic encryption. In: Pfitzmann, B. (ed.) EUROCRYPT 2001. LNCS, vol. 2045, pp. 280–299. Springer, Heidelberg (2001)
6. Damgård, I., Jurik, M.: A generalisation, a simplification and some applications of paillier's probabilistic public-key system. In: Public Key Cryptography—PKC 2001, pp. 119–136 (2001)
7. Damgård, I., Nielsen, J.: Universally composable efficient multiparty computation from threshold homomorphic encryption. In: Boneh, D. (ed.) CRYPTO 2003. LNCS, vol. 2729, pp. 247–264. Springer, Heidelberg (2003)
8. Fouque, P.-A., Poupard, G., Stern, J.: Sharing decryption in the context of voting or lotteries. In: Frankel, Y. (ed.) FC 2000. LNCS, vol. 1962, pp. 90–104. Springer, Heidelberg (2001)
9. Furukawa, J., Sako, K.: An efficient scheme for proving a shuffle. In: Kilian, J. (ed.) CRYPTO 2001. LNCS, vol. 2139, pp. 368–387. Springer, Heidelberg (2001)
10. Heathler, J.: Implementing stv securely in pret a voter. In: 20th IEEE Computer Security Foundations Symposium, pp. 157–169 (2007)
11. Furukawa, J.: Efficient and verifiable shuffling and shuffle-decryption. IEICE Transactions 88-A(1), 172–188 (2005)
12. Katz, J., Myers, S., Ostrovsky, R.: Cryptographic counters and applications to electronic voting. In: Pfitzmann, B. (ed.) EUROCRYPT 2001. LNCS, vol. 2045, pp. 78–92. Springer, Heidelberg (2001)
13. Kiayias, A., Yung, M.: Self-tallying elections and perfect ballot secrecy. In: Naccache, D., Paillier, P. (eds.) PKC 2002. LNCS, vol. 2274, pp. 141–158. Springer, Heidelberg (2002)
14. Lee, B., Kim, K.: Receipt-free electronic voting through collaboration of voter and honest verifier. In: JW-ISC 2000, pp. 101–108 (2000)
15. Lee, B., Kim, K.: Receipt-free electronic voting scheme with a tamper-resistant randomizer. In: Lee, P.J., Lim, C.H. (eds.) ICISC 2002. LNCS, vol. 2587, pp. 389–406. Springer, Heidelberg (2003)
16. Lipmaa, H.: On diophantine complexity and statistical zero-knowledge arguments. In: Laih, C.-S. (ed.) ASIACRYPT 2003. LNCS, vol. 2894, pp. 398–415. Springer, Heidelberg (2003)
17. Chong, S., Clarkson, M., Myers, A.: Toward a secure voting system. IEEE Symposium on Security and Privacy (2008)
18. Andrew Neff, C.: A verifiable secret shuffle and its application to e-voting. In: ACM Conference on Computer and Communications Security 2001, pp. 116–125 (2001)
19. Paillier, P.: Public key cryptosystem based on composite degree residuosity classes. In: Stern, J. (ed.) EUROCRYPT 1999. LNCS, vol. 1592, pp. 223–238. Springer, Heidelberg (1999)

20. Peng, K.: A hybrid e-voting scheme. In: Bao, F., Li, H., Wang, G. (eds.) ISPEC 2009. LNCS, vol. 5451, pp. 195–206. Springer, Heidelberg (2009)
21. Peng, K., Bao, F.: Correction, optimisation and secure and efficient application of pbd shuffling. In: Yung, M., Liu, P., Lin, D. (eds.) INSCRYPT 2008. LNCS, vol. 5487, pp. 425–437. Springer, Heidelberg (2008)
22. Peng, K., Bao, F.: Efficient vote validity check in homomorphic electronic voting. In: Lee, P.J., Cheon, J.H. (eds.) ICISC 2008. LNCS, vol. 5461, pp. 202–217. Springer, Heidelberg (2008)
23. Peng, K., Bao, F., Dawson, E.: Correct, private, flexible and efficient range test. Journal of Researchand Practice in Information Technology 40(4), 275–291 (2008)
24. Peng, K., Boyd, C.: Batch zero knowledge proof and verification and its applications. ACM TISSEC 10(2), Article No. 6 (May 2007)
25. Peng, K., Boyd, C., Dawson, E., Okamoto, E.: A novel range test. In: Batten, L.M., Safavi-Naini, R. (eds.) ACISP 2006. LNCS, vol. 4058, pp. 247–258. Springer, Heidelberg (2006)
26. Peng, K., Dawson, E.: Range test secure in the active adversary model. In: AISW 2007. ACM International Conference Proceeding Series, vol. 249, pp. 159–162 (2007)
27. Teague, V., Ramchen, K., Naish, L.: Coercion-resistant tallying for stv voting. In: EVT 2008, pp. 1–14 (2008)

RIES - Rijnland Internet Election System: A Cursory Study of Published Source Code

Rop Gonggrijp, Willem-Jan Hengeveld, Eelco Hotting,
Sebastian Schmidt, and Frederik Weidemann

Wij vertrouwen stemcomputers niet
Linnaeusparkweg 98, 1098 EJ Amsterdam, The Netherlands
rop@gonggri.jp
http://www.wijvertrouwenstemcomputersniet.nl

Abstract. The Rijnland Internet Election System (RIES) is a system designed for voting in public elections over the internet. A rather cursory scan of the source code to RIES showed a significant lack of security-awareness among the programmers which – among other things – appears to have left RIES vulnerable to near-trivial attacks. If it had not been for independent studies finding problems, RIES would have been used in the 2008 Water Board elections, possibly handling a million votes or more. While RIES was more extensively studied to find cryptographic shortcomings, our work shows that more down–to–earth secure design practices can be at least as important, and the aspects need to be examined much sooner than right before an election.

Keywords: electronic voting, internet voting, RIES, The Netherlands.

1 Introduction

The Rijnland Internet Election System (RIES) processed around 90.000 votes in public elections in The Netherlands in 2004 and 2006. Based on total votes processed in public elections, RIES is one of the largest internet voting systems worldwide. As an interesting feature, RIES offers cryptographic end-to-end verifiability. This enables the voter to use cryptography to verify that her or his vote was counted as cast. After some delay, the source code to RIES was published[1] on June 24th 2008. This paper describes the result of a few days of looking at the source code and documentation of a rather complex internet voting system. This study began when the source code for RIES was published, on June 24th 2008. The first preliminary results of this study were available to the Dutch media and members of parliament four days later on June 28th. This paper can by no means be understood as an exhaustive study. Such a study would require much more time, study and effort.

---

[1] http://www.openries.nl/downloads/broncode

P.Y.A. Ryan and B. Schoenmakers (Eds.): VOTE-ID 2009, LNCS 5767, pp. 157–171, 2009.

2   Permission

Verifying some of the problems we found in the source code on the actual system without permission from the people operating RIES would probably be prosecutable as computer crime. So in the early evening of Friday, June 27th we asked nicely and kindly got permission to attempt penetrating the RIES portal server at `https://portal.ries.surfnet.nl` from Simon Bouwman at "Het Waterschapshuis", a national cooperation of Water Boards that planned to operate the servers for the Water Board elections. He also kindly added one of our IP-numbers to the list of sites allowed to approach this server, a protection measure they were apparently just installing that very evening.

As a condition for getting permission, we accepted to print a brief reaction of "Het Waterschapshuis" along with our findings.

3   Sequence of Events

3.1   Water Boards

The Water Boards ("Waterschappen" in Dutch, sometimes also translated as "District Water Control Boards") are 27 different regional authorities dealing with water management in The Netherlands, a country that has long been highly dependent on a complex infrastructure of pumps and dykes to stay dry. Dating back to the 13th century, they are the oldest democratic structures in The Netherlands and among the oldest in the world. Since they are separate bodies of government the boards of these authorities are each directly elected by the people that live and/or own property in their area. In recent times these elections have been held by postal ballot, and in recent years turnout has been very low, often far below 30%.

RIES was developed by one of these Water Boards (Hoogheemraadschap van Rijnland) in conjunction with a number of private companies. It was used experimentally in the 2004 election by two of the Water Boards, and roughly 70 thousand voters cast their vote via the internet in that election.

3.2   2006 Parliamentary Election

RIES, in a version called RIES-KOA[2] was also used for the 2006 national parliamentary election as a complement to the postal voting available to Dutch citizens residing outside of the Netherlands. (The Netherlands do not offer postal voting to voters not residing abroad.) Roughly 20.000 votes were cast using RIES in that election. Because the Netherlands have proportional representation, these votes were added to the national totals for each candidate.

---

[2] KOA stands for "Kiezen Op Afstand" (Remote Voting), which is (was?) the Dutch government's remote e-voting project.

3.3   RIES-2008

A lot has happened with regard to electronic voting in The Netherlands in the past few years. The country was 100% e-Voting in 2006, and has since abondoned all electronic voting in polling stations. Our previous research [1] into the security of the Nedap system in use in 90% of the precincts played an important part in the decision making process. The use of RIES for these low-turnout Water Board elections would have made RIES the last remaining electronic voting system in use in The Netherlands.

The Water Boards would have liked to deploy RIES in its present incarnation, called RIES-2008, for the Water Board elections, which all took place simultaneously in November 2008. The ministry of Transport and Water Works had drafted legislation which, among many other things, also codified various procedures specific to the RIES system. Our foundation has lobbied with parliament to force rapid publication of the source code as well as for clear technical requirements and a procedure to formally test whether a proposed voting system meets these requirements. As a consequence the ministry created one and a half page of requirements [2] which for the greater part simply point to e-Voting recommendations issued by the Council of Europe [3].

The day after our preliminary findings were made available to the media and members of parliament, the ministry announced[3] that it would likely not approve RIES. As it turned out, the company hired to do the formal approval (Fox-IT) had also found very serious problems with RIES. They had concentrated on the underlying cryptography [4].

3.4   Post-2008

After the ministry's announcement, the Water Boards have expressed the intention to continue work on RIES for the 2012 elections. The Water Board elections of 2008 then ended in a fiasco. There were major problems with the postal ballot, mostly centered on the year of birth that people had to fill out coupled with the fact that the ballot forms were mixed inside households. Together with various other problems with scanning the ballots, this led to elections that saw more than 10% unintentionally spoiled ballots. Also, despite a massive advertising campaign and changes in the way the election was held, turnout remained very low, around 20%. After the election, the Water Boards have stated they would prefer not to hold direct elections again[4], making the future of this type of elections very unclear.

It is interesting to note that during the 2008 elections, RIES was also used for processing the paper ballots. Each ballot had a unique machine-readable code printed on it, and on one side of the process, files existed which coupled specific

---

[3] Announcement to parliament: http://wijvertrouwenstemcomputersniet.nl/images/9/98/Brief-VenW-geen-internetstemmen.pdf

[4] Source: Volkskrant interview available at http://www.volkskrant.nl/binnenland/article1100640.ece/Foutenmarge_bij_waterschapsverkiezingen_hoog

voters to this unique ID. On the other side of the process, there were files which coupled these IDs to votes. So though some of the vulnerabilities related to internet-voting were no longer in play, the vote secrecy related problems largely remained.

4 Known Security of RIES

4.1 Literature

The www.openries.nl website listed a large number of documents on RIES. On the page "What do others think?" we read (translated from Dutch):

Various prominent institutions have tested and positively evaluated RIES: TNO Human Factors from Soesterberg tested usability of the voting interface; A team of specialists from Peter Landrocks Cryptomathic (in Aarhus, Denmark) tested the cryptographic principles; Madison Gurka from Eindhoven tested the server and network setup and security; A team under supervision of Bart Jacobs (Radboud University Nijmegen) did external penetration tests.

Scientists [5, 6, 7, 8, 9, 10] as well as other parties [11, 12] have looked into various aspects of the design and/or security of (parts of) RIES.

Apart from purely scientific work, RIES has been subject to an accessibility test, a browser compatibility test, a modules test, a disaster recovery test, a functional acceptance test, a chain test, a regression test, a risk analysis, a security and usage evaluation, a server audit, evaluations of the various elections held with it and a report [13] to see how RIES matches up to the 112 recommendations of the Council of Europe with regard to e-Voting [3] and many, many more studies and reports.

4.2 Theoretical Upper Bounds

RIES, as well as many other internet voting systems, can only be as secure as the weakest parts of the system. With RIES, this means that if an adversary can steal data from specific parts of the process, vote secrecy is compromised. Also, election integrity and vote secrecy with RIES depend on cryptographic functions not being manipulated or observed while running on individual voter PCs. Since these circumstances place clear upper bounds on the amount of real-world security that can be obtained, it is good to mention the largest fundamental threats in a little more detail.

4.3 Limited Security against Insiders

Elections like the ones performed with RIES legally require secrecy of the vote. In RIES this requires the operators to destroy information they held at some stage during the process. If anyone manages to hold on to this information the publication of a verification file at the end of the election allows whoever has this information to tie every vote to an individual voter. Hubbers et al [7] conclude that the cryptography used in RIES offers no protection against insiders:

"RIES is built on certain cryptographic primitives, like one-time signatures. Keys for individual voters are generated centrally. There are no anonymous channels. The structural protection and safeguards offered by cryptography are therefore rather limited. Many of the guarantees in RIES thus rely on organizational controls, notably with respect to (voter) key generation, production of postal packages, insider attacks (especially at the server), integrity and authenticity of the software, and helpdesk procedures."

The CIBIT rapport [8] concludes (translated from Dutch): *"Vulnerability of the STUF-C10 file, all temporary variants hereof and KGenVoterKey. Using the STUF-C10 file one can influence the election and break vote secrecy. These objects need to be destroyed as soon as the necessity for the presence of these objects expires."*

Compared to a postal election performed in accordance with proper procedures, one must conclude that RIES created ways to surreptitiously violate vote secrecy on a scale never before possible. All that is needed for a massive breach of vote secrecy is a few people, or even a single individual, leaking critical files.

4.4 Household PCs Assumed Secure

Hubbers et al [7] also describe a central assumption during the design of RIES:

"RIES assumes that the voters PCs are secure. Attackers may however employ malware or even man–in–the–browser attacks to capture voters PCs. Powerful attackers may thus change votes, and so this involves a unique potential risk for Internet elections."

Given the prevalence of attacks against client PCs , for example with regard to electronic banking, it would seem inevitable for attacks to appear once electronic voting becomes common. The fact that candidates have apparently tried to submit faked signatures to be on the Water Boards candidate list in the past[5] proves that even for these election, there is already an apparent potential for fraud.

5   Security of RIES: A Look at the Code

We realise that previous researchers studying RIES had only design documents and not the source code to go by. So even though the source code had not been independently studied, the sheer amount of serious studies done on the security of RIES made us doubt if we would spot any problems, given the limited resources we had to study it. We were not able to perform a structured source code analysis, everything is this paper is based on a rather cursory look at the code. But even with our limited resources, we were able to spot quite a number of rather serious security concerns. We noticed a lack of input validation, creating verified opportunities for XSS and SQL injection, predictable random generation

---

[5] Hoogheemraadschap van Rijnland, Bestuursverkiezing Rijnland moet door fraude deels over, Persbericht 12 november 2004, http://www.rijnlandkiest.net/asp/get.asp?xdl=../views/rijnlandkiest/xdl/Page&ItmIdt=00001440

(for election management access tokens), hard coded values (for cryptographic keys, a CVS server, a mail server and an SMS gateway) as well as problems regarding exception handling.

5.1 Lack of Input Validation

XSS - Cross-Site Scripting. There are locations in the code where information supplied by the user is passed back on the page that is output by the system. For example we can see[6]:

```
document.location="start.jsp?elid= \
  <%= request.getParameter("elid") %>";
```

as well as[7]:

```
<c:set var="section" \
  value="<%= request.getParameter("section")%>"/>
```

By supplying this parameter in a specially crafted URL, the user's browser could be made to execute Javascript statements within the context of the user's session on the election site. In the case of RIES, the cryptographic routines that perform the actual act of voting are implemented as client-side Javascript, making it impossible for users to protect themselves against such attacks by turning off Javascript.

We found out that we were not the only ones who had spotted this problem. As mentioned above, the RIES website lists an impressive number of studies into various aspects of the system. Among them is a report by GOVCERT.NL, the Dutch government computer emergency response team. They found this problem and reported it in September of 2006 when they did a 'web application scan' [14]. They found the same **elid** variable to be vulnerable, and recommended that the input and parameters be validated to eliminate the risk of Cross-Site Scripting. They also ominously said (translated from Dutch):

REMARK: The lack of sufficient input validation can also lead to vulnerabilities such as SQL-injection which are more serious in nature. During the scan we have not found any such vulnerability.

We are surprised that the makers of RIES present a two year old report of a scan on their website, apparently without having implemented the recommendations contained therein.

SQL Injection. In 2006, GOVCERT.NL had warned RIES: if the programmer doesn't check the inputs to his/her code, the program may end up vulnerable to SQL injection attacks. During the interaction with the program, a user typically enters all sorts of text strings, such as her username when prompted. (See Fig. 1.)

---

[6] `riesvotewin_source_v1.0/admin/index.jsp`, line 29
[7] `riesvotewin_source_v1.0/admin/sectionlinks.jsp`, line 3

Login

Welkom

Voer uw gebruikersnaam in om in te loggen

Gebruikersnaam:

Verstuur

Fig. 1. Login screen

SQL queries involving user-supplied information in the RIES source code are all generated by simply inserting whatever the user entered into a query, without any checking. One of the queries that follows is the one where the code associated with the login box above tries to find the telephone number for a user to send a special SMS token to allow that user to log in[8]:

```
sbBuffer=new StringBuffer();
sbBuffer.append("select PHONE from OPERATOR where
   OPERATOR_ID='"+sUsername+"'");
oRs=oStmt.executeQuery(sbBuffer.toString());
```

As is visible from this code, the SQL statement to be processed by the database server is formed with the sUsername string. The code does not contain anything to sanitize that string first. If one enters `rop` in the username box the query to the SQL server would become:

```
select PHONE from OPERATOR where OPERATOR_ID='rop'
```

Since the program finds no corresponding entry in the `OPERATOR_ID` table it outputs "login failed" as shown in Fig. 2.

Inloggen mislukt

Login Fout

Het inloggen is mislukt.

- Heeft u de juiste gebruikersnaam ingevoerd?
- Is uw (mobiele) telefoonnummer al geregistreerd?

Probeer het nogmaals

Fig. 2. Login failed

However, we can make the SQL statement succeed by logging in with a string as shown in Fig. 3.

---

[8] `riesportal_source_v1.0.zip/WEB-INF/src/java/org/openries/portal/jaas/` `JAASHelperServlet.java`, line 347

Fig. 3. SQL injection

The resulting SQL statement now looks like:

```
select PHONE from OPERATOR where OPERATOR_ID='rop' OR 1=1; --'
```

And as a result we now get the output as shown in Fig. 4. The system has apparently sent the special not–so–random access code via SMS. Since the SQL statement succeeded on the first user in the user table, we suspect this user will have received such an SMS.

Fig. 4. Please enter SMS code

To actually enter the system and prove further vulnerabilities, one needs to play around a little more. We were still experimenting with this when the system suddenly said: *"Service Unavailable"*. A few minutes later it said *"Technical Problem"*, and then it finally said *"Closed For The Weekend"*. We guess that since we were testing on a Friday night, indeed the system could be down for the weekend. It did however briefly re-open on the following Saturday, but after a few more carefully crafted attempts it was again *"Closed For The Weekend"*.

5.2 Errors/Problems in Code

Predictable Random Tokens. The code contains a method of authenticating a user via her/his mobile phone. The code calls this challenge/response, however it is technically a response only. When a user wants to log in, the system generates a random password which is sent to the user via SMS. The user must than enter this password via the internet. Below is the piece of code[9] that does the actual generation of that 'random' token:

---

[9] `riesportal_source_v1.0.zip/WEB-INF/src/java/org/openries/portal/jaas/`
`JAASHelperServlet.java`, line 280

```
Random rGen=new Random(new Date().getTime());
String sResult="";
int i=0;
while(i<6) {
    sResult+=rGen.nextInt(10);
    i++;
}
```

Random() will present the same output when given the same output of Date() and getTime(). Even though the latter is in milliseconds, an attacker would only need a few thousand guesses to figure out the key sent to a phone that she does not own. Since the code does not prevent someone from trying a few thousand tokens, this would not prevent the attacker from gaining access.

Note that an attacker can probably acquire a very accurate idea of system time from the http headers provided by the system or, if the goal is privilege escalation, from the token received by SMS following a valid login.

Insufficient Exception Handling. Often when exceptions are handled in the code, a message is logged, but no action is taken. For example, in _sendResponseSMS[10], the exception handlers are (in pseudo-code) very often structured like the one in sendResponseSMS:

```
_sendResponseSMS()
{
  try {
    executeQuery
    if result {
      try { sendsms }
      catch(all) { return false }
    }
    else { return false }
  }
  catch (sqlexception) { logmessage }

  return true
}
```

Since the code contains no return false with the catch(sqlexception), an exception from the executeQuery will still cause the calling function sendResponseSMS to succeed and cause the server to display the 'enter-SMS-response' page. One of the possible reasons why executeQuery would throw an sqlexception would be a syntax error in the SQL statement, for instance, caused by an SQL-injection attempt. But given that SQL syntax errors are ignored, an attacker can carry his manipulations beyond the point where the program should

---

[10] riesportal_source_v1.0.zip/WEB-INF/src/java/org/openries/portal/jaas/
JAASHelperServlet.java, line 332

abort. This makes constructing more complex SQL-injections significantly easier. An attacker can now target specific SQL statements, without the need to keep all the other statements free of errors.

The problem is that RIES tries to trap exceptions from the library functions, and translate them in true/false but often fails to do a `return false`. In the case of the SQL exceptions, it might be even better not to trap these exceptions at all, but let the JSP server handle this. In most cases an exception should be a reason to abort any pending operations, not to 'log message and continue'.

5.3   Code Mixed with Configuration Information

Test Key. Then there's a part in `org.openries.ripocs.config.ConfigManager` where the code is apparently retrieving a stored 'salt' value from a file to create, through XOR, a smartcard key of some sort. The final lines of the code[11] that is supposed to be generating the value are:

```
// derive AbelPiKey (16 bytes)
return PKCS5.PBKDF1(sPassPhrase, abSalt, PKCS5_ITERATIONS, 16);
```

However, the entire function is commented out and instead it now reads:

```
//temp for ketentest 1 because of existing keys in smartcards
return Utils.stringToHex
  ("0123456789ABCDEF FFFFFFFFFFFFFFFF0123456789ABCDEF");
```

By interweaving (highly dangerous) testing code and production code in this way, the designers are waiting for accidents to happen. If this should be done at all, it needs to be done with `#IFDEFs` or other more suitable mechanisms.

CVS Server. The code exposes a development CVS server that appears to be running on a regular home ADSL connection[12]:

```
:pserver:arnout@cozmanova.xs4all.nl:4202/usr/local/cvs-ries-rep
```

Mail Server. Also, a hardcoded public mail server is used[13]:

```
private static String EMAIL_SERVER = "smtp.xs4all.nl";
```

It is not clear under what circumstances the system sends mail and whether one could perform attacks if one could destroy, intercept, modify or interject batches of these e-mails. The concept of 'phishing' for voting credentials comes to mind.

---

[11] `riesripocs_source_v1.0.zip/src/org/openries/ripocs/config/` `ConfigManager.java`, line 23

[12] `rieslogin_source_v1.0.zip/org/CVS/Root`

[13] `riessystem_source_v1.0.zip/source/org/openries/system/messaging/` `EmailMessage.java`, line 52

SMS gateway. The code also contains an SMS gateway with a valid account[14]:

```
private String _sServiceURL="https://secure.mollie.nl/xml/sms/";
private String _sUsername="mdobrinic";
private String _sPassword="riesdemo";
private String _sGateway="2";
  // development default; 1=more reliable; 2=cheaper
```

Assuming the authors want their voting system to be 'more reliable' as opposed to 'cheaper', the setting of the sGateway value shows how easy it is for undesirable development artifacts to make it into production code, especially if the programmer doesn't separate code from configuration.

5.4   Current Status Regarding Fixing These Problems

The URL supplied to download RIES still points to an overview page, but the links to the actual source code zip files give Microsoft IIS "The page cannot be found" error messages. There appears to be no way to verify progress, if any, on fixing these problems.

6   Conclusions

These are all issues stemming from general poor code quality and a lack of secure design principles. The cross-site scripting problem, the SQL injection problem and the token generation problem are especially serious problems that could, each in and by itself, lead to compromises of the entire system. When the RIES portal is compromised, all election management functions can be performed by the attackers and all data passed through the portal can be destroyed or manipulated, clearly placing election integrity at risk.

Computer security appears not to be part of the mindset of the people programming RIES. For example, in the case of the SQL-problems, it would have been better to use prepareStatement in addition to sanitizing user input. Normal best-practice secure design principles prevent most if not all of these problems from occurring. All problems can be repaired relatively quickly. However, given the general questions this quick study raises about overall code quality in the RIES project, such fixes would by no means yield a secure system. We plucked the low-hanging fruit in the part of the system which was facing the internet, many other parts of the code have not yet been studied.

We were amazed to find a system so apparently well-studied yet so fundamentally and undeniably insecurely programmed. This is not so much criticism of the people studying before us; it mostly shows how little one can say about security of a system without access to source code. Scientific studies of RIES seem to have concentrated on the more scientifically 'sexy' theoretical security offered

---

[14] `riessystem_source_v1.0.zip/source/org/openries/system/messaging/` `SMSConfig.java`, line 22

by the inventive cryptographic protocols. Only source code review can efficiently examine some of the threats posed by very straightforward and down–to–earth attack methods that are much more likely to be used in the real world.

The scope of this paper is not to completely understand the RIES system but only to outline a number of immediately-visible security problems. As a reality check, we are happy to have proven that SQL injection actually works on the live system. Further examination of RIES, including actually attempting to disturb/manipulate elections would likely require further study of the inner workings of RIES and is beyond the scope of this first examination.

Given what we found in the scope of this quick study, it is very worrisome that a previous version of RIES has actually been used in the context of a real-world parliamentary election. If society decides to go ahead with internet voting (thus implicitly deciding that the advantages of remote e-voting outweigh more fundamental problems with vote secrecy and lack of transparency/observability) it is clear that more attention should be given to secure programming. Internet voting suppliers seem reluctant to allow independent study of their source code. The Water Boards had to be forced by the Dutch Parliament to open the source code, and code review has also been controversial[15] in the recent Austrian national student body elections where an internet voting system made by voting technology supplier Scytl was used. Our findings clearly show that society cannot afford to merely study the outside-world interfaces of an internet voting system, even if there are "nice" cryptographic tricks involved.

To create a system that appears secure, there are two approaches. The proper approach is to design a system with security in mind. The other approach is to retrofit an insecure system with security-measures that make a system look secure but which in fact add little security. Such measures are usually intended to impress onlookers. There are situations where adding an SMS-token is a useful addition to other security measures. However in combination with the proven lack of security awareness during the implementation of the system, RIES' SMS-token appears to fall in the impress-the-onlookers category.

The www.openries.nl site says: *"Various prominent institutions have tested and positively evaluated RIES"*. This research shows that one must be very wary if scientific and other studies into some part of a not yet published and changing system are used to implicitly claim the entire system is secure. No amount of voluntary studies of some part of a voting system - often paid for by stakeholders wanting to see the system in use - can ever replace clear and stringent government-imposed requirements that include independent source code review. Such reviews need to pragmatically and 'holistically' look for security problems as well as test the code against more formal coding standards and practices.

In their 2004 article 'Stemmen via Internet geen probleem' [6] Hubbers and Jacobs "vote in favour" of use of this system when they state (translated from Dutch): *"Summarizing, [RIES] is a relatively simple, original and understandable system that has been implemented with the appropriate care and transparency. [...]*

---

[15] Source: description of source code review procedures at http://papierwahl.at/ 2009/05/19/details-der-sourcecode-einsicht

When the use of RIES during these Water Board elections is involved, we clearly vote in favour!". We pose that RIES has quite clearly not been implemented with "appropriate care". Given the dependence of society on their judgment, scientists should probably refrain from endorsing electronic voting systems until the entire system is open for public examination and at least until they have seen independent studies of all parts of the systems involved.

Despite obvious code quality and apparent quality management problems, the Water Boards need to be commended for the publication of the source code and documentation as well as for allowing outside researchers to study the security of the system. It seems that they are at least trying to do the right thing.

The amount of problems we found, as well as the class of problems, imply that If RIES were ever to be used again in elections, it must undergo much more testing and quite possibly partial code rewrites. Use of RIES in real-world elections without allowing independent source code review was, in retrospect, irresponsible. The attempt by the Water Boards to use RIES in the 2008 election even after our findings were known to them shows how deep government can become entrenched once the e-Voting train is in motion. Recent events in The Netherlands and Germany seem to indicate that government bodies are over-reliant on information provided to them voting technology providers. The Dutch government commission that studied past decision-making with regard to electronic voting stated in its report [15] (translated from conclusions on p. 51): *"Decennia of trusting the information provided by suppliers Nedap, Sdu and certivication agency TNO has placed the ministry at a disadvantage."*

The Dutch government had to be forced by a majority in Parliament to develop any standards at all for internet voting. The resulting half-hearted and minimalist legal requirements [2] (covering a whole page and a half) or the recommendations of the Council of Europe [3] that these requirements point to contain no provisions that would have prevented any of the problems we found.

Acknowledgements

The authors would like to thank Simon Bouwman of "Het Waterschapshuis" for giving permission to test some of our attacks against the system. Furthermore they would like to thank the entire crew of "Wij vertrouwen stemcomputers niet" and Zenon Panoussis for their insight and for helping in proofreading this paper.

7   Reaction Het Waterschapshuis

As stated in the introduction, we agreed with "Het Waterschapshuis" to include a brief reaction with our findings. They responded as follows:

"An advantage of open source is that the code can be reviewed and improvements of the code can be made. The published code of RIES is not yet the production code. Internal reviews and tests have to be made. Recommendations from

external - as in this paper - are welcome. New versions of the code will be published in the coming weeks.

As mentioned in the paper, RIES is a rather complex (internet) voting system. RIES contains several sub-systems. Each sub-system is a combination of software, configuration and administrative procedures. Each sub-system has very different tasks and settings and also different security requirements. For instance, the VoteWindow is the only sub-system which is public to the world-wide Internet. All other sub-systems are limited access only, not accessible through the internet. The RIES-Portal access will be controlled by VPN, RIES-RIPOCS is only accessible via RIES-Portal, and RIES-ROCMIS is an offline machine used within a proper set of administrative procedures. Therefore, RIES cannot be evaluated from source code alone to measure the security strength.

Keep in mind; this part is NOT production code yet. Many of the issues are related to proper input validation. And we agree that proper input validation is required and we will fulfill that requirement. Mainly Struts input validation mechanism will be used. In the published source packages and the development system investigated, the feature was not switched on for development reasons. Therefore again: were in a state of functional sequence test (ketentest) and not yet in production."

The original response was slightly longer and added a list where each issue we found was discussed separately. Since this was a little too long to be included in this paper, we agreed to include a link to the full response, which will be available on the RIES website at `http://www.openries.nl/wvsn-paper`

There is a lot to be said regarding this reaction, but that would turn this paper into a discussion forum. Suffice it to say that we stand by our original conclusions and recommendations. Despite RIES not being used in 2008, the debate on whether or not RIES is suitable for public elections may well continue at some point in the future.

References

[1] Gonggrijp, R., Hengeveld, W.-J.: Studying the Nedap/Groenendaal ES3B voting computer, a computer security perspective. In: Proceedings of the USENIX/Accurate Electronic Voting Technology workshop (2007)

[2] Ministerie van Verkeer en Waterstaat: Regeling waterschapsverkiezingen 2008. 15 mei 2008/Nr. CEND/HDJZ-2008/587, Staatscourant 23 mei 2008, nr. 97 / pag. 11 (2008),
`http://www.wijvertrouwenstemcomputersniet.nl/images/e/e7/SC85731.pdf`

[3] Council of Europe: Recommendation Rec. (2004) 11 of the Committee of Ministers to member states on legal, operational and technical standards for e-voting (2004),
`https://wcd.coe.int/ViewDoc.jsp?id=778189`

[4] Gedrojc, B., Hueck, M., Hoogstraten, H., Koek, M., Resink, S.: Rapportage Fox-IT - Advisering toelaatbaarheid internetstemvoorziening waterschappen (2008), `http://www.verkeerenwaterstaat.nl/Images/20081302%20Bijlage%201%20rapport_tcm195-228336.pdf`

[5] Hubbers, E.-M., Jacobs, B., Pieters, W.: RIES - Internet Voting in Action. In: Bilof, R. (ed.) COMPSAC 2005, Proceedings of the 29th Annual International Computer Software and Applications Conference, COMPSAC 2005, July 26-28, pp. 417–424. IEEE Computer Society, Los Alamitos (2005), http://www.cs.ru.nl/~hubbers/pubs/compsac2005.pdf

[6] Hubbers, E.-M., Jacobs, B.: Stemmen via internet geen probleem.Automatisering Gids #42, p.15 (October 15, 2004), http://www.openries.nl/aspx/download.aspx?File=/contents/pages/77743/stemmenviainternetgeenprobleem.pdf

[7] Hubbers, E., Jacobs, B., Schoenmakers, B., Van Tilborg, H., De Weger, B.: Description and Analysis of the RIES Internet Voting System (June 24, 2008), http://www.win.tue.nl/eipsi/images/RIES_descr_anal_v1.0_June_24.pdf

[8] Van Ekris, J.: CIBIT, Beoordeling KOA, Een beoordeling van de integriteit van "Kiezen op Afstand" (September 11, 2008), http://www.openries.nl/aspx/download.aspx?File=/contents/pages/77743/eindrapportcibit.pdf

[9] Nijmegen University - Security of Systems:?Server Audit van RIES, (July 23, 2004), http://www.openries.nl/aspx/download.aspx?File=/contents/pages/77743/reportkun.pdf

[10] Jonker, H., Volkamer, M.: Compliance of RIES to the proposed e-Voting protection profile, VOTE-ID 2007 (2007)

[11] Groth, J.: CryptoMathic: Review of RIES (v 0.3), Cryptomathic A/S (January 21, 2004), http://www.openries.nl/aspx/download.aspx?File=/contents/pages/77743/reviewofries.pdf

[12] Kruijswijk, L.: Internetstemmen met RIES onder de loep (2006), http://www.wijvertrouwenstemcomputersniet.nl/Internetstemmen_met_RIES_onder_de_loep

[13] Unie van Waterschappen: Aanbevelingen van de Raad van Europa, Evaluatie voorziening internetstemmen RIES, conform artikel 5 onderdeel b Regeling waterschaps-verkiezingen 2008, version 6 (June 2008), http://www.openries.nl/aspx/download.aspx?File=/contents/pages/77726/evaluatieaanbevelingenraadvaneuropa.pdf

[14] GOVCERT.NL: Webapplicatie-scan, Kiezen op Afstand (September 1, 2006), http://www.openries.nl/aspx/download.aspx?File=/contents/pages/77743/webapplicatie-scan.pdf

[15] Ministerie van Binnenlandse Zaken en Koninkrijksrelaties: Stemmachines, een verweesd dossier (April 17, 2007), http://www.minbzk.nl/contents/pages/86914/rapportstemmachineseenverweesddossier.pdf

Combatting Electoral Traces: The Dutch Tempest Discussion and Beyond*

Wolter Pieters

Faculty of Electrical Engineering, Mathematics and Computer Science
University of Twente
P.O. Box 217, 7500 AE Enschede, The Netherlands
`w.pieters@utwente.nl`

Abstract. In the Dutch e-voting debate, the crucial issue leading to the abandonment of all electronic voting machines was compromising radiation, or tempest: it would be possible to eavesdrop on the choice of the voter by capturing the radiation from the machine. Other countries, however, do not seem to be bothered by this risk. In this paper, we use actor-network theory to analyse the socio-technical origins of the Dutch tempest issue in e-voting, and we introduce concepts for discussing its implications for e-voting beyond the Netherlands. We introduce the term *electoral traces* to denote any physical, digital or social evidence of a voter's choices in an election. From this perspective, we provide a framework for risk classification as well as an overview of countermeasures against such traces.

Keywords: actor-network theory, electoral traces, electronic voting, risk classification, tempest.

1 Introduction

In the Netherlands, electronic voting machines were introduced in the 1990s without much controversy. A major debate was started by an activist group in 2006. As in the US, the discussion seems to revolve around correctness and verifiability.

In the Dutch e-voting debate, however, the crucial issue leading to the abandonment of all electronic voting machines was tempest (also written TEMPEST, supposedly being an acronym for Telecommunications Electronics Material Protected from Emanating Spurious Transmission or something similar), related to the secrecy of the ballot. Tempest involves listening to so-called "compromising emanations", i.e. radio emission from the device, in this particular case the display. In this way, it would be possible to eavesdrop on the information shown on the display, and thereby deduce a relation between the vote cast and the identity of the voter. Whereas the secrecy of the ballot is anchored in law in many other

---

* All the information in this article is based on publicly available documents and scientific analysis thereof.

P.Y.A. Ryan and B. Schoenmakers (Eds.): VOTE-ID 2009, LNCS 5767, pp. 172–190, 2009.

countries, they generally do not seem to be bothered much by this risk. The issue has only been mentioned incidentally, and without implementation details [7,13,3].

In this paper, we ask the question why tempest became so prominent in the Dutch debate. We analyse the emergence of the Dutch tempest issue from the point of view of actor-network theory, and discuss its possible consequences for e-voting beyond the Netherlands. As far as we are aware, this is the first systematic account of this discussion. In order to place it in a broader scientific context, we introduce the term *electoral traces* to denote any physical, digital or social evidence of a voter's choices in an election. From this perspective, we provide a framework for risk classification as well as an overview of countermeasures.

In section 2, we provide an overview of the electronic voting controversy in the Netherlands. In section 3, we zoom in on the tempest issue from the point of view of actor-network theory [17]. We investigate how the tempest issue was constructed in the debate, and why the issue could not be resolved. In section 4, we place the tempest issue in the context of electoral traces, and suggest guidelines for analysing such risks in different voting systems. In section 5, we discuss the possible consequences of the tempest issue for e-voting beyond the Netherlands, in terms of means to combat electoral traces. The final section draws conclusions from the presented analysis.

2   The Electronic Voting Controversy in the Netherlands

2.1   Background

The Netherlands are a constitutional monarchy, and have a system of proportional representation for local and national elections. Since 1928, the option of "stemmen bij volmacht" (voting by proxy) exists: one can authorise other people to cast one's vote. One is only allowed to have two authorisations. Since 1983, Dutch citizens living abroad, or having job duties abroad during the elections, are allowed to vote by postal ballot. Postal voting is not allowed within the country.

The Netherlands have been ahead in electronic voting for some time. In 1965, a legal provision was put in place to allow the use of machines, including electronic ones, in voting. In the late 1980s, attempts were made to automatise the counting, and the first electronic voting machines appeared. From 1994, the government actively promoted the use of electronic voting machines in elections. Since then, voting machines have been used extensively. The most widely used voting machines were produced by the company Nedap. These were so-called full-face DREs, with a button for each candidate. There was no paper trail. More recently, touch-screen based systems marketed by the former state press Sdu were also used, notably in Amsterdam.

In 1997, detailed regulation on voting machines was introduced, including an extensive list of requirements that voting machines have to meet ("Regeling voorwaarden en goedkeuring stemmachines"). The full requirements specification, consisting of 14 sections, existed as an appendix to the regulation. We quote and translate some items from section 8: Reliability and security of the voting machine:

- The storage of the cast votes is made redundant. The vote is stored in such a redundant way in the vote memory, that it can be proved that the failure rate is 1 x 10E-6. If there is a discrepancy in the redundant storage, the machine will report this to the voter and the voting station;
- The voting machine is able to avoid or reduce the possibilities for accidental or intended incorrect use as much as is technically feasible in fairness;
- The way of vote storage does not enable possibilities to derive the choice of individual voters;
- The voting machine has features which help to avoid erroneous actions during repair, maintenance and checks, for example by mechanical features which preclude assembly in wrong positions or in wrong places.

The possibility of recount or other forms of verification are not mentioned. Furthermore, most of the requirements in section 8 concern correctness under normal circumstances, and not especially security against possible election fraud.

An experiment with Internet voting took place during the European elections in 2004. Participation was intended for expatriates, who had the option to vote by mail before. For this purpose, the KOA system was developed by LogicaCMG in 2003–2004, and a law regulating the experiment was passed through parliament [19]. A somewhat more sophisticated system, called RIES, was developed by the water board of Rijnland together with two companies cooperating under the name TTPI [11]. An experiment with election via the Internet was conducted in the water board regions Rijnland and Dommel in 2004, with 1 million eligible voters. 120,000 people voted online, but turnout did not increase. RIES was also used in the second remote voting experiment for expats during the national elections in 2006, instead of the KOA system from 2004.

2.2 "We Don't Trust Voting Computers"

Criticism of the obscurity of the election procedure when using voting machines increased after 2000. Main reasons were the secrecy of the source code and the evaluation reports, and the lack of verifiability. After Ireland had insufficient confidence to use the Nedap machines they bought in the elections [6], Dutch politicians started asking questions about the safety and verifiability of such machines. At first, the government responded that everything was OK and not much happened.

In Fall 2006, the pressure group "Wij vertrouwen stemcomputers niet" ("We don't trust voting computers"), founded around June, managed to get hold of a couple of Nedap voting machines. They took them apart and reverse-engineered the source code. They made the results of their analysis public in a national television programme on October 4, with the general elections scheduled for November 22 [9]. The first main problem they identified was the easy replacement of the program chips, allowing the attacker to have the machine count incorrectly, or execute any other desired task. The second one was the possibility to eavesdrop on the voting machine and the choice of the voter via a tempest attack. Also, they found problems with the security of the storage facilities where the machines were kept in between elections.

The tempest attack was particularly successful because there is a special (diacritical) character in the full name of one of the parties. This required the display to switch to a different mode with a different refresh frequency, which could easily be detected. The minister responded to the findings of the activists by having all the chips replaced with non-reprogrammable ones (a questionable solution, because the chips had been *replaced*, not *reprogrammed*), seals on all the machines, and having the intelligence agency look into the tempest problem.

The fix for the diacritical character problem was easy (don't use special characters). With that implemented, the signal emitted from the Nedaps was fairly limited. However, the intelligence agency also looked into the other type of voting machine, the touch-screen based system produced by the former state press Sdu. They found that the tempest issue was much worse there, and someone outside the polling station might be able to reconstruct the whole screen from the signal.

The technical requirements only stated that voting machines should maintain the secrecy of the vote *in storing the vote*, not in casting. Nonetheless, the minister suspended the certification for the Sdu machines three weeks before the elections. This affected about 10% of the voter population, including Amsterdam. Some districts got spare Nedaps, but others had to use paper ballots, especially because the certification of one of the older Nedap types was suspended later.

2.3   Commissions and Reports

On September 27, 2007, the Election Process Advisory Commission – headed by former minister Frits Korthals Altes and consisting of both political and technical experts – reported on the future of the electoral process in the Netherlands [1]. The report stated that the primary form of voting should be voting in a polling station. Internet voting for the whole population would not be able to guarantee transparency, secrecy and freedom of the vote sufficiently. It was advised to equip polling stations with "vote printers" and "vote counters" instead of electronic voting machines, providing a paper vote in between the two stages. Vote printers would *only* print the voter's choice, which would then be verified by the voter and put in a ballot box. The vote would not be stored electronically. After the close of the polls, the vote counter would scan the votes by means of optical character recognition (OCR) and calculate the totals.

A technical expert group – headed by computer security professor Bart Jacobs – was formed to investigate the practical issues involved in the commission's proposal. Because of research into the tempest issue [15], the option of a vote printer was judged not to be feasible. Machine counting of manually cast paper votes was not considered, for unclear reasons. It might be that the government did not want to reconsider the design of the ballot for this purpose (the huge present Dutch ballots are impossible to feed automatically into a machine). Besides, problems in the United Kingdom with this type of e-counting were a reason for the Election Process Advisory Commission not to recommend this option. It was tried to propose to use machines similar to the Nedaps for counting by the poll workers. They would then enter the choices on the paper votes manually into the machine. Because of the separation between the voter and the electronic processing of the vote, this would resolve the tempest issue. However, parliament could not be convinced that this would reduce the other security problems involved in electronic voting, and rejected the option.

Finally, the planned Internet voting for the water boards in 2008 was also cancelled after independent investigations reported security problems [8]. Electronic counting of postal ballots for the water boards was continued, though.

3   The Construction of Tempest

In this section, we investigate how tempest came to be the crucial factor in the Dutch electronic voting controversy. We take the perspective of actor-network theory (ANT) [17], which focuses on social dynamics in terms of the forming of associations between different entities, both human and nonhuman. We start with an introduction to the perspective and terminology of ANT. The second part of the section discusses how a coalition emerged supporting the seriousness of the tempest problem in electronic voting. The third part analyses how the Netherlands ended up with a norm stating that the radiation should not reach beyond 5 metres from the machine. The final part discusses the emergence of consensus about the impossibility of solving the problem.

3.1   Actor-Network Theory

Actor-network theory is an approach in sociology starting from a generalised symmetry between social entities, both human and nonhuman. It was initially developed in the context of science studies, where it was argued that scientific and technological developments should be understood by following the intricate connections between scientists, their social relations, and their laboratory equipment [16]. Later, is was applied in various fields, including environmental science [4] and information systems research [27]. It has also influenced developments in philosophy of technology [26].

A central theme in ANT is that social developments should be understood as developments of actors *in relation to each other*, not in relation to some abstract social context. Every connection in a social analysis should point to other "local" entities, which are again connected. For example, instead of explaining the trust a politician has in electronic voting from the fact that the culture in the country has a "high trust context", ANT would require to trace back where the trust of this particular politician in electronic voting came from. ANT is also described as a "sociology of associations".

Actor-network theory perceives agency in both humans and nonhumans. For example, when a man with a gun shoots someone else, we are used to say that the man makes the gun shoot, but conversely, it is also the gun that makes the man shoot, because he would not have shot if he would not have had the gun.

Actions are thus joint efforts of collectives of entities – networks – in which each of the actors may *mediate* the contributions of the others.

Actors – usually called *actants* to denote that they need not be human – may be such diverse entities as texts, molecules, buildings, and electronic voting machines. Their general characteristic is that they *resist* certain actions of their environment, and as such seems to push social developments in a certain direction. In this process, the possibilities for action are *translated* to fit all the restrictions of the involved actants.

As with all somewhat counter-intuitive frameworks, there remains discussion on both theoretical and practical aspects of the approach, for example on whether ANT can take ethical considerations into account [28]. However, it can safely be said that ANT has at least proved itself from a pragmatic perspective, by providing useful insights in the interplay between science, technology and society.

Used in the context of electronic voting, ANT provides a particularly rewarding approach for socio-technical analysis because there are so many different types of entities involved. The Dutch tempest discussion was framed as much by politicians, activists and journalists as by particular design features of the machines and the physical properties of radiation. Instead of explaining the prominence of tempest in the Netherlands as a matter of culture or social context, ANT points out precisely which actants contributed to the construction of this difference. We will see this in the following analysis.

3.2   The Association of Tempest Supporters

It is important to start the analysis with the observation that there did not exist any social means to support the tempest issue before the start of the activist group's campaign. In the requirements, it was stated that the secrecy of the ballot needed to be ensured in storing the vote, not in casting. The risk of compromising radiation had thus been hidden in the requirements. Only from 2006, a social coalition emerged to support the tempest issue.

From the perspective of ANT, the tempest issue is a complex association between different types of beings. First of all, there is the activist group, trying to put e-voting on the political agenda. Secondly, there is a seemingly innocent design feature of the Nedap machines, allowing special characters to be displayed. Thirdly, there is a major Dutch political party which actually has a special character in its name. Fourthly, there is another type of electronic voting machine, using a much larger screen (touchscreen). Fifthly, there is a legal framework demanding a secret ballot, but not verifiability of election results. Sixthly, there is an intelligence service with all kinds of measurement equipment for radiation.

The forming of a coalition between these apparently incompatible entities goes roughly as follows. First of all, the possibility of special characters in names of political parties forces Nedap to enable the display of these characters in their machines. The particular solution chosen consists of a different display mode, amplifying the distinction between "normal" parties and those with special characters in their names. This feature is actually used in Dutch elections, because one of the Dutch parties has such a character. Here, the naming of the party and the design of the machine form an alliance, and make the potential problem actually appear in the operation of the machine.

Since the activist group wants to put e-voting on the political agenda, they are looking for problematic features of the machines to be demonstrated to the public and politicians. Accidentally, they find out that a radio antenna receives signals from the Nedap machines, which sound differently depending on the party selected. An alliance now forms between the name, the design, and the intention of the pressure group to *demonstrate* problems. Enter the TV programme, which is interested in news that can be easily showed to the public. The tempest issue meets this criterion,[1] and is therefore included in the programme on the activist group's findings. It is thereby translated from a technical detail into a public problem.

At this point, had there been no expertise, the issue might have been resolved by just ignoring the special character in the name. However, there is both an intelligence agency with expertise on this matter, as well as a different type of voting machine. An extended alliance is created here, where the intelligence service can show that even if the Nedap special character issue can be resolved, there are still problems with the other type of machine. Moreover, both the government and the activist group are looking for legal foundations for taking action against the machines: the activist group to enforce the abolishing of the machines, the government to respond to public pressure. Since there is nothing in the law about verifiability, which was the main topic of the activists, it is convenient for both to turn to the secret ballot instead. Based on the legal demand of the secret ballot, something can be done against unverifiable voting machines, even if the concrete voting systems requirements state nothing about verifiability or secrecy of the vote *in casting*. The tempest issue is translated from a problem of a particular machine to a problem with electronic voting in general. The coalition is now complete.

This coalition stands for the now undeniable fact that e-voting machines cause trouble with compromising emanation. The government, by acknowledging the tempest issue, may actually have a chance to save the electronic voting machines and their efficiency benefits if the issue can be solved. The question then becomes what the consequences should be, especially in terms of which levels of radiation are acceptable and which are not. At some point, the consensus seems to be that it should not be possible to capture radiation from beyond 5 metres distance [10]. From a measurement perspective, this still does not solve the question, as radiation decreases quadratically with the distance, but only reaches zero asymptotically. Everything thus depends on the size of the antenna used, but the 5 metre norm does not specify this. Where, then, did this norm come from?

3.3 The Association of 5 Metre Measurers

In order to understand the origins of the 5 meter norm, let us quote some longer fragments by the responsible minister from the parliamentary reports on the issue:

---

[1] See http://www.youtube.com/watch?v=B05wPomCjEY

"The possibility that the choice of a voter can be assessed outside of the voting booth is a source of concern, and all possible efforts will be made to find a solution. The possibility can never be completely excluded though, even when voting with paper and pencil. After all, with a small camera in the voting booth observation of the voter's choice is also possible. This can never be prevented completely, but if there were any indication of such a thing happening, extra supervision is of course possible. Something similar must happen now as well. The problem consists of two parts. Radiation can be captured up to tens of metres of distance from the voting machine, i.e. outside the polling station too. This is not the first concern, for someone outside only knows which vote has been cast, but not by whom. That does not diminish the necessity of investigating possibilities for prevention. The greatest concern, however, is the possibility of someone inside the polling station finding out who casts the vote. The question is if, with whichever advanced technical means, it is possible to capture radiation within the polling station without somebody noticing. This is now being investigated." [24, p. 7, translation by the author]

The first step in the construction of the 5 metre norm is the drawing of a distinction between outside and inside of the polling station. In the above statement, the radiation *inside* the polling station is seen as the most dangerous. However, now that this distinction has been mobilised as a member of the tempest issue, it can also be used differently:

"The radiation range of the Sdu machines is 40 metres. With relatively simple equipment, the voting behaviour can even be read from the screen of the voting machine within this distance. The radiation range of the three Nedap machines that have been tested is approximately five metres at maximum, the dimension of a polling station itself. [...] The radiation, however, does not only concern the diacritics, but is also about the intensity of the radiation and the equipment necessary for capturing the signal. Weak radiation can indeed be captured by advanced equipment within a distance of five metres, but this implies that one would have to stay in the polling station with this equipment for a longer period. Such behaviour will draw attention in a polling station, and will be acted against. A 100 % guarantee can not be given though. The actions and measures taken must be seen within the proportions of the reliability that can be offered." [25, p. 5, translation by the author]

In this more recent comment of the minister, the inside/outside distinction has been translated into a radiation range. From a technical point of view, this is understandable, since this is more amenable to standardised measurement, using the devices the intelligence agency possesses. Note, however, that the distance of 5 metres is introduced here as the *actual radiation range of the Nedap machines*. This range is thus descriptive rather than normative. Also note that, as opposed to the earlier statement, the problem of capturing *outside* the polling station is now considered the most important one, because this is less likely to draw attention. In the earlier statement, capturing *inside* the polling station was considered more dangerous. This may be a reversal in the problem perception based on what can be physically measured: a maximum range can be tested against, but a minimum range ("only outside the polling station") does not make sense from what physicists know about radiation. The physical properties of radiation *mediate* the political perception of the problem: what the politicians see as problematic about tempest meets the resistance of what is physically possible. A new alliance forms between the radiation expertise of the intelligence agency and the political formulation of the problem. This formulation of the problem is reconfirmed in a later statement by the minister:

> "As I said before in parliament, there remains as a residual risk the possibility that radiation from the machine can be captured and the display reproduced within a range of maximum 5 metres. This, however, requires very advanced devices. As I stated in the AO [discussion with parliament] of 31 October 2006, I hold the opinion that this residual risk is acceptable." [18, p. 1, translation by the author]

In this statement, the beginning can be noticed of a transformation of the descriptive range into a normative range. Especially noteworthy is the role of the term "maximum". Although used in a descriptive sense before (the maximum range that was measured), this concept clearly has a normative connotation, and this may have invited the transformation into a norm (the maximum range that is acceptable). Here, the text produced about the measured radiation *mediates* the formulation of the normative requirement. In this respect, the text is an actor in the ANT sense. There is now agreement on the acceptability of radiation within a range of 5 metres, whatever that may mean exactly for the measuring equipment of the intelligence agency, and this political agreement is convenient for future government action: if one sticks to the 5 metre norm, the acceptability does not need to be renegotiated. This norm had major consequences for the outcome of the discussion, as we will see next.

3.4   The Association of Impossibility

After all the problems had revealed themselves, it was up to the Election Process Advisory Commission to propose a new way of voting that would (at least partly) solve them. Concerning the tempest problem, the report of the Election Process Advisory Commission considers the following:

> "It might be wondered how great the need is to protect voting equipment against compromising TEMPEST radiation. There are both matters of principle and pragmatic aspects here. The rules and regulations require the secrecy of the ballot to be protected. The question, however, is: how great is the risk of the compromising radiation emitted by the voting equipment being misused? Sophisticated TEMPEST expertise is currently well protected, but a motivated, technically knowledgeable

amateur can go a long way. Ignoring the phenomenon is not an option, especially now that the subject is commanding wide attention. It is not desirable, for example, for the political leanings of Dutch celebrities to be published on the web. Theoretically it is even conceivable that real-time election results could be obtained on election day and published on the Internet. This, however, would involve eavesdropping on the ballots in at least enough polling stations for the results to be representative of the totality, and it is highly doubtful whether anyone would be willing to go to that much expense and trouble." [5, p. 34]

The Commission did not seem to be convinced that the problem really needed (technical) solving in general, but given the attention that the topic received, it could not be ignored: the risk of misuse had increased by the widespread coverage of the issue. The Commission recommended reactive measures, and was doubtful about the feasibility of preventive ones:

> "The Commission recommends that reactive measures be taken, by making such practice a criminal offence and reaching clearly defined agreements with the Public Prosecution Service on investigation and prosecution. If the additional cost of protection against compromising radiation is not prohibitive, the current NATO SDIP-27 Level B standard should also be applied." [5, p. 35]

The NATO norm, however, is confidential, which conflicts with the demand for transparency in the election process. This created a new problem hindering simple technical measures. Still, the Electoral Council (Kiesraad) strongly advised against solving the tempest issue by legal measures only:

> "From the point of view of the Electoral Council, safeguarding the secrecy of the ballot should be a self-evident topic in this accreditation procedure. This guarantee is incorporated in various international treaties and in the Dutch Constitution. This means that potential problems with radiation found in the ballot printer (the TEMPEST issue) cannot only be dealt with repressively by making eavesdropping an offence. For this problem a preventive solution should be sought, protecting the secrecy of the ballot to the greatest possible extent. It appears to the Electoral Council that minimally, a norm should be enforced according to which radiation is not allowed to reach further than a few metres from the device." [14, translation by the author]

This led the government and the new expert group to give an assignment to the German company GBS (http://www.gbs-tempest.de/) to draw up a public norm for radiation in electronic voting machines. This resulted in the document mentioned earlier [15]. In the report by GBS, the 5 metre norm finally materialises in a physically meaningful form: 5 metres means 5 metres with an antenna aperture of 1 square metre [15, p. 6]. This seems to complete the translation of the inside/outside distinction that was coined to make a distinction between problematic and unproblematic radiation. The physical relation between antenna aperture and possibility of capture seems to be more or less randomly chosen: one could also have said 0.5 square metre, as long as it could be justified that anyone with a larger antenna inside a polling station would draw attention. However, if one gets closer to the voting machine, the signal may be captured by a smaller antenna. It is thus assumed that smaller antenna sizes closer to the machine are also infeasible for the eavesdropper.

The document also provides procedures for testing and re-testing. Two types of measurement are defined: an accreditation measurement (for a type of machine) and a compliance measurement (for each machine). The accreditation measurement would take 4 hours, the compliance measurement 25 minutes. It is calculated that with normal working hours in a single lab, the compliance testing of the 10,000 machines necessary to cover all of the Netherlands would take 50 weeks. The compliance measurement needs to be repeated every two years. It is noted that transport and wear and tear can change the tempest properties of the machines.

For the test, it would be required to run test software on the machines, maximising the possible radiation during the test. The rationale behind this may be that emulating real voting during the tests would lead to strong fluctuations in radiation depending on the state of the device. This would not lead to repeatable results. Thus, the specific software used for voting would *not* be included in the test. First of all, this means that special software techniques would not improve the measured tempest behaviour. Secondly, this means that the device should allow software different from the normal voting programme to be run, introducing a security risk.

The report by GBS also provided for requirements on polling stations, including:

 - placement of the machine opposite the windows;
 - no other technical equipment (mobile phones switched off);
 - procedure for checking seals on the machines.

According to a member of the expert group, a prototype ballot printer satisfying the requirements was built as well, weighing over 100 kg, due to the heavy metal case [12].

By means of the report, the idea of a technical norm had now been translated into a whole range of measurement procedures. Whereas it might have been hoped that a technical norm would be easily enforceable, these testing procedures form part of the final translation of the inside/outside distinction, and complicate its political acceptability. In a way, technical measures are translated back to the organisational burdens of elections. Now it was the turn of the government and the Expert Group to respond to the contents of the report. The Electoral Council had indicated clearly that organisational and legal measures alone were not acceptable. The technical norms, though, would lead to high costs and heavyweight devices, and most importantly, a host of additional organisational measures, including test logistics and polling station design. These organisational burdens were not considered acceptable. In response to the report, the Expert Group states the following:

> "In fact, the issue of compromising emanations demands a process such as exists in military circles, where all factors can be controlled. According to the Expert Group, this is not realistic for the election process, and not desirable either." [23, p. 2, translation by the author]

The fact that the GBS report was even written already reinforced the perception that the issue should be resolved technically, which was also advised by the Electoral Council. The request for the report pulled new entities, GBS and their report, into the network. Apart from the contents of the report, this already changed the network in such a way that the problem was *translated* into a technical one. Thus, a coalition had emerged supporting the idea that technical measures were necessary. At the same time, the report showed clearly that even if technically acceptable devices could be built, the testing procedure would be impractical. This initiated a second coalition, namely one that judged the tempest problem to be insolvable. As we have seen, this coalition came out as a winning one in the discussion.

Relaxing the technical tempest requirements was not an option either. Knowing that the activist group was closely following the developments – and would be prepared to demonstrate any possible attack – and that parliament would see no reason to abandon the firmly established 5 metre norm, the government could not afford to take any risks, and decided not to introduce the ballot printer. One might be tempted to analyse this as a capitulation to a public perception issue that had got out of hand. The tempest issue, however, was not only a matter of perceived security; because it had been revealed so clearly, the likelihood of people actually attempting to find out the vote of someone, especially celebrities, had increased considerably.

> "In case it would still be decided to introduce the ballot printer, discussion on this topic will remain, possibly undermining trust in the new voting method. The government considers this not desirable, and therefore decides not to introduce the ballot printer." [23, p. 2, translation by the author]

Thus, from the perspective of ANT, the prominence of the tempest issue in the Dutch debate can be explained in terms of shifting associations between humans, devices, distinctions, norms etc., and the mediations between those. Interestingly, the tempest issue has not been discussed much in other countries, and neither in the Dutch debate on Internet voting. In the major Belgian e-voting study, it is mentioned as a requirement, but without explanation or a realistic estimation of costs: "The embedded computer system is made resistant to tampering and is shielded to prevent advanced attacks, e.g., tempest and electromagnetic radiation." [3, p. 98]. This technical guideline is seen as an implementation of the requirement of "System integrity & Voter anonymity: the remote observation of an electronic voting machine may compromise the privacy of the voter. Shielding the embedded computer system so that such information cannot easily be derived from side channels (e.g., electromagnetic radiation and power consumption) improves the trustworthiness in the eVoting system." [3, pp. 98–99] Note that any practical considerations regarding residual risk and measurement are omitted. In this section, we explained how different actants formed the particular association that supported the tempest issue in the Netherlands. The fact that this configuration can be quite different in other countries may account for the absence of focus on the issue there. See [22] for an analysis of the differences between the British and Dutch e-voting discourse.

As Internet voting is performed on electronic equipment as well, it is potentially affected by the same threats. Still, the Dutch debate on Internet voting did not include tempest. We will come back to this curiosity in the next section.

The lesson to be learnt here is that perceived security is not an innocent naiveté of the public towards security issues. Rather, the entire battleground of attackers and defenders in a society can be changed by relatively minor details happening in the domain of perceived security and the forming of associations between different types of people and things. In such a case, the political options for the government may be extremely limited. Whereas the traditional distinction between actual and perceived security may be useful in some types of analysis, the symmetry of humans and nonhumans of ANT provides a richer vocabulary for understanding the emergence of seemingly major security problems that might not even have been considered if the situation would have been slightly different.

4   Risk Classification

Considering this – from a computing and information sciences point of view – rather disappointing conclusion, what can these sciences do to contribute to the discussion on voting and tempest? Probably the best option is to widen the blinkers of the risk assessment a bit, enabling governments to make well-founded decisions in case the tempest discussion spreads to other countries. The question to ask, then, is of what type of risk in voting tempest is an instance, and how it compares to other instances of the same class.

There are similar threats to the secrecy of the ballot in voting systems. For example, what is the risk of attacks on the secrecy of the ballot by comparison of fingerprints with those on paper votes? In general, we can speak of *electoral traces* as a general term to denote physical, digital or social evidence of choices made by voters in elections. Physical evidence can be present in the form of fingerprints, recognisable handwriting, physical remainders in receipt printers, et cetera, Digital evidence can consist of compromising radiations, images in computer or printer memory, or cookies in case of Internet voting. Social evidence may be related to voter behaviour, exit polls.

Definition 1. *An* electoral trace *is a piece of information (partly) revealing the connection between voter and vote.*

Electoral traces can appear in various ways:

1. The vote is marked such that it can be traced back to the voter;
2. The voter is marked such that she can be traced back to the vote;
3. A different medium is used to emit or store the relation between voter and vote.

Examples of the first category are fingerprints or markings on paper ballots, or electronic storage of votes in sequential order. Examples of the second category are proxy voting or a receipt that carries a proof of the voter's choice. Tempest, fingerprints on keys/touchscreen and camera recordings constitute examples of the third category. In the British system, a registration is kept of the relation between voters and ballot numbers, which also constitutes an electoral trace. An interesting overview of additional privacy risks is found in [13]. Apart from the traditional risk attributes of probability and effect, electoral traces can be characterised along a number of dimensions:

Added value. Benefits of the system causing the electoral traces. The British system allows for easier corrections in case of fraud. The US elections are much more complicated than the Dutch, so there will be a higher added value of voting electronically. In Internet voting, some traces may be allowed to increase verifiability;

Context. Likelihood of the electoral trace being exploited given the social context. In the Dutch context, the tempest issue had become riskier due to media coverage;

Domain. Digital, physical, social;

Effort. Effort required to reconstruct vote-voter relation from trace (e.g. breaking weak crypto, matching paper ballot numbers with their registration in the British system);

Information content. Amount of information that the trace reveals about the vote. The tempest attack due to the special character only revealed whether the voter voted for a specific party or not;

Intentionality. Unintentional electoral traces are related to the secrecy of the ballot. Intentional electoral traces are related to the freedom of the vote, and may enable coercion or vote buying [21]. Intentional traces may include video recordings of casting the vote or markings to make a ballot recognisable;

Overtness. Overt (designed communication) vs. covert (not designed channel) [13];

Persistence. Transitory (e.g. tempest) vs. long-lasting (e.g. fingerprints).

In each case where the risk of electoral traces is considered, a comparison should be made of the various traces that are possible and their properties along the mentioned dimensions, leading to a balanced view on their relative importance. In this way, the alliance of entities focusing on a particular type of trace can be placed in a wider context, such that appropriate measures can be taken not only for the risk that has the public's attention, but for similar risks as well.

We can now understand why tempest has not been considered important for Internet voting. Other electoral traces are already present in this voting method, e.g. the verification option in the RIES Internet voting system (digital, intentional, long-lasting) and shoulder surfing (social, unintentional/intentional, transitory), making the tempest issue relatively low-risk. If one allows people to check for which candidate their vote has been counted, this may constitute a high-risk electoral trace. Still, prominence of the tempest issue in the discussion on voting machines was harmful for the Internet voting efforts in a different way. The tempest issue put the requirement of the secret ballot high on the agenda, and because of the inherent secrecy problems in remote voting, this may have worsened the perspectives for success of the Internet voting effort of the water boards.

Still, the tempest discussion and the associated awareness of the secret ballot has not led to major discussion on the future of proxy voting in the Netherlands, which also has problems with the secrecy of the ballot in terms of social electoral traces. The risks of this feature of the Dutch electoral system have apparently been well-hidden, and there was no association of actors that was strong enough to put this back on the agenda.

Comparing different electoral traces thus leads to a more balanced view on voting system issues related to the secrecy of the ballot. Only if different dimensions of electoral traces are identified for each possible electoral trace in a voting system can electoral traces be subject to a more rational analysis and comparison, and can the Dutch tempest discussion be placed in a context fruitful to other countries. Other case studies of electoral traces may provide additional dimensions for the framework presented here.

5   Combatting Electoral Traces

Given the framework provided in the previous section, how can we counter the threats of electoral traces in elections? Based on the estimated importance of the risks, several countermeasures can be proposed. We will first give some suggestions with respect to the tempest issue, based on the discussion in the Netherlands, and then broaden the view to other electoral traces.

The tempest issue arises from the *simultaneity* of the casting of the vote and the electronic processing thereof. Only in that case is it possible to derive the relation between voter and vote from the signal. Therefore, the following types of e-voting are affected by the tempest issue: DRE, precinct-count optical scan (where the voter enters the ballot into the counter), and Internet voting. Central-count optical scan, where e-counting starts after the close of the polls, is not affected, because there is no simultaneity of the casting and electronic processing of the vote.

For all the affected types, the tempest risk needs to be compared to other threats of electoral traces. An assessment should be performed in which it is made clear how much higher the risk of a breach of the secrecy of the ballot will be in case the particular e-voting system is used. Several technical measures can help to reduce this risk: the type of screen, the type of printer, shielding of the machine and cables, software measures (e.g. randomised display), and jamming stations (if legally allowed). In particular, touch-screen based systems with large screens are problematic.

Technical measures need to be applied in combination with some form of certification. Certification requires a) a norm and b) testing procedures. To guarantee tempest behaviour, each individual machine should be tested, but governments may want to relax this requirement because of organisational burdens. In that case, the type of machine is tested and the government accepts the risk of individual machines not conforming to the norm. A decision should be made on whether a secret norm is acceptable, both for the public and for the manufacturers. As we have seen, the question should also be asked whether a norm should only address hardware requirements or also software. This may have major consequences for the testing procedure.

Next to or instead of technical measures, organisational and legal measures may be applied to reduce the risk of breaches of the secrecy of the ballot through tempest:

- physical requirements for polling stations (e.g. size of the room, placement of the voting machine);
- organisational requirements for polling stations (measures to prevent people from capturing signals both inside and outside the polling station);
- (criminal) law.

It is not possible to combat electoral traces only by addressing the tempest problem. As we have seen in the section on risk classification, similar risks may appear, and in their presence expensive tempest measures may not achieve their goal. Risks associated with other electoral traces need to be compared to the tempest risk, and an integrated approach to managing these risks should be applied, based on this comparison. Especially in the situation where people carry all kinds of devices capable of recording the environment, high-risk traces may appear. Additional technical measures to combat electoral traces may include:

- use e-voting in order to prevent markings on ballots, both unintentional (fingerprints) and intentional (text, symbol, fold);
- use a pen for the touchscreen instead of fingers;
- use printers that do not keep traces of what was printed and when (memory usage, physical traces in print technology, "yellow dots");
- use "privacy folders" to protect machine-readable ballots carried by voters from eavesdropping [13].

Again, certification may be necessary for more complex technical issues, such as the printer requirements. Organisational measures may include:

- disallow electronic equipment in voting booth to prevent intentional traces like video recordings;
- limit proxy and remote voting to prevent social traces;
- in Internet voting, only allow voters to verify *that* their vote has been counted, not how, such that voters will not have proof of their vote (receipt-freeness [2,20]);
- separate ballots for different races, to prevent using unique combinations to prove one's vote [13].

These measures may reduce the risk of several electoral traces, but they may not be able to completely eliminate them. It remains to be seen whether a combination of such measures is sufficient to restore trust in the secrecy of the ballot in the age of electronics. As we have seen in the Dutch situation, the problems may not even be regarded solvable in practice. This may hold both for problems induced by the automation of the voting process and for problems induced by the increasing number of recording devices carried by voters. In the end, political choices need to be made here, and risk analysis can only hope to assist in making these choices.

6   Conclusions

In this paper, we analysed the Dutch tempest issue in the e-voting controversy. We gave an actor-network account of the emergence of both the tempest problem and the associated 5 metre norm. We followed the translation of the distinction between tempest inside and outside the polling station to a complex measurement procedure, which was finally judged to be infeasible for election systems.

To place the discussion within a broader framework and allow for risk classification, we introduced the notion of electoral traces, of which the tempest issue is an instance. We used our risk classification framework to explain why the tempest issue did not come up in the discussion on Internet voting in the Netherlands. Based on the Dutch situation and the analysis thereof, some recommendations were given on which topics to consider in similar discussions elsewhere. Case studies in other countries may illuminate the current socio-technical landscape around electoral traces there, and can lead to country-specific recommendations.

Most importantly, tempest should be considered as a particular instance of electoral traces. In this context, it becomes subject to comparison to similar risks, rather than a completely separate problem. To avoid the Dutch situation, where the tempest risk overshadowed other and possibly more serious risks, it would be wise to incorporate tempest into risk analysis, requirements and legislation around electronic voting. If manufacturers at least consider the problem, major vulnerabilities like the Nedap special character may be prevented.

As far as we are aware, this paper is the first to give a systematic account of the Dutch tempest discussion. It remains to be seen whether the discussion on electoral traces and tempest emerges in other countries, but if it does, the framework devised here may be helpful in guiding the scientific and political analysis. Otherwise, it is just a scientific contribution, both on the social dynamics of risks of information technology and on risk assessment of electronic voting systems.

References

1. Adviesommissie Inrichting Verkiezingsproces. Stemmen met vertrouwen (September 2007), http://www.minbzk.nl/contents/pages/89927/advies.pdf (consulted November 3, 2007)

2. Benaloh, J.C., Tuinstra, D.: Receipt-free secret ballot elections (extended abstract). In: Proc. 26th ACM Symposium on the Theory of Computing (STOC), pp. 544–553. ACM, New York (1994)
3. BeVoting. Study of electronic voting systems, part i of the "studie geautomatiseerde stemming def. vs 18122006, version 1.1 (April 15, 2007), http://www.ibz.rrn.fgov.be/fileadmin/user_upload/Elections/fr/presentation/bevoting-1_gb.pdf
4. Burgess, J., Clark, J., Harrison, C.M.: Knowledges in action: an actor network analysis of a wetland agri-environment scheme. Ecological economics 35(1), 119–132 (2000)
5. Election Process Advisory Commission. Voting with confidence (September 27, 2007), http://www.kiesraad.nl/nl/Overige_Content/Bestanden/pdf_thema/Voting_with_confidence.pdf
6. Commission on Electronic Voting. First report of the commission on electronic voting on the secrecy, accuracy and testing of the chosen electronic voting system (2004), http://www.cev.ie/htm/report/first_report.htm
7. Fairweather, B., Rogerson, S.: Technical options report (2002), http://www.communities.gov.uk/documents/localgovernment/pdf/155484.pdf (consulted March 24, 2009)
8. Gedrojc, B., Hueck, M., Hoogstraten, H., Koek, M., Resink, S.: Rapportage advisering toelaatbaarheid internetstemvoorziening waterschappen. Fox-IT (August 12, 2008), http://www.verkeerenwaterstaat.nl/Images/20081302rt_tcm195-228336.pdf
9. Gonggrijp, R., Hengeveld, W.-J., Bogk, A., Engling, D., Mehnert, H., Rieger, F., Scheffers, P., Wels, B.: Nedap/Groenendaal ES3B voting computer: a security analysis (October 6, 2006), http://www.wijvertrouwenstemcomputersniet.nl/images/9/91/Es3b-en.pdf (consulted March 16, 2007)
10. Hermans, L.M.L.H.A., van Twist, M.J.W.: Stemmachines: een verweesd dossier. Rapport van de Commissie Besluitvorming Stemmachines (April 2007), http://www.minbzk.nl/contents/pages/86914/rapportstemmachineseenverweesddossier.pdf (consulted April 19, 2007)
11. Hubbers, E., Jacobs, B., Pieters, W.: RIES – Internet voting in action. In: Bilof, R. (ed.) Proc. 29th Annual International Computer Software and Applications Conference, COMPSAC 2005, pp. 417–424. IEEE Computer Society, Los Alamitos (2005)
12. Jacobs, B.P.F.: Practical issues in electronic voting. Slides of FOSAD summer school presentation (August 30, 2008), http://www.cs.ru.nl/B.Jacobs/TALKS/fosad08.pdf
13. Keller, A.M., Mertz, D., Hall, J.L., Urken, A.: Privacy issues in an electronic voting machine. In: Strandburg, K.J., Stan Raicu, D. (eds.) Privacy and Technologies of Identity: A Cross-Disciplinary Conversation, pp. 313–334. Springer, Heidelberg (2006)
14. Kiesraad. Reactie op rapport stemmen met vertrouwen over inrichting verkiezingsproces (commissie-Korthals Altes). Kiesraad advice 2007-0000406046 (October 15, 2007), http://www.kiesraad.nl/nl/Overige_Content/Bestanden/Advies-Adviezen/reactie_15_okt_2007.pdf
15. Kuhn, M., Friedrichs, G., Aksoy, A., Koch, E., Friedrichs, L.: Tempest specificaties en testmethoden voor elektronische stemapparatuur. Appendix BLG15766 of Kamerstuk 2007-2008, 31200 VII, nr. 64, Tweede Kamer (May 21, 2008)
16. Latour, B.: Science in Action: How to Follow Scientists and Engineers Through Society. Open University Press, Milton Keynes (1987)

17. Latour, B.: Reassembling the Social: An Introduction to Actor-Network-Theory. Oxford University Press, Oxford (2005)
18. Minister voor Bestuurlijke Vernieuwing en Koninkrijksrelaties. Vaststelling van de begrotingsstaten van het Ministerie van Binnenlandse Zaken en Koninkrijksrelaties (VII) voor het jaar 2007; Brief minister over stemmachines. Kamerstuk 2006-2007 30800 VII, nr. 13, Tweede Kamer (November 3, 2006)
19. Ministerie van Binnenlandse Zaken en Koninkrijksrelaties. Project kiezen op afstand. report BPR2004/U79957 (November 1, 2004),
    http://www.minbzk.nl/onderwerpen/grondwet-en/verkiezingen-en/
    kiezen-op-afstand/kamerstukken?ActItmIdt=12800
    (consulted March 13, 2007)
20. Pieters, W.: What proof do we prefer? Variants of verifiability in voting. In: Ryan, P., Anderson, S., Storer, T., Duncan, I., Bryans, J. (eds.) Workshop on e-Voting and e-Government in the UK, Edinburgh, February 27-28, pp. 33–39. e-Science Institute, University of St. Andrews (2006)
21. Pieters, W., Jonker, H.L.: Vote buying revisited: implications for receipt-freeness. In: 2nd Benelux Workshop on Information and System Security (WISSec 2007), Luxembourg city, Luxembourg (September 20–21, 2007)
22. Pieters, W., van Haren, R.: Temptations of turnout and modernisation: E-voting discourses in the UK and The Netherlands. Journal of Information, Communication and Ethics in Society 5(4), 276–292 (2007)
23. Staatssecretaris van Binnenlandse Zaken en Koninkrijksrelaties. Vaststelling van de begrotingsstaten van het Ministerie van Binnenlandse Zaken en Koninkrijksrelaties (VII) voor het jaar 2008; Brief staatssecretaris met oordeel kabinet over uitkomsten nader onderzoek naar haalbaarheid stemprinter en stemmenteller. Kamerstuk 2007-2008 31200 VII, nr. 64, Tweede Kamer (May 21, 2008)
24. Vaste commissie voor Binnenlandse Zaken en Koninkrijksrelaties. Vaststelling van de begrotingsstaten van het Ministerie van Binnenlandse Zaken en Koninkrijksrelaties (VII) voor het jaar 2007; Verslag algemeen overleg van 12 oktober 2006 over beveiliging van stemmachines. Kamerstuk 2006-2007 30800 VII, nr. 18, Tweede Kamer (November 28, 2006)
25. Vaste commissie voor Binnenlandse Zaken en Koninkrijksrelaties. Vaststelling van de begrotingsstaten van het Ministerie van Binnenlandse Zaken en Koninkrijksrelaties (VII) voor het jaar 2007; Verslag algemeen overleg van 31 oktober over stemmachines. Kamerstuk 2006-2007 30800 VII, nr. 19, Tweede Kamer (November 28, 2006)
26. Verbeek, P.P.C.C.: What things do: Philosophical Reflections on Technology, Agency, and Design. Pennsylvania State University Press (2005)
27. Walsham, G.: Actor-network theory and IS research: Current status and future prospects. In: Lee, A., Liebenau, J., DeGross, J. (eds.) Information Systems and Qualitative Research, pp. 466–480. Chapman Hall, London (1997)
28. Winner, L.: Upon opening the black box and finding it empty: social constructivism and the philosophy of technology. Science, Technology and Human Values 18(3), 362–378 (1993)

Author Index